RUNCIE:

The Making of an Archbishop

£1·50

Also by Margaret Duggan

Padre in Colditz (ed.)
Through the Year with Michael Ramsey (ed.)

RUNCIE:

The Making of an Archbishop

Margaret Duggan

HODDER AND STOUGHTON
LONDON   SYDNEY   AUCKLAND   TORONTO

British Library Cataloguing in Publication Data

Duggan, Margaret
  Runcie: the making of an Archbishop. –
  (Hodder Christian paperback)
  1. Runcie, Robert   2. Church of England –
  Bishops – Biography
  I. Title
  283'.092'4   BX5199.R8/

ISBN 0-340-37318-0

Contents

	Introduction	9
1.	Crown Appointments	13
2.	The Role and the Church	30
3.	Choosing an Archbishop	40
4.	Early Days	50
5.	Growing Up	63
6.	The Scots Guards	81
7.	Oxford, Cambridge and Ordination	102
8.	Back to Cambridge	122
9.	Cuddesdon – I	139
10.	Cuddesdon – II	164
11.	St Albans – I	189
12.	St Albans – II	212
13.	Lambeth – I	238
14.	Lambeth – II	264
	Postscript	292
	Index	314

Illustrations

Robert Alexander Kennedy Runcie
Wedding Day, 5 September 1957
Lieutenant R. A. K. Runcie
The newly-consecrated Bishop of St Albans with Archbishop Michael Ramsey and Bishop Frank Cocks[1]
Captain of the Bishop of St Albans' XI[4]
Anglican-Orthodox conversation at St Albans
With Lindy, James and Rebecca in 1979[2]
Enthronement at Canterbury on 25 March 1980[3]
With Cardinal Basil Hume and the Bishop of Bedford
Meeting the Pope for the first time in Accra in 1980[5]
Visiting Northern Ireland with Richard Chartres and Terry Waite
In China, the first visit of an Archbishop of Canterbury[6]
Greeting HRH the Duchess of Kent in St Paul's Cathedral after the Falklands service[3]
With a patient at St Joseph's Hospice for the dying
Silver Wedding Anniversary in 1982[2]

ACKNOWLEDGEMENTS
1 Keystone Press Agency
2 Robert Miles
3 Press Association
4 Echo & Post Ltd, Hemel Hempstead
5 Church Information Office
6 Central Press Photos Ltd

Acknowledgements

One cannot write a book like this without drawing on the help of a great number of people, and it would be impossible for me to list everyone who has responded with kindness and generosity to my requests for information. Many are mentioned in the text, and I hope they will take that as an acknowledgement of the debt I owe them. But there are some whom I must specially thank.

The Archbishop's two sisters and brother, Mrs Kathleen Inglis, Mrs Marjorie Barker, and Mr Kenneth Runcie, all gave me invaluable help without which the early chapters of their brother's life would have been very thin indeed. I am also grateful to the Headmaster of Merchant Taylors School, Crosby, not least for providing me with a history of the school; and another book of great help in the first chapter was *Cantuar* by Dean Edward Carpenter.

Sir Hector Laing was splendidly kind in persuading former Scots Guards officers to contribute their memories of the young Lieutenant Runcie, while Mr William Whitelaw invited me to tea at the Home Office to add his memories. Even so, it would have been almost impossible to do justice to the Archbishop's war-time years without being able to draw on Mr David Erskine's history of *The Scots Guards 1919–1955* lent to me from the regimental headquarters archives.

Among the several bishops who have helped me I must particularly mention Bishop Hugh Montefiore of Birmingham, and Bishop Mark Santer of Kensington; while among the clergy Dr Owen Chadwick, Canon Eric James, Arch-deacon Peter Coleman, Canon David Paton, Peter Cornwell, Nicholas Coulton, Peter Goodrich in Crosby, and John Little in Gosforth, have all shown great patience. My thanks also go to Mr Derek Pattinson, the Secretary-General of the General Synod, Dr David Carey, former Registrar of the Province of Canterbury, and to Mr Christopher Martin of the Independent Broadcasting Authority.

Mrs Rosalind Runcie and James and Rebecca all kindly agreed to talk to me, and I met with friendly helpfulness from all the staff at Lambeth Palace. My debt is particularly great to Deaconess Inez Luckraft who tried so hard to keep spaces for me in the Archbishop's diary, to her successor, Ann Shirwill, who became an ally in the same cause, and to the Revd Richard Chartres and the Revd Christopher Hill. My friends in the Church Information Office (es-pecially Mrs Jackie Robinson who faithfully kept me sup-plied with press cuttings and texts of the Archbishop's addresses) and on the staff of the *Church Times* were also always ready with their help.

My special thanks go to my friend, the Revd Peter Wyld, who read the manuscript and suggested many detailed improvements; and to my brother, Peter Cansdale, for meticulously reading the proofs and helping me with the Index. Nor must I forget the Director of Church Army Housing, Mr Peter Naish, and my other colleagues, who generously put up with my preoccupation and absences in spirit and fact while working on this book. My husband has been consistently supportive; and I have had another sort of support from the Sister of the Community of St Mary the Virgin, Wantage, who has carried the writing of this book in her prayers.

Most of all, however, I am grateful to Archbishop Runcie himself who, even when he was obviously tired at the end of a long and demanding day, unfailingly met me and my ques-tions with kindness, humour, patience, and honesty. Without that honesty this would have been a much poorer book.

Introduction

One day a full and official biography will be written of Robert Cantuar: the one hundred and second Archbishop of Canterbury, Primate of All England, and spiritual leader of the world-wide Anglican Communion of Churches. This is not that book. It is the story so far of Robert Runcie, who was born in 1921 in the small Lancashire town of Crosby, and grew up with the natural abilities and wide experience which eventually led to his taking his place in the historical line of the Archbishops of Canterbury at a time when church, nation and the world at large were undergoing great stress, change and uncertainty. Such times cause many people, not only Christians, to cry out for moral and spiritual leadership and, whatever misgivings Robert Runcie the man might have, Robert Cantuar the archbishop must try to meet this need, and in a very different way from his predecessors. Never has the task been more personally demanding.

For thirteen centuries the Archbishops of Canterbury have had a leading role to play in the English nation, and for several of those centuries they were one of the most powerful influences in the land. Their history has been entwined with that of the English monarchy. When kings and queens ruled England, the archbishops were at their side advising, supporting and often quarrelling with their royal and earthly masters. On occasions the relationship between them led to dramas which shook the nation. The love that Henry II had for Thomas Becket, whom he made first his chancellor and then his archbishop, later turned to rage and resulted in Becket's murder. Five centuries later, Charles I and Archbishop William Laud were executed within three years of each other for their shared belief in the absolute authority of kings and bishops.

Those days are long past. The sovereign is now a constitutional monarch whose only political power is that of personal influence and the right to be consulted, to encourage and to warn. Meanwhile, as professional politicians have moved to fill the centre of the national stage, and the country has grown ever more secular, the archbishop has, perforce, stepped back to his original role of spiritual leader with no more than the moral authority of his own personality. But like the sovereign and all public figures, he is at the mercy of the media of mass communication with their cult of the personality. The Queen has learned to use this searchlight of public interest to strengthen her influence – moral in every sense of the word – with her people, and recent archbishops have begun to learn from her example. In particular, Robert Runcie has recognised the importance of the media in public life and, while he is not yet sure how far they can be used in any direct way to preach the gospel of Jesus Christ, his positive response to their constant demands has given him many opportunities to speak about his beliefs to many millions of people: congregations beyond the wildest dreams of his predecessors.

The fact that he can speak with lightness of touch and is not afraid to entertain as well as to preach means that he is watched and listened to with increasing interest. And however much he may deplore this emphasis on individual personality, he knows that in this media-oriented age it is the means by which public attention is attracted. People respond to celebrity and are far more inclined to listen to those whom they feel they know rather than to those they have never seen or heard of, however good and wise the latter's words might be – a human weakness which thrusts a heavy responsibility on any church leader in the public eye.

And public curiosity grows about the person behind the familiar face. It is a natural human desire to want to know more about the man or woman who has become almost a family friend through the television screen. And when that particular person so often speaks of the deeper things of life, and is asked to make moral judgments on issues that concern us all, then there is a deeper curiosity to know what the real person is like, and what is his experience of life which has given him his special wisdom. It is to try to satisfy that very natural and proper curiosity that this book has been written.

And because it is no longer possible to assume that anyone who speaks the English language and takes such a book as this off the library shelves will also have a working knowledge of the Church of England, I have tried, with the utmost brevity, to put the story of Archbishop Runcie into the context of both his job and its history, even though that history is now changing minute by minute. My doing so will give those readers who are knowledgeable Anglicans the opportunity to demonstrate their Christian capacity for forgiveness. For it is with rash selectivity that I have attempted in the first chapter to sketch the place of the archbishops in our national history from the time of St Augustine to the present day. I have done it in the belief that only with some knowledge of what went before will readers be able to understand the magnitude of many of the changes taking place in the church today. It is, however, an entirely optional chapter, and those readers who are interested in Robert Runcie and not in his hundred and one predecessors are welcome to skip it.

In the second chapter I have been still more subjective in trying to describe the Church of England as it now appears. This will make even greater demands on the Christian charity of my Anglican readers, for many would describe it very differently. It may also puzzle non-English Anglicans from other parts of the world where their own version of our common church seems tidier and better ordered. For the much-vaunted comprehensiveness of the Church of England is both our glory and our embarrassment. Only those of us who know it and love it, and believe it to be our particular path to God, can explain why it is possible to feel so strongly rooted in something which, to people of other churches and other faiths, seems so amorphous, so undisciplined, so *woolly*. Yet, from within, the Church of England and the whole Anglican Communion feels like a strong, supportive framework of the ancient Catholic faith which has proclaimed the Lordship of Christ through the centuries and still allows, with tolerant discipline, the freedom for each individual soul to explore the meaning of religious truth. It is a freedom which has sometimes been taken to lengths that have scandalised the more conservative members of the church. But the Church of England has always demanded faith, hope, much charity – and intellect. This does not preclude the 'simple faith' which is the support and gift of many millions of simple people. But it recognises that God made us intelligent beings and requires us to use the full capacity of our intelligence to discover his purpose.

Robert Runcie is right in the centre of this tradition. In the strange nuances of English churchmanship he is known as a radical Catholic, holding firmly to the Catholic faith and often conservative about its traditional practices, yet always with a questioning mind that is open to new insights about God and his meaning, and the interpretation of Christ's teaching in the modern world.

Chapter One

Crown Appointments

Portraits of nearly forty of his predecessors look down on Archbishop Runcie as he walks the wide corridors of his London home. He has learned to live with them, and the lives of many of those earlier archbishops fascinate him. He knows them so well that they are almost personal friends. Yet he has never quite lost his astonishment that he has joined their historic line and that one day his own picture will take its place among them.

The portraits hang on the walls of Lambeth Palace which has been the London residence of the Archbishops of Canterbury for eight hundred years. But the line of archbishops goes back six centuries more, to the year 597 when Pope Gregory the Great realised what had long been one of his dearest ambitions and sent missionaries to Britain. Their leader was Augustine, the prior of a Roman monastery. He came because he was told to and, half-way across France, he panicked and turned back rather than face the fierce barbarians that he and his small party of monks feared they would meet. But Gregory was firm and Augustine and his monks were obedient. They set out again and eventually landed at Thanet on the Kent coast.

After an exchange of messages the King of Kent came to meet them and good fortune was with the missionary enterprise. King Ethelbert's French wife was already a Christian, and Ethelbert was ready to listen to the claims of this mature and modern religion. Augustine's preaching met with overwhelming success. He converted the king and his followers, and he and his monks were allowed to establish themselves in Ethelbert's capital city of Canterbury where, said Bede, the ecclesiastical historian who wrote of these events a century later, they converted many who admired 'the simplicity of their innocent life and the sweetness of their heavenly doctrine'. A report was sent to Gregory that at the following Christmas they baptized no less than ten thousand new Christians.

As the city was the capital of the kingdom and the scene of this most promising start, it was natural that Augustine should make it his base. He briefly returned to France to be consecrated Archbishop of Canterbury. There were already three churches in the town, for Christianity had first come across the Channel in the second century, probably brought by the Roman army of occupation. But the Saxon invaders of the intervening centuries had brought their own gods, and had pushed the Christian remnants to the western and northern fringes of the British Isles and into Ireland. The Celtic church flourished but, over most of England, Christianity almost disappeared except in a few places like Canterbury where it was probably kept alive by traffic with Christians from across the Channel.

From the time of Ethelbert's conversion the history of England became increasingly intertwined with that of the Christian church. The start was slow and uncertain. The brilliant promise of Augustine's first few months was not sustained and the Christian light flickered and almost went out before it began to burn steadily. Ethelbert's son was not baptized; there was opposition from the bishops of the Christian remnant in the north; and Gregory's hope of establishing an archbishop from the Roman mission in York took thirty years to achieve. Gradually, however, the Roman influence grew, and the bishops from the north submitted to its new ways at a synod called at Whitby in 663.

Even so, the church was deeply divided, disorganised, and decimated by plague. The sixth Archbishop of Canterbury, Deusdedit, died in 664, and for five years no willing successor could be found. Then came a most unlikely figure to sort out the church in Britain, sent rather doubtfully by Pope

Vitalian; but he was to prove exactly what was needed.

If Robert Runcie could ask just one of his early predecessors to dinner, his choice would fall on Theodore for
whom he has always confessed a fascination. Theodore was
already sixty-six when he first landed in England in 668. He
was an Asiatic Greek, educated in Tarsus and Athens, and
known as a philosopher and fine classical scholar. He had
never been further west than Rome, and knew nothing of
the language or the ways of the English people. Yet, within
two years of his arrival, he had made a thorough visitation
of the whole of England, and had put in hand a series of
reforms to divide the land into dioceses, to appoint new
bishops, and to regulate the discipline of the church. He laid
the first real foundations of the church in England as we
know it today, and created an ecclesiastical organisation
long before there was a political one. It was an astonishing
achievement for an elderly man, and he continued to rule
the church with wisdom and vigour until he died in 690.

As the several kingdoms of England gradually became
one, the church grew stronger. In 803, when the midland
kingdom of Mercia was at the height of its power, an upstart
archbishopric in Lichfield led Pope Leo III to confirm, once
and for all, the primacy of the Archbishops of Canterbury
over all the other bishops. 'We give this in charge, and sign
it with the Sign of the Cross, that the archiepiscopal see,
from this time forward, never be . . . in any other place but
in the city of Canterbury where Christ's Church is; and
where the Catholic faith first shone forth in this island; and
where holy baptism was first established by Augustine.'
Even so, this edict never quite obliterated the memory that
it had been the original intention of Gregory the Great
that, after the death of Augustine, whichever of the two
archbishops, Canterbury or York, had been longer in his
post should be senior in authority. On numerous occasions
in the ensuing centuries rivalry flared up between them.

But the Archbishops of Canterbury, because of their
learning and their spiritual authority, soon became influential advisers to the king, and it was very much in the king's
interest that the choice of archbishop should be his. As

from the earliest days the chapter of monks at Canterbury continued formally to elect the primate, but it was nearly always the king who nominated whom they should elect. The Pope's approval was sent in the form of the *pallium*, a Y-shaped vestment of lamb's wool that the archbishop wore over his shoulders as a mark of his authority; and on occasion the Pope had his own ideas about the candidate. Through several centuries there were numerous wrangles between King, Pope, and the Canterbury monks over who should be elected.

Robert Runcie will remark ruefully that each of the three Roberts who has preceded him at Canterbury has been something of a disaster. Certainly the first one started his stormy career as the subject of a quarrel over his appointment. At the death of Archbishop Eadsige in 1051, the Canterbury chapter hastily elected their own choice, Elfric, who was a relation of the king's most dangerous and untrustworthy subject, Earl Godwin. King Edward (the Confessor) had already decided that he wanted an old friend from his days in exile in Normandy and, at a meeting of the Witan in London, he set aside Elfric and nominated Robert, Bishop of London, formerly Abbot of Jumièges. Robert naturally supported the king and the Norman interest and, in a popular rising in support of Godwin, was driven out of London. In the *Anglo-Saxon Chronicle* it is recorded that he and his companions 'slew and otherwise injured many young men, and made their way straight to the Naze where he [*sic*] took an unworthy ship and went immediately overseas, forsaking his pallium and all Christendom here in this land'. His place was taken by Stigand, who was excommunicated more than once, and who was finally deposed when William of Normandy invaded England.

The Norman Conquest strengthened the continental hold on the English church, and the Pope increasingly became a force in English political and ecclesiastical life. The coming of the Norman king was followed by the appointment of a succession of Norman-French archbishops and bishops who were more inclined than their predecessors to look to Rome for their authority. But the king usually got the archbishop he wanted. There was, however, at least one occasion when popular acclaim and the power of the barons forced a choice on the king. William Rufus, one of the most irreligious of all monarchs, held the see of Canterbury vacant for four years so that he could pocket its considerable revenues. But pressure from his subjects made him accept Anselm, Abbot of Bec, as archbishop in 1093. Anselm was already sixty years old and reluctant to take the job, but he was one of the great spiritual archbishops, and Robert Runcie still uses the prayers that he wrote, and keeps a book of them at his bedside.

The interest from all quarters in the appointment of the archbishop was by no means purely spiritual. Throughout the medieval period the church was the source of educated men to fill the positions of government. Increasingly the bishops, especially the two archbishops and the senior bishops of London and Winchester, were as much secular statesmen as spiritual leaders; and the prince-bishop of Durham was expected to maintain his own army to keep the Scots at bay. From the middle of the fourteenth century until the Reformation two hundred years later, no less than ten out of the fourteen archbishops were also chancellors of England, next in power to the king himself; while nearly all the senior bishops held a variety of high secular offices. It was therefore politically essential to the king that these bishops, and the Archbishop of Canterbury in particular, should be men of his own choosing, whether or not his choice coincided with that of the Pope.

But the king's was not the only interest in the matter. The chapter at Canterbury had from the beginning traditionally elected the archbishop and occasionally they wanted more than just a formal part in the appointment. The bishops, too, were personally concerned in looking for a leader who would protect their ecclesiastical privileges and the church's fast-accumulating wealth from encroachment by the state. And the leading laymen of the time, the barons, the bureaucrats and the place-seekers, all had their preferences.

The various factions formed alliances with or against the king or Pope according to their interests. Occasionally there was a stalemate as the king maintained a long interregnum, not only as a way of delaying the election of a candidate not of his choice, but also because a large part of the archbishop's substantial income then reverted to the royal treasury. Sometimes the king simply insisted on having his way as, for instance, when Henry II chose his friend and chancellor, Thomas Becket, who was not even in priest's orders. Becket had very hurriedly to be ordained priest before he could be consecrated Archbishop of Canterbury.

On other occasions the Pope promoted his own candidate. When, in 1205, the Canterbury monks disagreed with King John's nomination, they secretly elected and dispatched to Rome a candidate of their own. But Innocent III refused to endorse either their choice or the king's, and ordered them to elect Stephen Langton, a distinguished English theologian at the University of Paris. The king was so enraged with the Pope's high-handedness that he refused to accept him, with the result that Langton spent six years in exile in France while the Pope put the whole of England under an interdict which deprived the people of all the sacraments and ministrations of the church until King John submitted.

In 1353 the Archbishop of Canterbury's precedence over the Archbishop of York was permanently established, bringing to an end years of sporadic quarrelling, even though the Archbishops of Canterbury had consistently claimed the primacy, not only as St Augustine's successors, but also because theirs was the privilege of crowning the king, which gave them a unique relationship with the monarchy. This claim of precedence had been regularly contested by successive Archbishops of York with constant appeals to Rome. The quarrel culminated in a disgraceful scene at a council in Westminster in the twelfth century when the Archbishop of York tried to squeeze into Canterbury's place and finished up in a scuffle sitting on his brother archbishop's lap. The matter was finally settled – to everyone's relief – when Simon Islip of Canterbury agreed with John Thoresby of York that the latter would bear the title of Primate of England while the Archbishop of Canterbury would be Primate of All England: and so the distinction has remained.

By the end of the fifteenth century the tensions which were to lead to the Reformation were already strong. Increasing numbers of educated men recognised the need for drastic reforms in the church. Too much of the church's great wealth went on fat livings for the clergy, and too little of the church's daily life seemed to have anything to do with its origins in the life, death and resurrection of Jesus Christ. Many of the monasteries which had once been centres of holiness and charitable work had become worldly and corrupt, and the commercial traffic in holy relics and indulgences, of which Luther was to complain to such great effect, was only one of the symptoms of a church that had lost its way.

When the storm of the Reformation blew up in England, precipitated by Henry VIII's desire to divorce the wife who had been unable to give him a son, and to marry again in the hope of securing the succession, the Archbishop of Canterbury, William Warham, was a sad and humiliated man. He was helpless in the hands of Thomas Wolsey, the most powerful subject England has ever known. As chancellor, Wolsey held the reins of secular government. As Archbishop of York, and at the same time holding the two senior bishoprics of Durham and Winchester, he had enormous ecclesiastical power (and wealth) which became supreme when he was also made Cardinal and Papal Legate. As the Pope's representative in England he claimed the right to supersede anything that Warham might do, even in Warham's own province. The Archbishop of Canterbury became little more than a cipher, and it is ironical that it was in an Archbishop of York that the arrogation of power and wealth by an archbishop should reach its apex and its culmination. By the time of Wolsey's downfall and his unhappy death, both the theological and the nationalistic forces of the Reformation were well under way.

The king was pushing through his divorce, not only from Catherine, but from the Pope; and it was all too much for the weak and traditionally conservative Warham to restrain. When, in 1531, Henry added to his title (granted by the Pope) of 'King and Defender of the Faith' the further title, 'Protector and only Supreme Head of the English Church', the most that the unhappy Warham could do was to add the saving clause, 'as far as the law of Christ allows'. The following year he unequivocally submitted to the king's demands that the ancient Convocation of the bishops and clergy could not be summoned without a royal writ, and no new canons could be promulgated without royal assent. Then he died.

The king's choice for a new archbishop fell upon Thomas Cranmer, an academic theologian for whom the principle of royal supremacy was part of his theological understanding. As a scholar he was in touch with the reformers in Germany, and also with the humanist and historical approach of Erasmus to the Bible. He was a scholarly, sensitive man, destined to be the first architect of the post-Reformation church in England, and its first archbishop-martyr. He was summoned back from Mantua where he had recently been sent as ambassador to the Emperor Charles V, and he was duly elected by the monks at Canterbury, and the necessary papal bulls were procured. But at his consecration, when he took the required oath of obedience to the Pope, he made a formal assertion that he did not consider such an oath binding if it was against the law of God and conflicted with his loyalty to the king.

In 1534 Parliament declared Henry to be the only 'supreme head on earth of the Church of England', an act which finally repudiated any allegiance to Rome. Henry appointed a layman, Thomas Cromwell, as his Vicar-General, and gave him political precedence over the archbishop. Cromwell set about methodically suppressing the monasteries, reorganising the dioceses, and issuing injunctions that a Bible should be placed in every church, that registers of births, marriages and deaths should be kept, and that the clergy should be more disciplined about their work. Cranmer, finding his authority usurped, set to work on translating the liturgy from Latin into English and compiling a new prayer book to be used by the common people. His *Book of Common Prayer*, though revised in detail several times, became the basis of Anglican belief for the next four centuries.

The portrait of Cranmer hanging in Lambeth Palace shows him with the long white beard which he grew after the death of Henry VIII. He looks an old and apprehensive man. Like Robert Runcie, he had been a university teacher at Cambridge, and he had never wanted to be in the public eye. But his theological opinions, once expressed over a dinner table, had brought him to the notice of an overweening king, and had catapulted him into a painful national role which led eventually to his martyrdom at the stake in the reign of Queen Mary.

He had been deprived of the archbishopric, and he was succeeded by the equally sensitive and scholarly aristocrat, Reginald Pole, who gazes serenely out of his portrait next to Cranmer's. Pole was ordained priest the day before Cranmer was burned at the stake, and was consecrated Archbishop of Canterbury the day after. His efforts to turn the clock back, and to reunite the English church with Rome, were not helped by Mary's political ineptitude and her ill-judged marriage with Philip of Spain, nor by the burnings of three hundred Protestants as heretics. Mary and Pole died on the same day in 1558, leaving the way clear for Mary's half-sister, Elizabeth, to become queen and the second architect of the post-Reformation Church of England. She also chose a scholarly, tolerant man as her first archbishop. Matthew Parker was the first Archbishop of Canterbury to be consecrated without reference to Rome. He was elected by the Canterbury chapter, and consecrated by four bishops in Lambeth Palace chapel on 17 December 1559. His bones are now interred in that chapel before the altar.

Elizabeth had a fierce regard for the mood, aspirations, and unity of the English people. Her overriding ambition was the harmonious well-being and prosperity of the nation. She moderated her father's claim from 'supreme head' to 'supreme governor' of the Church of England, and implemented a regime which, while requiring outward conformity in religious observance, did not question too closely the individual conscience. The Prayer Book published in her reign maintained the essential Catholic faith but, with its delicate ambiguity at the most controversial points of theology, contrived to be acceptable to the majority of the English people. And in Matthew Parker, and later in John Whitgift, she found Archbishops of Canterbury who could guide the church in a path that was as comprehensive as the strong religious passions of the time allowed.

But all did not go smoothly. In the following hundred years, under succeeding archbishops, the Church of England tried to work out its position as a happy mean between Roman Catholicism and Genevan Protestantism. When the pendulum swung too far to the rigidly high Catholic ambitions of Charles I and Archbishop Laud, the country exploded into civil war with a violent swing in the opposite direction, the execution of the king and archbishop, and the abolition of all bishops. But the strict joylessness of the Puritans did not suit the English temperament and, almost by common consent, the king in the person of Charles II was reinstated, and the Church of England restored. Two years later, in 1662, the *Book of Common Prayer* was revised and republished in the form that was to be used by the church for the next three hundred years. It enshrined the doctrine and ethos of the Church of England. Together with the Authorised Version of the Bible which had been published in 1611, it not only shaped the spirituality of the English people (and, as the years went on, a growing number of Anglicans overseas), but penetrated and enriched the English language as no other books have ever done.

The Church of England came to look upon itself as the 'middle way', keeping, as the Preface to the Prayer Book said of the liturgy, 'the mean between the two extremes, of too much stiffness in refusing, and of too much easiness in admitting any variation'. And when, in 1688, James II went too far in admitting variation by taking the first steps to re-establish the Roman Catholic Church in England in opposition to Parliament and the established law of the land, it was he who was defeated. Archbishop Sancroft, who looks so competent and strong in his Lambeth portrait, resisted him 'not from any want of tenderness towards dissenters, but because the (king's) declaration, being founded on such dispensing power as may at pleasure set aside all laws ecclesiastical and civil, appears to me illegal'. For this Sancroft was committed to the Tower, and later stood trial with six other bishops in Westminster Hall. But their cause was a popular one and, when they were acquitted, they were greeted rapturously by the people. However, after James II had fled the country, Sancroft's stern principles also led him to refuse to recognise William and Mary as joint king and queen in James's place, and in 1690 he was deprived of his archbishopric and lived his remaining years in retirement.

As the religious passion which had racked the previous two centuries subsided, the reaction was a national compromise in which religious 'enthusiasm' was to be avoided at all costs. The archbishops, Whigs to a man, took their place in society as well-to-do landowners of high moral principles, given to benevolence and hospitality, especially at Lambeth Palace. There, clergy and laity were lavishly entertained, and thirty poor people a day were given beef, bread, and twopence at the palace gate. The archbishops lived in the style of dukes and, at court, took precedence over all other peers but princes of the royal blood. In their Lambeth portraits they sit plump and complacent in their close-curled wigs and extravagant lawn sleeves.

Their family backgrounds were varied. Though a few were nobly born, the majority came from the trading and middle classes. They reached their high office through ambition and influence as much as diligence. Only a few of them maintained the Anglican tradition of sound learning and scholarship, though most of them were genuinely pious and conscientious according to the standards of the time. They sat, together with the Archbishop of York and (at that time) all the diocesan bishops, in the House of Lords and, though they no longer held the key positions of national influence that their predecessors had once known, because their votes were important to the government, so was their selection.

Ever since the reign of Queen Elizabeth, the sovereign had increasingly taken the advice of his or her chief minister in the appointment of archbishops and bishops and, at the coming of the Hanoverians (with George I who had no knowledge of the English language or the English church), the nomination had passed almost wholly to the Prime Minister, with the king doing no more than giving his consent. Only once did a king insist upon his own candidate for archbishop in opposition to his first minister's wishes. George III was determined to have his friend, Charles Manners Sutton, Dean of Windsor, at Canterbury. Before William Pitt could impose his choice, the king called for his horse and rode to Windsor to tell the dean that the archbishopric was his, thus pre-empting any action his Prime Minister could take.

The ancient forms were still adhered to. The sovereign commanded the dean and chapter at Canterbury to elect the nominated candidate by sending a Letter Recommendatory together with the *congé d'élire* (permission to elect), a custom which went back to the time of King John in the thirteenth century; and the chapter had to elect the king's nomination under pain of the ill-defined penalties of *praemunire*. Then the Royal Assent was given, the election formally confirmed, and only then could the archbishop be enthroned in the marble chair of St Augustine in Canterbury Cathedral. However, in the eighteenth and early nineteenth centuries several of the archbishops were enthroned by proxy and rarely, if ever, visited their archiepiscopal see.

The eighteenth century is not one of which the Church of England is generally proud, but during it began the great missionary expansion overseas as devoted Christians carried the gospel to the colonies, often at the cost of their lives. At home there was, as there always had been, much individual piety and Christian holiness which longed for a reform of the worldly and politically acquiescent church. John Wesley and the rise of Methodism brought a new seriousness to Christian belief and practice, and it was an indictment of the established church that it could not hold the new wine of the 'Methodists' within its structure but allowed them, contrary to all Wesley's own intentions, to break away and form a separate church. The Evangelicals of the 'Clapham sect' in the early nineteenth century fared better, with their renewed emphasis on biblical teaching, private prayer, and social caring. They not only stayed within the church, but exerted a national influence out of all proportion to their number. Their most famous member, William Wilberforce, led the twenty-year campaign to abolish slavery.

The rise of the Oxford Movement in the eighteen-thirties came as a Catholic reaction both to the torpidity of the ecclesiastical hierarchy, and to the Protestant emphasis of the Evangelical movements. It sought, against almost hysterical public opposition, to restore the high-church ideals of the seventeenth century and, later, many of the Catholic beliefs and practices of the medieval and primitive church.

The Archbishops of Canterbury did not readily respond to these winds of change. The bishops in general were at the nadir of their popularity with the people, who saw them as wealthy, complacent and resistant to reform. Archbishop William Howley, like most of the other bishops, was conservative by nature and opposed most of the political changes that were taking place, including the Reform Bill. But he was realistic enough to go along with the setting up of a commission in 1835 to enquire into ecclesiastical abuses, and he rapidly became, with the encouragement of Bishop Blomfield of London, its most energetic and determined member. The commission soon became permanent and established as the Ecclesiastical Commissioners. It was ruthless in its work of reforming the boundaries and administration of the bishoprics and cathedrals so that the money could be distributed more equitably to reduce the huge and scandalous discrepancies between the princely lifestyle of the bishops and that of the poverty-stricken parsons. Howley's own income of £30,000 was halved, and he made drastic cuts in his style of living. No longer did outriders trot beside his coach when he went out; and there was no more extravagant hospitality on public days at Lambeth Palace.

In 1852 the Convocations, the ancient provincial assemblies of bishops and clergy which had been prorogued since 1717, were again allowed to meet so that the church could discuss its own affairs. Everywhere standards were beginning to rise. Sunday worship in parish churches was taking on a new reverence and dignity, and Holy Communion was being celebrated more often. Religious orders were beginning again, many of them working among the very poor. Church schools were improved, and many new ones started. Training colleges were established to provide properly trained teachers. And the professional training of the clergy, which had been almost non-existent apart from their university degrees and the efforts of a few individual bishops, was for the first time put on a proper footing by the foundation of nearly a dozen theological colleges.

In the late nineteenth century the bishops were again men of ability and scholarship, determined to bring their flocks to a greater understanding of Christ and their social responsibilities. But there was a growing desire that the church should be able to choose its own bishops and archbishops. It gained strength in the twentieth century as church and state steadily separated and the number of churchgoers who had attended Sunday worship out of social convention began to drop away, leaving increasingly serious-minded and committed Christians.

As frank secularism grew, concern was voiced at the anomaly of a system in which a Prime Minister who might not be a church-goer, or even a Christian, was in a position to select the names of those who would be appointed by the sovereign to the high offices of church leadership. The anomaly was even more acute in the case of the Archbishop of Canterbury who was not only the English primate, but leader of a growing world-wide communion of churches. If it was inappropriate that an English Prime Minister, not necessarily an Anglican, should *de facto* choose the spiritual leader of the many millions of English Christians, it became as time went on even more of an anomaly that he should at the same time be choosing the *primus inter pares* of several hundred bishops of many colours and nationalities spread through sixty countries of the world.

That the system usually worked well, and that there were few disasters, was not enough assurance that the system would always work, particularly if, in a time of volatile politics, England were to have a succession of non-Christian or even anti-church and republican Prime Ministers. The church as a whole had been shocked into facing these issues when it had attempted to revise its own Prayer Book in 1927–8. The revision had been going on for twenty years with the intention of bringing more order to the church's worship, for it had fallen into a state of chaotic variety, with Anglo-Catholic churches aping Rome, Evangelical churches indistinguishable from Nonconformist chapels, and virtually every church taking its own way to shorten, simplify or modernise the seventeenth-century services as they were printed in the Prayer Book by leaving out the long homilies and exhortations which belonged to another age.

A modest revision and simplification, in line with current practice in most lively and non-extreme churches, was approved in 1927 by large majorities in both the Convocations and the Church Assembly, and eventually in the House of Lords. But, when it came to the House of Commons, a well-organised group of Evangelicals orchestrated its defeat in which even Nonconformists and non-churchmen voted. A few alterations were made to the book, but it was again defeated and the church humiliated in just the same way the following year.

This residual tyranny wielded by Parliament, especially in the appointment of the church's leadership, was also a growing embarrassment in ecumenical relations. Ever since the World Interdenominational Missionary Conference had been held in Edinburgh in 1910, Christian divisions had begun to break down and, as hopes grew that the churches would gradually lose their mutual suspicion and ancient bitterness and grow together in unity, it became clear that, for both the Protestant Free Churches and the Roman Catholic Church, eventual reunion within the Church of England would be a more viable proposition if the Church of England did not have its peculiar relationship with the state.

It was a long battle fought through the church's governing bodies. It had begun in the Convocations and then, when the Church Assembly of bishops, clergy and laity was brought into being by the Enabling Act of 1919, the debate continued there. By the time the Assembly's successor, the

General Synod, was inaugurated in 1970, with more real power delegated to it by Parliament than the Assembly had ever had, things had begun to move.

The first achievement in the field of episcopal appointments had come about with the institution of vacancy-in-see committees in the late 1960s. As soon as a bishopric fell vacant a committee was appointed of clergy and lay representatives of the diocese who met together with the Prime Minister's and the archbishop's secretaries for appointments. Together they discussed the needs of the diocese and the sort of man – perhaps even naming a candidate – who was required as its bishop. This gave the diocese, even in the case of Canterbury, the chance to speak corporately and directly to the men who were to advise both the Prime Minister and the archbishop in their separate recommendations to the sovereign. But it did not go far enough. Nobody doubted that the scrupulous care of the two secretaries and their discreet consultations, not only with the vacancy-in-see committees but with every interested party, would result in judicious and wise advice. The trouble was that there was no guarantee that their advice, in the last resort, would be taken. So the matter was again brought forward in the General Synod, and a legislative process started in 1973 by which the church was to ask for a direct say in the recommendation of its leaders to the Crown.

Alternative schemes were proposed. There were many clergy and laity who wanted the same straightforward election of a bishop by the clergy and people of the diocese as takes place (not always successfully) in other churches of the Anglican Communion. Others favoured some sort of electoral college. And there were quite a few who wanted to leave well alone a system that had always seemed to work tolerably well.

The legislative process ground on until, in 1976, a compromise was reached with the then Prime Minister, Mr James Callaghan, which was accepted by the General Synod. In addition to the vacancy-in-see committees, a Crown Appointments Commission would be set up consisting of the Archbishops of Canterbury and York, three clergy and three lay members of the General Synod, the two appointments secretaries and four representatives of the vacant diocese. The Archbishop of Canterbury would chair the commission except when his own post was under consideration. On those occasions the chairman would be a communicant lay member of the Church of England appointed by the Prime Minister and, to represent the interest of the other churches of the Anglican Communion, the Secretary of the Anglican Consultative Council would also be a member.

This commission would meet to consider each episcopal vacancy, and it would agree two names – in order of preference if the members wished – to submit to the Prime Minister. It was generally understood that the Prime Minister would then submit the preferred name to the sovereign. That meant that, in the future, any new bishop or archbishop would be the first (or possibly the second) choice of senior representatives of the whole Church of England meeting for discussion and prayer under the guidance of the Holy Spirit. For the first time in well over a thousand years the people of the English church were able, through their elected representatives, to choose their own bishops and archbishops.

Chapter Two

The Role and the Church

On 5 June 1979, Dr Donald Coggan, the hundred and first Archbishop of Canterbury, announced that he would retire the following January. He had just returned from an official visit to Eastern Europe, and had held a press conference in Church House, the administrative headquarters of the church in Westminster, to answer journalists' questions about his tour. But any news that he had brought back from Eastern Europe was entirely overshadowed and lost to posterity by the announcement that the press officer made as soon as the Archbishop had left the building and escaped from further questions. Dr Coggan, who would shortly be celebrating his seventieth birthday, was going to retire on 26 January 1980, five years and two days after he had taken office.

Speculation about his successor began immediately. The first short list of likely bishops appeared in the *Church Times* three days later, and was quickly taken up by the secular newspapers.

Top of the list was the Archbishop of York, Dr Stuart Blanch who, at sixty-one, was the oldest. In bookmaker's terms he was bound to be the favourite because, in the current century, no less than four of the six archbishops to be enthroned at Canterbury had come there by way of the northern primacy. The next most frequently quoted name was that of Bishop Robert Runcie, aged fifty-seven, who was known to be very popular in his diocese of St Albans, and to have strong links with the Eastern Orthodox Churches. The most distinguished intellect was that of Dr John Habgood, Bishop of Durham; while Dr Graham Leonard, Bishop of Truro, and one of the leading opponents of the ordination of women (an issue that was currently racking the church) was a favourite with the newly-invigorated 'Catholic' wing of the church. The well-liked Bishop Ronald Bowlby of Newcastle was rather more of an outsider, as was the Bishop of Liverpool, David Sheppard, beloved of the media because of his many good qualities and – not least – because he once captained England against the Australians in Test cricket.

The following Sunday the Dean of St Paul's Cathedral in London, Alan Webster, who was known to be a member of the new Crown Appointments Commission, preached from his pulpit about the need for both the Church of England and the Anglican Communion to find a man with a new vision. For the first time, he declared, the church itself had a responsibility for its own choice. For the first time since the Reformation, men from outside England would be considered. The challenge was enormous.

The church needed a leader, he said, 'to turn the attention of Christian people to the great human needs of courage in the face of suffering and death, to a dynamic concern over injustice, human rights, and the dangerous poverty of so much of the world'. He talked of the major causes of division in the church at that time: of the defeat of the scheme for reunion with the Methodists in 1972 and the heavy weather that had been made of all subsequent negotiations for unity with other churches. He spoke of the bitter defeat of the proposal to ordain women in the Church of England, despite the fact that they were already being ordained in the Anglican churches in New Zealand, Canada, the United States, and Hong Kong.

'Men and women of goodwill have much more in common than the denominational divisions suggest,' the dean said.

We must remain a church and not become a tight sect. Can a new leader be found who will inject into the Anglican Communion a dynamic tolerance so that the provinces and dioceses which do ordain women can work in trust and goodwill alongside dioceses which do not? Can the Crown Appointments Commission find an outstanding man who can hearten the church, respond to the intellectual vitality of the modern world, and fire our country and our Commonwealth, where the Anglican Communion is still strong, with the conviction that God needs his church for the sake of his kingdom?

As the world moves from a technological age, where for the first time we all recognise that science alone cannot provide the answers, to a gentler and more humane ecological age, we need a man who can unite not only Christians, but millions of people who never occupy pews. They, too, hope that from the Christian tradition there may come vision and action.

It was a tall order. The dean was asking for a man who could fulfil three quite distinct roles and bring a fresh updated vigour to them all. He had forcibly made the point that the church needed a leader to guide it through a time fraught with serious dissension on a number of emotional issues which were provoking stronger party feelings than there had been for some years. The ordination of women, reunion with various other churches, remarriage in church after divorce, and the acceptance of homosexuality as a natural, if minority, sexual orientation, were all issues on which church members were deeply divided. In addition, there was a groundswell of restiveness about the new services which had been authorised as an alternative to the much-loved *Book of Common Prayer*, and there was also the increasing strain of inflation which was putting severe pressure on every part of the church's organisation.

Overseas there was the archbishop's role vis-à-vis the independent world-wide churches of the Anglican Communion. The Archbishop of Canterbury no longer has jurisdiction over most of them, but he is recognised as the focus of unity. By his visits he maintains the family links between the churches, and he is presiding chairman of the Lambeth Conference, the ten-yearly meeting of the bishops from all four hundred Anglican dioceses.

But the Archbishop of Canterbury is also one of the handful of church leaders in the world who still has – if he has the personal qualities to claim it – a moral influence beyond the members of his own communion. Increasingly in recent years, with daily secular life filled with tensions and the apparently insoluble problems of political, social, and personal relationships, the mass media have looked for prophets and spokesmen capable of speaking with some authority on the intransigent issues of the day. The archbishop, regarded as the leading churchman in England, is in constant demand to say something of significance on all manner of occasions; and if he himself wants to take the initiative in a way that is genuinely newsworthy, he can be sure of a wide audience. Nor is he a prophet only in his own country. He is readily accorded the status of an international statesman and can expect, if he so wishes, to be welcomed by national leaders in almost any part of the world, and to have ambassadors and diplomats calling regularly at his front door.

The time could come, and some people predicted that it would be on this occasion in 1979, when a non-Englishman would be brought from overseas to Canterbury. A name frequently suggested as Dr Coggan's successor was that of Archbishop Ted Scott, Primate of the Anglican Church in Canada. But, as many people pointed out, if such an appointment were made, it would be appropriate to separate the role of the Archbishop of Canterbury as focus of the Anglican Communion from that of the Primate of All England. The principle of having indigenous bishops has now been firmly established in those countries which were once British colonies with British expatriate bishops. The same principle of having a primate who shares the culture of his people should hold good in England, where only a native could begin to understand the web of historical complexities in which the church is caught.

For, in any human terms, the Church of England is a most awkward institution either to guide or to lead. Within its membership there is a divergence of belief which passes the understanding of almost any other ecclesiastical organisation. Its comprehensiveness has long been a cherished tradition, and it was firmly established at the time of the sixteenth-century Reformation that the Church of England was both Catholic *and* reformed, meaning to retain what was good and true of the old, but discarding many of the accretions which seemed to be distorting the Christian gospel as it had been handed on by the early church. There was a determination to keep the Catholic faith in a form that would both be understood by contemporary people, and be recognisable to the Christians of the first four centuries of the Christian era. And this was very carefully spelt out in the small print of the prefaces to the *Book of Common Prayer*, with their emphasis on tradition, unity and concord rather than on 'innovation and new-fangleness which is always to be eschewed'.

This determination to be both Catholic and Protestant, with changing emphases on one or the other during the history of the last four centuries, has led to a wide variety of churchmanship among Anglicans. At one extreme there are still Anglo-Catholics maintaining traditional Catholic practices which have long disappeared from the Roman Church. At the other extreme are ardent Protestants, suspicious of all taints of 'popery', and clinging passionately to the Thirty-Nine Articles, the sixteenth-century doctrinal formulae of the Prayer Book, as though they were written yesterday. (For most Anglicans, certain of the Articles which were written at the height of the anti-papal controversies of the Reformation are now an embarrassment: for the last century the clergy have been required to assent to them only in a very general way. As they are bound into the *Book of Common Prayer*, which remains sacrosanct, there is no immediate possibility of revising them; and so they are left, perhaps in the hope that, if they are ignored long enough, they may disappear of their own accord!)

But both extremes are small minorities. Most Anglican churchgoers are to be found somewhere between the two, usually falling in quite happily with whatever practices in the spectrum of churchmanship their parish church happens to favour. For the English are not a theologically-minded people and, though there is a wide variation in theology behind most of the variations of practice, the majority of Anglicans accept it as quirks of habit that some of their parish churches call the Holy Communion service the Mass, light candles in front of saints' statues, use private confession, incense, and have six candles on the altar; while others speak of the Lord's Supper, prefer non-liturgical family services with lots of vigorous hymns, and have no incense or candles at all. Most parish churches, however, settle for the middle way: they call their main Sunday service the Parish Eucharist, they use one or other of the new authorised alternative services, and settle for two candles on the altar.

But variations in church practice, as demonstrated by these outward, visible and largely unimportant symbols, form only one of the spectra in the Anglican church. When it comes to belief, the range is as wide. At one extreme are academic theologians, clergy and laity, whose Christian thinking has followed the radical path so far that almost every item in the Creed, the basic statement of belief, has become intellectually unacceptable as it stands; yet they would still claim their place in the Church of England. At the other extreme are fundamentalist Evangelicals, who believe in the Bible as the literal word of God by which all belief and practice must be tested. But again these two extremes are tiny minorities, and the great bulk of Anglicans hold to a personal and real belief (albeit rather woolly in its theological definitions) in the existence of God; the life, death and resurrection of Jesus Christ as told in the Bible; and in the sacraments and traditions of the church. It is the essence of Anglicanism (a view that was shared by Queen Elizabeth I) that the church offers a broad and stable framework inside which each mature Christian conducts his own spiritual search for the meaning of religious truth and the reality of Christian love.

Different again is the spectrum of moral views. Faced with human problems, particularly those to do with sexuality, the radical will put his emphasis on the importance of loving human relationships, and might condone fornication or homosexual practice where he believes true and self-giving love to be concerned. But the conservative will stand doggedly by the traditional moral rules that a sexual relationship is only permissible within marriage and nowhere else; and he tends to have a similar black-and-white attitude towards other traditionally listed sins.

Meanwhile, in and out of the pews, there is a deep political diversity. Many of the laity – and clergy too – regard the church as a bastion of conservatism in all senses; not only of moral duty, law and order, and the values of middle-class family life, but of Cranmer's Prayer Book, polished brass, and an exclusively male priesthood. They look to the church to preserve a secure and familiar world, and they are made uncomfortable and unhappy by a generation of Christians who believe Jesus to have been a social revolutionary proclaiming justice for the underprivileged, and arguably ready to countenance violence in achieving that justice. The Jesus of such Christians is often no stranger to the teachings of Marx, and his followers are ready to repudiate the traditional church with its beautiful buildings, its treasures, its ancient liturgy and its ordered ministry. For them the Christian Aid poster is a more important aid to worship than stained glass, and folk hymns and guitars more 'real' than an organ and traditional choir. But again, such Christians represent the other end of a spectrum, and the Anglican consensus falls somewhere in between.

This great diversity of Anglicanism suggests that it is the religious expression of English culture, a wide variety of views and eccentricities held together by a broad tolerance, respect for the individual, a liking for a certain formality of ceremony, and – until recent years, anyway – a love for the literary as well as the spiritual qualities of the *Book of Common Prayer* and the Authorised Version of the Bible.

So it is all these practising Anglicans, with all their shades and nuances of practice and belief, together with all the English people whose church allegiance rarely goes further than 'C of E' on official forms and a vague attachment to their parish church for weddings and funerals, who come under the jurisdiction and guidance of the Archbishop of Canterbury. It is no wonder, then, that those who are responsible for the good order of the church hope and look for a man who will have a light but sure touch as he stands in the middle of these many tensions. The diversity of the Anglican church, both in England and overseas, is perhaps the one distinctive characteristic that all its members hold equally precious. The Archbishop must cherish this tradition while being the centre of its unity.

But those who are to select the next Archbishop of Canterbury must take his wider responsibilities into account. Not only is he generally regarded, particularly by the mass media, as the spokesman for the nation's morals; he is an important figure on many royal and state occasions. At times of national thanksgiving or mourning he will be expected to play a leading role. He has a special relationship with the royal family, and the assumption is that he will officiate at their baptisms, weddings, and funerals as well as being called upon for his spiritual advice.

And there is his international role. For it is a curious fact that the distinctively English church which grew out of the sixteenth-century Reformation has transplanted remarkably well all round the world.* To a large extent it followed the flag: missionary work was strongest and the resulting churches largest in those countries that were once part of the British Empire. But, even there, the Anglican churches have since become naturalised, with their own liturgies (based on the *Book of Common Prayer*) and their own government and bishops. While in North America, Australia and New Zealand there may still be cultural characteristics which link Anglicans with the England from which many of their ancestors emigrated, the same can hardly be said of the Anglican church in Korea, in Polynesia, in the countries of East Africa where the numbers of Anglicans are growing faster than anywhere else in the world, or in the tiny Anglican church in Iran whose bishop and members bravely

* But not in the European countries where the numbers of Anglicans have always been tiny, and mostly confined to embassies and chaplaincies where expatriates from England are gathered. This is because of the long-held Anglican view that the Church of England has no business proselytising in countries where another Christian church is active.

withstood persecution in the revolution which followed the expulsion of the Shah in 1979. What holds them all together is that they are 'in communion with the See of Canterbury', and they hold the Archbishop of Canterbury in a special esteem.

With this responsibility, and with the increasing ease and speed of modern travel, Archbishop Donald Coggan and his predecessor, Archbishop Michael Ramsey, travelled extensively during their primacies. They not only visited Anglican dioceses, but met the leaders of other churches, including the Pope and the Orthodox patriarchs, and the national and political leaders of many diverse countries. When Dr Ramsey was travelling in South Africa in 1970 he had a private interview with Prime Minister Vorster in which he spoke his mind on the injustices of *apartheid* in that country. On another occasion, when he was in Chile, he tackled President Pinochet about the number of political prisoners held in Chilean gaols. Dr Coggan similarly had private conversations with many heads of state, including Mrs Ghandi of India, President Bhutto of Pakistan, and the President of Ghana.

With such precedents in mind, therefore, it is important that any Archbishop of Canterbury should not only have a grasp of worldwide affairs, but should also be capable of learning the arts of diplomacy, and the skill of choosing the right moment to speak his mind about peace and international justice. There is the negative requirement of knowing how not to put a diplomatic foot wrong, and there is also almost unlimited scope for the gifted spiritual leader to intervene on the side of righteousness in areas of international human conflict. The role, played to its full, is an almost superhumanly demanding one, especially when one considers how small a personal staff and how tight a budget he must work with.

Those who were responsible in 1979 for the selection of Dr Coggan's successor were aware of all these needs, but inevitably they concentrated on the part that he must play as leader of the Church of *England*. Among the possible candidates they were looking for someone with outstanding qualities of leadership, and within the 'right' age-range. He must be neither so old that his years and energy would be limited, nor so young that – should he prove to be less than a paragon – he would wear out his welcome to the lasting damage of the church of which he was guardian. Broadly speaking, all the virtues of tact, strength, holiness, worldly wisdom, great physical stamina, and charisma were required in a man probably in his middle or late fifties. It was then necessary that he should be acceptable to the Prime Minister and the Queen.

Chapter Three

Choosing an Archbishop

The *Church Times* was very modest in its hopes for the next archbishop. In a leading article on 22 June 1979 it looked with gentlemanly envy at the personal triumphs of Pope John Paul II who had been in office for ten months and had just made his momentous first visit to his homeland of Poland.

> It is not an unmitigated tragedy [it said with just a tinge of sour grapes] that there does not appear to be any Anglican of the stature of the present Pope available for appointment. In these days an Archbishop of Canterbury would probably be doomed to frustration if he adopted the lifestyle of an ecclesiastical superstar. He is expected to be, and to be seen to be, a diocesan bishop among diocesan bishops, a chairman among chairmen, a preacher among preachers; not another Pope, not even another William Temple.

Meanwhile the secular press were giving their own advice. Even those papers which rarely carried church news except when it was bizarre or scandalous had views on the sort of primate the country needed.

> Pope John Paul has set a new standard [said the London *Evening News*]. Already Roman Catholics in this country have a charismatic leader in the person of Cardinal Hume. Anglicans, though led by worthy men who commanded

great respect, have not been blessed with exciting leadership since Archbishop William Temple died 35 years ago. The Queen and her advisers ... must go beyond the closed purple-clad circle. They must search the schools and parishes, the colleges and monasteries for one outstanding man with the fire and the vision to stir souls and move masses.

While the newspapers indulged in rhetoric, the church was taking its own steps. On 22 June the Standing Committee of the General Synod held a special meeting at the Church Commissioners' offices on Millbank, across the road from the Houses of Parliament. The Standing Committee is virtually the Cabinet of the church, and it is normally chaired by the Archbishop of Canterbury (though not on that occasion). Its membership consists of the chairmen of the houses of clergy and laity in the General Synod, the chairmen of all the church's main boards and committees, and eighteen elected members, all of whom are distinguished members of the Synod. They were joined by the Prime Minister's and archbishop's appointments secretaries, and the committee discussed and recommended what manner of man they hoped for as the next archbishop.

Early in July the General Synod met at Church House, Westminster, for its regular summer session. Its 560 members include all the diocesan bishops, certain elected suffragan bishops, cathedral deans, archdeacons, and clergy and lay people elected from each of the forty-three dioceses of the Church of England. (The Church of Wales and the Scottish Episcopalian Church are independent Anglican churches and have their separate synods.) Its powers to legislate in matters of church law have been delegated to it by Parliament, and it works by parliamentary processes, its measures eventually requiring parliamentary approval and the Royal Assent to become law. But the Synod is also the central and most important forum for the church, and the great meeting-place of all those most keenly interested in ecclesiastical appointments.

It was inevitable, therefore, that there should be much

discussion in corridors and the tea-room (as, indeed, such discussions had been going on wherever two or three clergy gathered together) about the possible choices. The Archbishop of York's and Bishop Runcie's names were heard most frequently, though the Bishops of Derby and Wakefield were suddenly being tipped as the most likely dark horses. The known candidates were closely watched through the debates on the agenda, especially the one that touched on the divisive issue of the ordination of women.

Four years before, in 1975, the Synod had agreed that there were 'no fundamental theological objections' to ordaining women to the priesthood, but had been unwilling to take the matter further at that time and, after a procedural muddle, had put the whole matter into the hands of the bishops to bring it back to the Synod when they should 'judge the time for action to be right'. The church was deeply split on the issue, with the publication of scores of books and pamphlets rehearsing the conflicting arguments, much preaching and praying for and against, and demonstrations by groups of women who were deeply convinced that they had vocations to the priesthood and that it was only traditional male prejudice that was holding them back.

The crunch question came back to the Synod in 1978 at its November session. Was it prepared to set in motion the legislation that would be required for the Church of England to ordain women? The Synod met in a packed house with a record turn-out of members and, while the bishops voted substantially and the laity voted narrowly for the motion, the proposal was heavily defeated by the clergy. It was a bitter disappointment for the women to whom it mattered so much.

For the time being that finished that; and it would be for the protagonists of women's ordination to gather their forces to make a fresh moral assault on the clergy's intractability at some future date. Meanwhile there was the difficult question about how the Church of England should regard those women who had been legally ordained in those churches of the Anglican Communion that now permitted it. If they came to England, would they or would they not be recognised as priests and allowed to celebrate Holy Communion in English parish churches? It was this problem that was before the Synod in July 1979.

Like the church they represented, the members were divided. The conservative Catholics, together with a small number of conservative Evangelicals, were on one side, totally opposed to the change because there was no biblical or theological precedent for it. The liberals and radicals were on the other side, convinced that the great sociological change in the status of women, and the new psychological understanding of human gender and the enormous overlap of abilities and characteristics between the two sexes, could no longer be ignored – in common justice – by the church. In the light of the pending appointment, everyone concerned was anxious to observe how the possible candidates for Canterbury would declare themselves.

In the event the only one on the 'short list' to speak in the debate was Bishop Runcie. It was known that in the 1978 debate he had been very much influenced by the fact that he was the chairman of the International Commission for Anglican–Orthodox Conversations, and had voted against the ordination of women on the ground that the Orthodox churches of Eastern Europe would be deeply dismayed and puzzled if the Church of England, which they had come to regard as a bridge between Rome and the rest of Christendom, should depart on such a fundamental issue from the traditional Catholic practice. Since then Bishop Runcie had taken five months' sabbatical leave and had spent most of it touring the Orthodox countries. His views had not changed, and they were still based on a diplomatic view of the ecumenical scene.

'It is this synodical fidgeting which makes our church the despair of our ecumenical partners,' he said. He thought the ecumenical arguments against making any move towards ordaining women were even stronger than in the previous November because the Synod had not given the other churches time even to respond to that debate before coming up with this new issue. 'I believe this is one of those cases where to do nothing is correct,' he concluded.

In this he was out of line with most of the bishops who, like the laity when it came to the vote, were massively in favour of allowing women ordained overseas to officiate as priests in England. But a majority of the clergy once more voted against the motion by 113 to 87. No progress had been made.

The synod agenda ranged over a wide variety of subjects. There was revision of some of the new services to go in the *Alternative Service Book*. There was a debate on disarmament which was brought to an early end because the Synod thought that the report it was based on, though good on politics, was lacking in theology. A report on evangelism in England was sharply criticised; and a debate on sexual ethics brought by a private member was stopped short when it was discovered that the bishops were so bored with the subject that they had not left a quorum on the episcopal benches. In between these unsatisfactory items there was a good deal of necessary but finicking legislative business. No public reference was made to Dr Coggan's impending retirement because he would not be making his official farewell to Synod until the following November.

The meeting of the Crown Appointments Commission was a very well kept secret. The only hint that it was in the offing was a mention in the church papers that one of the two diocesan bishops who were members, Colin James of Wakefield, was being replaced by John Waine, the new Bishop of St Edmundsbury and Ipswich. Such hints as these were eagerly seized by the Lambeth-watchers, and this was taken as evidence that Bishop James would be one of the candidates under discussion.

Unknown except by the most select few, the Commission met for two days starting on 9 July, the Monday following the week of the General Synod. They gathered at Launde Abbey in Leicestershire and so secret was the meeting that John Waine was greatly embarrassed at having to cancel a visit to one of his diocesan primary schools at short notice without being able to give a reason. In the chair was Mr (now Sir) Richard O'Brien, at that time Chairman of the Manpower Services Commission, who had been nominated as chairman-in-waiting by Mr Callaghan when he was Prime Minister, and the appointment had not been changed by Mrs Thatcher. He fulfilled all the requirements. He was an active communicant layman of the Church of England and, according to a member of the Commission, he had a 'quiet down-to-earth attitude to the Church of England as the church of the English people; and was sufficiently knowledgeable not to be taken in by any of the elaborate manoeuvrings to satisfy parties and factions'.

There was a fairly long list of names for the Commission to discuss, including several from outside the Church of England. The proceedings were informal and totally confidential. The Eucharist was celebrated and the daily offices said in the chapel, with periods of private prayer. But discussions were relaxed in the abbey drawing-room and, in between the informal sessions, members walked about the garden in twos and threes continuing their exchange of views.

Monday and Tuesday passed without any decision, and the last morning came. By lunch-time they had decided on the two names required of them, and the total confidentiality of the proceedings has kept one of those names secret. Was it that of the Archbishop of York? Or was it an overseas bishop to be doubtfully regarded by the Prime Minister and the Queen? Or was it a little-known suffragan bishop from the north of England? Gossip has suggested all three possibilities, but so far the secret has been kept. Nor is it known in which order the two names were placed.

Two days later O'Brien and Bishop David Say of Rochester, the senior bishop on the Commission, went to 10 Downing Street to present the two names to Mrs Thatcher. None of these events was known by any but those most closely involved. Public speculation went on in ignorance that the decision – as far as the church was concerned – had already been made and, increasingly in church circles, it was Robert Runcie's name that was most frequently heard. Some were still predicting the translation of the Archbishop of York, even though Dr Blanch had said in public that he had no wish to move south. But there were many who believed that the church could hope for a change of style in its leadership, and that it was 'Bob' Runcie who had the dynamic potential that they hoped for.

In contrast to the Evangelicalism of both Dr Coggan and Dr Blanch, Runcie was a moderate Catholic inclined towards radical views, though occasionally more conservative – as in the matter of the ordination of women – than might have been expected. That was as great a swing in churchmanship as most Anglicans wanted to see. It was broadly in line with many of the church's younger leaders. In addition, Runcie was popular. He had a freshness of manner and approach, a ready sense of humour, and a great talent for listening to people. There were other bishops also able to think clearly and to speak well but, in the 1980s the rarer gift of intelligent listening might be more important.

However, any discussion of the likelihood of Bob Runcie being appointed to Canterbury turned to speculation about his wife's reaction. It was generally known that Lindy Runcie was by no means the complaisantly orthodox clergy wife. She had a mind determinedly her own, and had made it clear that she had no wish to leave St Albans where she had established a circle of pupils to whom she taught the piano, and a regular engagement as music correspondent for the *Hertfordshire Advertiser*. It was rumoured that she had been behind her husband's refusal of York in 1975. Might her will be strong enough also to persuade him against Canterbury?

These misgivings were strengthened in the very week that the Crown Appointments Commission was meeting in Leicestershire. Mrs Runcie was asked by a reporter of the *St Albans Review* what she thought of the possibility of her husband going to Canterbury and she roundly declared, 'I don't know what on earth we should do if he got the job. The only way I ever want to leave St Albans is feet first in a coffin.' She suggested it had far better go to the Archbishop of York who was 'used to being an archbishop and would probably be very good'.

The weeks passed and July became August and still neither the church nor the public knew if any decision had been made. The fact that it was the height of the holiday season went some way to explaining the delay, but it still left many people on tenterhooks. John Miles, the Chief Information Officer in Church House, had not dared take his family on holiday earlier, but now took the chance that nothing would happen until life returned to normal in September, and prepared to go to Cornwall. On the very day before he was due to leave he was summoned to Downing Street, to the Appointments Secretary's office, and was told that the announcement would be made on Tuesday 4 September when the man who had been chosen would have come back from holidaying abroad. Miles went to Cornwall not even allowed to warn his colleagues.

On 27 August the British nation and much of the Western world was shattered by news of the murder of Lord Mountbatten while sailing his boat on holiday in Ireland. For several days, and until after his funeral on Wednesday 5 September, the British media could think of little else. But during that week, following a telephone call from John Miles who had been able to extend his holiday in Cornwall by a few days, Joy Meacham, the press officer in Church House, rang round the news agencies and news editors in Fleet Street. An important announcement, she said, was to be made at a press conference in Church House on Friday morning, 7 September. The newsmen did not need three guesses to know what it would be.

They were scooped by the *Hertfordshire Advertiser* that appeared in St Albans that Friday morning with the front-page headline: 'Runcie for Canterbury'. The news flashed round Fleet Street. The press conference was packed with reporters, photographers, and television camera crews hoping for interviews. Punctually at eleven o'clock John Miles led the Bishop of St Albans into the room, followed by his wife and their two children, nineteen-year-old James and seventeen-year-old Rebecca, and the bishop's domestic chaplain, the Revd Richard Chartres.

The bishop stood before them, tall, crinkle-haired, with the precise and easy elegance of an athlete. He had many friends among the journalists in the room, and it took only a few minutes for his apprehension to relax, even though he told them that his main feeling was one of trepidation. He began by making a statement, and it was clear that he had already given a lot of thought to his future job. After a courteous appreciation of the work of Dr Coggan, and pleasure at the thought of returning to the diocese of Canterbury where he had been stationed during the war before crossing to Normandy, he told the journalists that, above all, he hoped to avoid the trap of becoming a platitude machine. He knew that as archbishop he would be expected to have views on everything, but he was determined to avoid 'the hollowness of ringing declarations and general moralising divorced from a direct experience of the doubts and difficulties of ordinary people'. To this end he had already planned to build up a small team of assistants with a varied experience of contemporary life to enable him to make informed and searching comment on events and controversies.

He went on to speak about the church. He was wary of it becoming ghetto-minded and spending 'too much of its time firming up the centre, and tightening up passport regulations to font and altar'. There was no wisdom in the church becoming a dull echo of fashionable, liberal notions but, 'we have nothing to contribute to building a better world unless we speak in a simple and human way from the heart of our tradition, and unless we are serious about the study of scripture, and serious about prayer. We cannot be radical unless we are rooted in tradition.'

After that, all four members of the family answered questions. The bishop was asked about his views on marriage and divorce, on abortion, and about his much-publicised hobby of keeping pigs. He was asked about the ordination of women, and he tried to turn the question by saying that he would welcome women clerics from overseas to his enthronement. But, pressed by reporters, he admitted, 'At the moment I am against the ordination of women in this country'. On the other hand he was quite positive that he wanted to see it made possible for divorced people to be remarried in church; and he parried questions about his views on homosexuality by saying that he was waiting to see the report of the church's current working party on the subject. As for relations with the Roman Catholic Church, he said that he looked forward to meeting the Pope, and that he might even take up squash so that he could play with Cardinal Hume.

Mrs Runcie was asked about her music, and whether she was now resigned to leaving St Albans. James, tall like his father, with a mop of red curls, said that he was reading English at the college where his father once taught in Cambridge. Rebecca told the reporters she was still at Haileybury School, and admitted that she had known about her father's new appointment for nearly a month, but had managed to keep it secret even from her boy-friend.

The reporters were interested in the whole attractive family, but most of all they wanted to know about the new archbishop himself: his early life, his parents, his education, his war experience, and what he had done since he had been ordained. Every detail of the story of his life had suddenly become of interest to the public.

Chapter Four

Early Days

The birth of a baby brother one Sunday morning in the autumn of 1921 came as a complete surprise to the three Runcie children. It was the second day of October with the weather turning cold, and they were having their breakfast in front of the warm fire in the kitchen range. Great-aunt Leily was looking after them. She had recently come from Dublin to help their mother who had not yet appeared that morning, and the children were vaguely wondering where she was. But while they were eating their breakfast their father came into the kitchen and told them, in his soft Scottish voice, that she was staying in Little Crosby, and had a new brother to show them.

Not even twelve-year-old Kathleen had known that her mother was pregnant; it was not a subject to be talked about in that respectably restrained household. She and her sister Marjorie had noticed her recent enthusiasm for knitting small garments but had been told they were for 'Mrs Morris's daughter'; Mrs Morris being a rather shadowy figure said to live the other side of the Mersey river in Wallasey. Eight-year-old Kenneth had not noticed the knitting. He had hardly wondered, and certainly not dared to ask, where babies came from, and he was no wiser now. But all three children were excited at the news, and their father promised that they would go to Little Crosby that afternoon to see their mother and the new baby.

The Runcies lived in Great Crosby, once a village listed in the *Domesday Book*, but now a flourishing small town in the process of being absorbed as a prosperous suburb in the sprawling conurbation of Liverpool. They lived at 6, Moor Lane, a roomy apartment behind two shops, close to what was still recognisably the village centre. There was plenty of space for the children, with a big yard at the back for them to play in, and a glass-roofed nursery on the top floor large enough for Kenneth to play football with his father and for a swing to be suspended from the rafters.

Though Great Crosby was developing fast, spreading outwards as speculative builders put up more and more red-brick houses for middle-class business people moving out of Liverpool, the fields and lanes of genuine countryside were not far away. It was not very attractive country; the flat marshy land was swept by the wind from the Irish Sea. But to the children it offered plenty of open space to roam at will and, when they tired of the fields, they could always go down to the sand-dunes that stretched along the coast to Southport, and watch the liners and merchant ships steaming through the grey sea into the mouth of the Mersey where the Liverpool docks were still some of the busiest in the world. They could also bathe and paddle, though that coastline was notorious for its quicksands and, like all local children, they had been brought up on spine-chilling legends of people who had been sucked into them and never seen again. But in fine weather the temptations of sand and sea were stronger than the cautious warnings of their elders.

It was a mile and a half to Little Crosby, and the family had often walked there before that afternoon. They found Mrs Runcie in a bedroom in the local midwife's house, and rather fretful because her husband had let so many hours elapse before coming to see their latest offspring. When Kenneth, who had been missing his mother, climbed on to her bed, he was told quite sharply to be careful not to squash the new baby. But nine-year-old Marjorie was enchanted with her bald-headed brother, even though he was slightly yellow with jaundice and cried a lot. Very soon after he was brought home he had to go to the local hospital for a small hernia operation. After that he stopped crying and, years later, Marjorie said, 'I think that during those early weeks he must have got rid of all his resentment at being born because, for ever afterwards, I remember him as a happy, good-tempered little boy.'

Six weeks later, on 22 November, he was christened in the parish church of St Luke which stands at the centre of Great Crosby. His parents were not church-goers. His father, from a Scottish Presbyterian family, had little religious inclination, and no love for the Church of England. But his mother, of Protestant Irish parents, had been brought up in the conventions of the English church and, for a common mixture of reasons – part religious, part socially conventional, part superstitious – she would not allow her baby to go unbaptized.

So, with a sprinkling of holy water and signed with the cross, he was received into the Church of England and given the names Robert Alexander Kennedy. Robert was after his father; Alexander was in compliment to his godfather, Alexander Fisher, who, nearly twenty years before, had come with Robert Runcie from Greenock to Liverpool; Kennedy was after another family friend. When the service was over they all went back to the house in Moor Lane to a family tea-party to celebrate the occasion. Nancy Runcie had baked the cake herself in the oven of the kitchen range. As the oven was heated by the coal-fire at its side, her cakes usually came out lop-sided; but the christening cake had been a triumph. Marjorie observed that, for once, it was perfectly shaped.

Robert Alexander Kennedy Runcie was soon called Robin by his family. He had been born into an easy-going household. Both parents were kind and affectionate and, for the most part, even-tempered, though just occasionally Nancy would flash with Irish fire. They were not demonstrative in their love, or ever really intimate with their children; but they created a pleasant well-mannered home background in which relationships were tolerant and unquestioning rather than close. There was not much money. Their income was adequate in that they could afford a house large enough for their needs and live comfortably within it. But, with three children at school and a new baby, there was little to spare. Nancy did most of her own housework with a woman coming in to help. Holidays or visits away from home were rare, and certainly not annual events. And the family had no car, but that was not surprising for few of their middle-class neighbours had one either.

Robin's father was out most of the time. He was the chief electrical engineer at the Tate and Lyle sugar refinery in Liverpool which had its own generating plant, and the generators were his main responsibility for twenty-four hours of every day. Even when he was not at the factory he was still responsible for their working, and every evening at ten o'clock there would be a telephone call from the night-shift engineers to report that all was well. But Mr Runcie was rarely there to answer the telephone. He was nearly always with his friends at the Burlington Club where he played bowls. Almost any sort of game or sport fascinated him. He played golf, he followed the racing with regular small flutters, he was president of the local Waterloo Park Football Club, and also of the Crystal Baseball Club where the baseball that was played – a very popular game in Liverpool at that time – was more akin to rounders than to modern American baseball. And when he was at home, he was always ready to play cricket or football with his children in the garden.

Robert Dalziel Runcie had been born in 1879 in Kilmarnock where his father, James Runcie, had a draper's shop. The family had previously come from Greenock where his grandfather, also James, had married Catherine Dalziel. James Runcie, the draper of Kilmarnock and grandfather to the new baby in Crosby, had married Isabella McKellar from Tarbet, a village on the shore of Loch Lomond. Robert Dalziel was the first of their children, and he was quickly followed by two sisters, Catherine and Florence. While these three children were still very young, their mother died, and James employed a housekeeper, Sarah Picken, whom he later married. She also produced three children, all girls, and died when the youngest was only three years old. Her death was soon followed by that of her husband so that Robert was left as the older brother of five orphaned sisters. Fortunately there were two uncles, both prosperous flour merchants, who took care of the girls and arranged for

Robert to be apprenticed to an engineering firm in Greenock. It was from there that he moved to Liverpool, some time around 1904, to work at Tate and Lyle's.

He was a slim, good-looking man of medium height, and he kept his soft Scottish accent and his fondness for Burns's poetry all his life. He had been in Liverpool three years when he went with a friend to the theatre where they met two girls, one of whom his friend knew. The other girl immediately attracted Robert. She was very pretty, slim and shapely, but it was her vivid auburn curls that made men look twice. She was introduced as Nancy Benson (her Christian names were Ann Edna), and she had recently come from Norwich to live with friends at Rock Ferry and to finish her training as a hairdresser in Liverpool.

Though she had been born and brought up in the shadow of Norwich Cathedral, Nancy's family was Irish. Her father, Henry ('Paddy') Benson, had married Sarah Gunning in Dublin, and they moved to Norwich where Mr Benson was employed by the organ-builders, Norman and Beard's, as a 'voicer', a skilled job requiring a good musical ear for the tuning of organ pipes. He had travelled widely, including a prolonged visit to South Africa, to supervise the installation of organs. He also built small instruments of his own: in his spare time he collected and reassembled parts of old organs and built smaller ones, some of which – known as 'Paddy Bensons' – are believed to be still in existence.

Robert and Nancy were married in August 1908 at Holy Trinity Church in Norwich, and from then on seem to have had little contact with Nancy's family. They lived in the Anfield district of Liverpool where their first three children were born at two-yearly intervals, and it was when Kenneth was a year old in 1914 that they moved out to Crosby and the house in Moor Lane. It was the first year of the Great War, but there was no question of Robert Runcie going into the army. Not only was he already thirty-five, but his job at Tate and Lyle's was too essential for him to be spared.

Soon after Robin was born they moved again, to 26 Queen's Road to the south of the village. The new house was plain, Victorian, semi-detached and built of red brick, with one bay window for the sitting-room. The porch, with its front door, was at the side of the house, stuck on rather like an afterthought. The building had no aesthetic merit, but there were five bedrooms and two bathrooms, and a garden back and front for the children to play in.

Queen's Road was lined with similar substantial houses, each one slightly different in style. It was an area of rising middle-class families, conventional, conservative and respectable. Many people in the area were of Irish Catholic stock, and sent their children to the local convent schools. For the non-Catholic families who wanted the best available education for their children, hopes were fixed on the two Merchant Taylors' grammar schools half a mile away on the Liverpool Road.

It was to these two schools that all three of the older Runcie children went, and to which Robin himself would later go. The schools were of great influence in the district. The boys' school had been founded in 1618 by John Harrison, whose father, a woollen cloth merchant, had left his Crosby home (probably in Moor Lane) in 1556, and had gone to London where he had prospered and been made a member of the Merchant Taylors Company. John Harrison had inherited his father's new-made wealth and position, and had prospered even more. He, too, became a Merchant Taylor, and was infected by the contemporary enthusiasm for education.

In the early part of the seventeenth century it had become a philanthropic fashion for rich men to endow schools in their home areas; and John Harrison, who had never set eyes on Crosby, decided, at the age of forty-nine, to visit his father's birthplace and to found there a grammar school in his father's memory. He made the journey north and chose a site for his school on the track leading to the village of Liverpool eight miles away, and left instructions with the local rector to supervise the construction of the building. A year later, back in London, he died, leaving five hundred pounds in trust to the Merchant Taylors Company to pay for the building of 'one free grammar school for the teaching, educating and instructing of children and youth in the

55

grammar and rules of learning for ever'. He also left the rents of some of his extensive London property to pay for its maintenance and for one schoolmaster and one usher.

But the trustees in London had little idea of what was going on two hundred miles away in Crosby. The school got off to a poor start and for two hundred and fifty years it had a chequered and occasionally scandalous history until it was virtually refounded in the middle of the nineteenth century. From then on it gained rapidly in numbers and academic prestige until it outgrew its seventeenth-century building, and a site for a larger school had to be found. So land was purchased further along the Liverpool Road, and a Victorian Gothic school was built in dark red brick, with single-storey classrooms, and a lofty clock-tower. It was finished in 1878, and the boys ceremoniously moved in. Ten years later the Merchant Taylors' Girls' School opened in the original seventeenth-century building which had been renovated and extended.

Kathleen was already going to the girls' school when her youngest brother was born, and Marjorie started soon after. The fees were modest, about fifteen pounds a year, but they were still a drain on an engineer's salary. However, their mother had her own resources. During the war she had begun to supplement the family income by resuming her hairdressing profession and offering a hairdressing service in her own house to the wives of army officers from a nearby camp, and she followed this up after the war by a very unusual venture for a married woman of her time and conventional background.

Nancy Runcie had more determination and courage than her dreamy, sentimental and normally placid exterior might have suggested. As a housewife she was not a very good manager. Her creative and artistic instincts found their outlet in dressmaking and needlework, and she dabbled in various handicrafts. But she had a romantic imagination. She read novels avidly. Her husband's Highland ancestry through his McKellar mother inspired her to read everything the public library could offer about the Scottish Highlands. Hollywood, in later years, also fed her imagination. And it might have been this craving for adventure, as much as the need for extra family income, that led her to sign on, with a woman friend, as a freelance hairdresser on two Cunard Line cruises to the Mediterranean.

These cruises took place before Robin was born. But when he was two years old she ventured further and had her final fling, going as a hairdresser on a world cruise that lasted a whole six months. Great-aunt Leily came to stay again to look after the children, together with a young woman who was confusingly called Lily. Surprisingly, Robert Runcie seemed to have no objections to his wife's travels, though they must have caused raised eyebrows among his friends and colleagues. But whatever he thought, and whatever the reasons for Nancy's adventures, they were not discussed with the children.

Of the older three, Kenneth missed his mother most, and was unhappy at her absence. Two-year-old Robin, as far as anyone could see, seemed hardly to notice that she had gone. But her return from overseas brought excitement, exotic presents and colourful stories. And there was the continuing benefit of visits from her Cunard friends who came to see her, bringing foreign chocolates and occasional presents and left behind them the lingering scent of Turkish cigarettes.

Perhaps it was because her mind was so often elsewhere that Robin was never very close to his mother. Being so very much the youngest of the family, with an eight-year gap between him and Kenneth, he was more isolated than the rest of them realised. From the viewpoint of his parents and his sisters he was the petted and indulged baby brother; they did not observe the frequency with which he was told to go away and stop being a nuisance. So he learned to depend on his own company, playing games by himself and with his imaginary friend 'Bonner'. Nobody knew where Bonner had got his name, but he had to be considered and catered for until he became almost real to the rest of the family. Robin insisted that a place was always laid for him at table.

Sometimes Robin was allowed to join Kenneth and his friend in the attic where the two older boys had combined their Hornby train sets in a splendid layout. Robin also had a large red bus. This particularly pleased him because buses had recently come to the district, supplementing the trams and making it easier to get to Liverpool: a ride on a bus was still a special treat. And Robin was delighted with his toy bus that he trundled round the garden from stop to stop while Kenneth, when he could be persuaded, rode the family tricycle as a bus in the opposite direction. The more muddy puddles they could find to splash real mud on the bus's wheels, the better Robin was pleased.

More important for his future career than bus-driving was the encouragement he got, from both his father and Kenneth, to play cricket. This began as soon as Robin could hold a bat, and it quickly became clear that he had a natural eye for a ball. The cricket practice went on for many years as his batting proficiency improved. His quickness of eye and reaction – perhaps for more than cricket balls – owed something to the constraints of the lay-out of house and garden. As Robin grew older, beyond the pat-ball stage, and demanded to hit proper balls, there was no path long enough for a straight run up to bowl. So the bowler, usually Kenneth, had to run up one side of the house, turn a sharp right-angle, and bowl down the other. Robin, getting no clues from the run-up to the type of ball he might expect, had to react as the ball came upon him.

Before he was quite old enough for the local primary school, he had his first – brief – experience of Sunday school. It was Kathleen who took him. She had discovered the youth club and Sunday school run by the Methodist church in Mersey Road. The church was a popular one, it was the centre of a strong middle-class community which catered for all age-groups, and had a purposeful sense of mission both overseas and in the local area. Missionaries newly returned from far-off lands were a regular attraction and inspired the local congregation, and the minister was assiduous in his determination to attract young converts.

Kathleen had started going to the youth club regularly, and to the family services on Sundays, and her new sense of Christian responsibility suggested that she should take her younger brother to Sunday school. It was not a success. He went willingly enough but, once there, was terrified by a picture he was shown of Abraham about to sacrifice Isaac. Nothing would induce him to go again. The minister came round to the house specially to try and persuade him, but four-year-old Robin remained adamant. It was several years before he went near another church.

Real school, half a mile away at the Coronation Road Primary School, was a very different matter. The two-storey building, close to the village centre, was typical of its generation, and schools just like it, with their distinctive style of architecture, are still to be found in every town and suburb in the land. Solidly built in red brick with stone quoins, it stood in an asphalt playground surrounded by green-painted iron railings. Under its steeply-pitched slate roof each classroom was allotted three tall windows, the upper panes of which were opened from inside by a dangling cord: as much part of the standard school classroom equipment as the battered double desks with their joined benches and china ink-pots, and the chalk-dusted blackboard.

From the beginning Robin responded to the new stimulation and enjoyed learning. He was in Miss Jessie Gale's class. Miss Gale was herself in her first year as a probationer teacher, and she knew Bobby Runcie as a quiet little boy, already tall and leggy for his age, with tightly-curled auburn hair the same colour as his mother's. He was bright and learned quickly. School gradually cured him of his painful shyness with children of his own age which had been so acute that, when he had once been taken to a children's party, he had been unable to speak or to join in any games. But at school he overcame it and developed his normal share of naughtiness, and was caned more than once. He had an early lesson in the fallibility of feminine advice when he was summoned, with his girl partner-in-crime, to see the headmistress about some now-forgotten misdemeanour. While they were nervously waiting to be called into the presence, his companion assured him that if he put a hair across his hand while being caned it would not hurt so much. Trustingly he accepted the offer of one of her long hairs and carefully wound it round his palm. He was painfully disillusioned.

At home the imaginary Bonner had deserted him 'to go to another school', but he continued to spend a lot of time on his own. He became adept at playing football for two sides at once, scoring goals in both directions. He gave concerts with himself as the applauding audience. He developed his talent for mimicry and would take both parts in a double act. He talked to himself and argued with himself and, in this, probably set the pattern for his later years of arguing every proposition in his mind, and always seeing at least two sides to any matter under discussion.

The eight-year gap between him and his brother and sisters did much to shape his personality. The Benjamin of a family, the child who is youngest by many years, often spends as many solitary hours as an only child, but he is under a different set of pressures. His position is more ambivalent in that he is a generation apart from, yet under compulsion to identify with, his older siblings. Yet they, from his viewpoint, have already reached the wholly desirable adult world where all appears exciting and important, and its members are listened to and taken seriously, while he finds himself usually laughed at, indulged, or dismissively told to go away and play. So he longs to be accepted as one of them on their level.

This observation by the youngest child probably exaggerates the true state of affairs, and the view of the older members of the family, that the youngest appears to be the petted and spoiled focus of concern, may also be inaccurate. What matters is what is perceived, and the youngest child comes to believe that real life begins with being grown up and accepted by the adult world. So he tries hard to make his behaviour and his conversation acceptable to older people. He not only learns to please, he also learns the social skill of adapting to the company he is in, particularly to those more sophisticated than himself. From an early age his social antennae are stretched towards the adult world, away from his peers and contemporaries. Such a child caught in this syndrome may have difficulty in relating to children of his own age, though time inevitably cures this as the contemporaries themselves grow up beside him and all become adult together.

Robin's sunny disposition and aptitude for sport of all kinds saved him from this separation from friends of his own age, but his peculiar position in his family forced him to depend upon his own resources, and to adapt to his social surroundings. Both these lessons were to stand him in good stead in the years to come. In addition, his early habit of arguing with himself became ingrained, making it difficult for him ever to accept any statement uncritically. In fact by instinct and training he became critical and analytical, primarily of himself. He became a perfectionist in all he did, which probably led directly to the 'workaholic' regime he set himself in later life. His critical judgment also extended to others, but it was mitigated by a natural sympathy and – as he grew older – charitable understanding. It gave him a keen eye for character.

As a child, however, he was ready to play with whoever was available, and there were other young children living in Queen's Road. The Templeton family had come from Scotland to live next door, bringing two little girls of much his own age. One day the younger, Jean, heard him calling over the garden wall to come and see the performing worms he had been busily training. It was the beginning of a friendship in which they shared the Templetons' sturdy tricycle which had a footplate at the back for a passenger, and on it they took turns pedalling up and down the road with the other clinging on the back. The Templeton parents approved of the quiet, well-mannered small boy, and continued to be impressed by his polite ways as he grew up, and the way he always touched his school cap in greeting when he met them in the street.

While he was still at primary school both his sisters left home. Kathleen had done well at Merchant Taylors' and, at a time when university was not readily thought of for girls, had won a place at Liverpool to train as a social worker. While in the sixth form she had come under the strong Christian influence of Emily Fordham, the headmistress, and had been confirmed in the Church of England. It was with a sense of Christian vocation that, when she qualified in 1930, she went to London to work in the slums at a Bermondsey settlement.

Marjorie, who had not enjoyed her school years, terminated them when she was sixteen to stay at home and help her mother. A year or more later she went on a visit to her father's youngest sister, Aunt Nettie, in Ayrshire. While she was there her aunt took her to visit a children's convalescent home in Prestwick (where she had worked before her marriage), and Marjorie was immediately attracted to the place. She loved children, had doted on her youngest brother while he was little, and this seemed exactly the sort of work she was best suited for. She went there as soon as she was nineteen, and was very happy looking after children from the slums of Glasgow, seeing them arrive sickly and undernourished, and watching them being transformed by the good food and open-air regime of the convalescent home. Apart from holidays, she did not return to live with her family until Robert had completed his first year at Merchant Taylors'.

With a Harrison Scholarship, one of those which perpetuated the founder's original intention of providing free grammar school education for local boys of ability, Robert – now known to his contemporaries as Bob – began his secondary education in 1932, the year that his brother, Kenneth, left school. Like Marjorie, Kenneth had not enjoyed his education. He had got off to a bad start because his mother had decided that, rather than Merchant Taylors', he should go to a small private school. He was not happy there and when, after a year, the school suddenly closed and he was abruptly transferred to Merchant Taylors', he felt himself at a permanent disadvantage. Without any very clear idea of what he wanted to do, he left when he was sixteen for a clerical job in a Liverpool engineering firm and, within a year, moved to Manchester.

This left Robert the only one of the four children living at home with his parents; although once he started going to the grammar school he, too, began to centre his life elsewhere. For him, Merchant Taylors' School was to prove a natural environment, exactly suited to a boy with his combination of academic and athletic talent.

Chapter Five

Growing Up

Robert was in his second year at Merchant Taylors' when Marjorie came home from Scotland, persuaded by the matron of the Prestwick children's home to start proper nursing training. Six months at the Royal Liverpool Hospital were enough to convince her that she had made a mistake and would be happier back in Scotland, but while she was at home she was able to renew her acquaintance with her young brother and was delighted to find that he was not only doing well at school, but excelling on the sports field. It was no surprise to the family that he was proving himself good at cricket: all that practice in the garden had paid off and he was a promising batsman. In athletics he was beginning to shine in the high jump and hurdling; and the winter terms were given to rugby and hockey, both of which he enjoyed. On the winter Saturday afternoons not occupied by school games he still went with his father to football matches. That was when he enjoyed his father's company most. They followed the fortunes of the local clubs, and would come back to a family tea, happily discussing the play. Marjorie and their mother would be there, and often Kenneth home from Manchester; and tea on Saturdays became the occasion for family gossip.

Robert was a thoroughly normal adolescent boy, regularly to be found with his friends and their bicycles, riding round the local streets, hanging round the public library, and occasionally going to the Odeon or the Regal cinema to watch Laurel and Hardy, Harold Lloyd and, later, the Marx brothers. Those were also the years when the wireless was coming into its own as family entertainment, and the whole Runcie family would listen to the comedy shows together. Robert began to develop his gift for mimicry and, with his friend, David Molyneux, would turn the kitchen into a BBC studio, 'broadcasting' the shows of well-known comedians, and putting on his own news programmes. Marjorie, coming one day into the kitchen, found herself face to face with her own photograph and a carefully printed announcement that the beautiful Miss Runcie would be giving an interview Miss Runcie flatly declined, but Kenneth was more obliging. He and Robert were both keen on jazz and on the famous dance-bands of the time such as those of Jack Hilton, Jack Payne, and Henry Hall. While Kenneth was away, Robert had the free use of his gramophone and his large collection of records, and these he added to their 'broadcasts'.

But he was growing up and, by the time he was fourteen, he had begun to take an interest in girls. He and David both became keen on the same one and, when they learned that Betty was planning to attend confirmation classes at the parish church, David decided to go too. Robert, who was not going to be cut out by his friend, did the same, and the three of them met each week at the classes held by the vicar, the Revd Powell Miller.

A condition of the classes was the obligation to go on Sundays to St Luke's, the church in which Robert had been christened. It was of the Evangelical tradition, with very plain services which Robert found as tedious and unattractive as the confirmation classes. But having started, and because they kept him in the company of David and Betty, he persisted, and in Lent 1936 he was confirmed in St Luke's by Bishop A. A. David of Liverpool. He made again, on his own behalf, the promises that had been made for him by his godparents at his baptism; and the bishop laid his hands on his head and prayed – as every bishop prays over every individual he confirms – 'Defend, O Lord, this thy child with thy heavenly grace, that he may continue thine for ever, and daily increase in thy Holy Spirit more and more, until he come unto thy everlasting kingdom.' In essence it was a short and simple service, made long by the large number of adolescent boys and girls, together with a sprinkling of adults, who went up two by two to kneel at the bishop's feet. Robert found that this rite, by which he was made a full and responsible member of the Church of England, moved him more deeply than he expected.

By long Anglican tradition confirmation was the preliminary to admission to Holy Communion, the central sacrament of the church; and the following Sunday Robert was expected to make his first communion at St Luke's with his friends. But Kathleen was home from Nottingham where she was now working, and as she usually went to St Faith's Church, which she clearly preferred, Robert decided he would go with her.

Writing many years later to his own godson – Kathleen's son – who was about to be confirmed, he recalled this time:

I clearly remember my own Confirmation day and my first communion which I made beside your Mummy. It didn't seem to be so much then (and, of course, you will be warned not to expect to *feel* too much), but looking back at that time I see it as a decisive stage and landmark in my life. It was soon after that that I decided to be ordained; but that was something that emerged gradually. There was nothing sudden or dramatic about it. In any case, I was more concerned in those days about getting into the first XI for cricket and passing my exams: a double and immediate problem which rightly left me no time for too much planning or even dreaming about the future.

His first communion in St Faith's Church was indeed a landmark, for he suddenly found a church full of colour, ritual and Catholic devotion which attracted something deep inside him. It offered a form of Christian practice and discipline to which he could respond. In its own way it was a conversion experience; not a sudden meeting with the Lord Jesus Christ like that so often recounted by Evangelicals, but a deep and indescribable awareness that he was where he should be, following the path that he should take.

St Faith's was a big Victorian Gothic building in the familiar dark red brick of the area, with a grey slate roof and an apology for a tower surmounted by a green copper steeple. It stood on the corner of the Liverpool Road not far from Merchant Taylors' School, a plain, unlovely suburban church. But the strength, vigour and attractiveness of its life can only be understood in the context of its history, time, and place. In 1975, when it was celebrating its seventy-fifth anniversary, Mr Christopher Price, a local historian, wrote:

For better or worse, St Faith's has always stood for something distinctive in Crosby: an uncompromising and unavoidable building, standing for a special order of worship and an emphasis which for many years set it well apart from the mainstream of Anglican worship in the area. As a result it must often have seemed something of a citadel set in hostile territory, and its successive priests and congregations saw themselves as Defenders of the Faith, an embattled minority witnessing to a style and pattern of worship generally conspicuous only by its absence, not only in the local area, but also in the Liverpool diocese as a whole.

For when St Faith's was built, the Oxford Movement was little more than half a century old ... The new emphasis on order in worship, authority in the church, regular celebration of the Eucharist and a limited use of vestments and ornaments in the church, moderate though it seems by today's standards, was sufficient at the turn of the century to inflame the tempers of loyal Protestants who, deeply suspicious of Rome and all its ways, saw in the Anglo-Catholic movement not merely a devoted attempt to deepen spiritual life and restore some of the ancient principles and practices of Anglicanism into a church which seems sadly to have neglected them, but a sinister campaign to sell out to the Pope and restore rule from Rome by the back door. And in ultra-conservative Protestant Liverpool, though there were fewer of the dramatic battles for the faith, vicious lawsuits and personal attacks, than happened so often in London and elsewhere at the time, there was nevertheless a strong and genuine feeling which showed itself in hostility and bitterness at the time of the foundation of St Faith's, which had left a legacy of suspicion and isolation for the first half century of the new church's life and beyond.

St Faith's had had its noisy times. In its early years, Protestant demonstrators had regularly appeared outside the church as worshippers were arriving for the Sunday services. 'Change here for Rome,' they liked to shout; and on one occasion they stoned a visiting priest from Toxteth. In 1931, only five years before Robert went there for the first time, a contingent of twenty Protestant 'Orangemen' had arrived to disrupt a service, but their courage failed when they discovered that news of their coming had preceded them and that every male member of St Faith's congregation had turned out to pack the church with a formidable array of muscular Christianity.

The spasmodic persecution through the years had drawn the congregation into a close-knit determined community, standing strongly for its beliefs. In the late 1930s, when Robert began going there, the church was in its heyday under its fourth priest, Father John Schofield, whom Mr Price described as 'a saintly man of great charm'. More than three hundred people attended the main Sunday services and, on Easter Day 1938, it was recorded that four hundred and sixty people made their communion. The church had a splendid musical tradition, and the choir was considered second only in the diocese to Liverpool Cathedral. The Holy Communion service, called 'Mass' at St Faith's, was celebrated every day; and on Sundays and feast-days there was the full Catholic ritual with all the colour of vestments, processions, bells, candles, and incense as the outward and visible panoply of a strong sacramental life of prayer.

For a susceptible fourteen-year-old schoolboy, the attraction was immediate. The colour, the solemnity, the sense of purpose, provided all that he had found lacking at St Luke's. And Kathleen, who had been a committed and conscientious

Christian ever since her own confirmation, was anxious that her brother should be encouraged in his new religious faith. Before she returned to Nottingham she called on Fr Schofield to ask him to keep a special eye on Robert, and, possibly as a direct result of that intervention, within a matter of weeks Robert found himself in a cassock and lace cotta serving at St Faith's altar. Catholic ritual had suddenly become exciting and important. He recalled many years later how he and his fellow-servers quickly became 'tremendous sanctuary-wallahs, all gossipy about birettas and incense'. It was heady, esoteric stuff; but at the centre of it, under Fr Schofield's direction, there was a strong and genuine religious life. Within its discipline Robert grew spiritually just as he was growing intellectually at school.

Life had become very full and stimulating, but there was increasing anxiety at home. For several years Robert's father had been experiencing periods of unexplained and random pain in his arms and legs which had been getting steadily worse. In the early stages it was thought to be rheumatism, but eventually his condition was diagnosed as neuritis and, as the pain had become unbearable, a drastic form of treatment was begun. Mrs Runcie was warned that there could be side-effects which might include temporary loss of sight. The treatment lessened the pain and improved Mr Runcie's general health but, as the doctors had warned, his eyes had begun to be affected.

Early in 1937, when Robert was fifteen, Kathleen had become engaged to Angus Inglis, curate of St Mary's Church, Nottingham, and they were planning to be married in October. With her father's ill-health, it was clear that a wedding at home in Crosby would be a great strain on her mother and, in any case, Kathleen had been away from the area for so long that she had few friends left there. So her choice fell on All Hallows-by-the-Tower, the London church where she had been very happy during her three years working in Bermondsey. Angus took over the organisation of the wedding, and persuaded his vicar from Nottingham, Neville Talbot (previously Bishop of Pretoria), to perform the ceremony on 20 October.

Marjorie was bridesmaid, and she, with Robert and their parents, travelled to London the day before the wedding to stay at the Waldorf Hotel where the reception would be held next day. There had been considerable anxiety about whether Mr Runcie would be well enough to make the journey, but in the event he managed quite well with the help of the rest of the family. They were joined at the Waldorf by Kenneth, who by this time was working in London, and he and his father were highly amused – and Angus embarrassed – when they found the hotel full of clergymen who were attending a conference and were more than ready to assume that Angus was one of their number. It was Robert's first visit to London, and the first time he had stayed in a hotel, and he enjoyed the whole experience. After the wedding the guests returned to the Waldorf for the reception and then Marjorie, Kenneth and Robert, together with the best man, accompanied the bride and groom to Victoria Station to wave them off to Paris for their honeymoon before Robert and his parents returned to Crosby.

Very soon afterwards Mr Runcie was forced, by his failing health and eyesight, to retire early from Tate and Lyle's, and life became difficult for the family both financially and emotionally. Robert often came home from school to find his mother in tears, and his reaction became an unhappy mixture of irritation, guilt and compassion at the ease with which she wept. Her husband depended on her, but increasingly he turned to Robert to read to him and take him out. All his chief pleasures had been connected with sport which he could no longer see, and it was here that he felt the deprivation most. His wife once accompanied him to a football match when Robert was occupied with his own affairs, but he got so frustrated at her inability to follow and describe the play that the experiment was not tried again. Thereafter it was Robert who took him. Their companionship was as strong as ever, and they still enjoyed their mutual sporting interests as Robert faithfully read aloud the sports and racing pages of the daily papers as well as the political news. But he was now so fully committed at school and at St Faith's, that he carried a constant burden of uneasy guilt at not devoting still more time to his father.

By this time he was working hard with the hope of going to university. He had come under the eye of the headmaster, the Revd Charles Russell, a distinguished mathematician and a Fellow of Pembroke College, Cambridge. A former headmaster of King Edward VI School in Southampton, Russell had also been an assistant master at Harrow, and it was to the tradition of the great public schools and of the ancient universities that he turned for models on which to run the school now in his charge. He was a formal, courteous, shy man, always in a dark suit with a high clerical collar. He expected his staff to wear their academic robes at all times, and the monitors to wear undergraduate gowns. He had a jealous eye for the school's traditions and history, and promoted and made the most of them; commemorating all awards and distinctions won by past and present boys of the school on honours boards, and hanging photographs along the corridors of old Crosbeians who had achieved renown. He divided the school into houses, and games and athletics flourished. There were clubs and societies, concerts and plays, and the speech day was an important local event. On one of those speech days in Robert's early years, Russell had persuaded his friend, William Temple, at that time Archbishop of York, to come and present the prizes.

Less able boys found Russell remote, and their parents knew and resented the fact that he had no real interest in Crosby or its local trade and industry. All his own gifts were academic, and his concern was to encourage his most promising boys in the direction of scholarship and the professions. During his time a steadily increasing number of boys stayed on into the sixth form to prepare for university, and Robert's academic ability made him exactly the sort of boy that Russell could understand and encourage.

In the summer of 1938 Robert sat for his School Certificate and also won his cricket colours as opening bat for the First Eleven. By this time, too, he was adding steadily to his collection of athletics cups for high jump and hurdling. In the winter months he played in goal for the school's hockey team, and on the wing in the rugby fifteen. The first glimpse that Angus Inglis, his brother-in-law, ever had of him was on the rugby field, 'playing wing forward, quite appropriately on account of his height, rather lazily and casually, then switching to speedy and concentrated action when required. There was a delightful "zoom" about him.'

In the sixth form he was concentrating on classics for his university entrance. It was the year of the Munich crisis when the probability of war with Germany came very close. Gas-masks were issued and air-raid shelters dug – only to be filled in again when Chamberlain brought Hitler's signature back from Munich proclaiming 'peace in our time'. Robert's growing political awareness made him despise the 'agreement' with fascist Germany, for he had come under the communist influence of one of his schoolmasters, and it was a time when the country was deeply divided.

His parents, like most of their Crosby neighbours, had always been unwavering Conservatives. But the years of the depression and unemployment in the late twenties and thirties had drawn many socially-minded intellectuals to communism as a solution to the evils of a class structure in which the complacently rich could ignore the desperate poverty of the depressed areas. This communism, with its threat to the traditional social order, was deeply feared by the conservative majority, and the political emotions of the British people were further polarised by the civil war in Spain. Never had the country been so divided by a conflict in which it was not directly involved, and many volunteers went to Spain to fight on opposing sides. Those who feared the rise of Marxist communism fought with Franco's rebels, and saw their allies newly arrived from Nazi Germany and fascist Italy as champions against the communist threat. Those on the other side, with socialist ideals and a horror of fascism, supported the Spanish left-wing coalition, and welcomed the military aid that was coming from the Soviet Union.

Intellectual left-wing thinking was being fuelled in Britain by Victor Gollancz's Left Book Club which was known to have a wide circulation among schoolteachers. So it is not surprising that there was a communist schoolmaster at

71

Merchant Taylors'. R. F. Parr, Robert's classics master, exerted a good deal of influence on some of the older boys and could easily be distracted from the lesson in hand to talk about Munich and the iniquities of the Chamberlain government. He provided an intellectual excitement and a way of looking at society that was far removed from the conventional conservatism of most of the boys' homes. For a time Robert was dazzled. The communist ideal of social justice seemed to relate strongly to his growing understanding of the Christian gospel. He was of an age to throw off the conventions of his home background and experiment with revolutionary ideas. His flirtation with communism was brief, but it fundamentally shifted the pivot of his politics away from his family's unquestioning tradition. Even when, for a short period after the war, he became an active member of the Conservative Party as a gesture against the threat of left-wing totalitarianism, he still clung to the ideals of social justice.

His father's sight was growing worse. By Christmas he could only just see, and early in 1939 he went completely blind. Kathleen had had a baby daughter on New Year's Day and could not immediately come to help, but Marjorie was summoned home from Scotland and found her mother frantic. Mr Runcie was in hospital where efforts were being made to restore his sight; but it was too late. The family were numbed with shock when the verdict came that the optic nerves had been damaged beyond repair and he would never see again. There was no question of Marjorie returning to Scotland. With the family in a state of crisis, and war again threatening, she stayed at home to help and support both her parents. Kathleen came as often as she could, and Robert was glad of her frequent visits because she, more than any other member of the family, could understand his ambitions, sympathise with his new interests, and encourage his broadening horizons.

By the summer air-raid shelters were again being dug in the school playing-fields, and Robert's membership of the school cadet force took on a new meaning as he worked for his 'A' certificate for basic proficiency in army drill and handling a rifle. War was declared in September, and Angus, who had been in the Territorial Army, was immediately called up as an army chaplain. Tony Otter, vicar of nearby Lowdham, was a close friend, and he and his wife urged Kathleen and baby Rosemary to go and live with them for the duration of the war, rather than stay alone in Angus's vicarage at Wilford. Kathleen gratefully accepted the arrangement, and it worked well. Kenneth, who had been working in London, joined the army and was soon commissioned in the Royal Engineers. Marjorie began training in the post office censorship department in Liverpool.

A family decision was made to sell the Queen's Road house and to move to something smaller in the neighbourhood. It was a great upheaval in those months of continuing crisis. They found a small house further up Moor Lane from their original home and, early in 1940, Marjorie helped her mother to move house before she herself was posted to Belfast where she remained for the rest of the war. There were already occasional air-raids over Liverpool, and during them Mrs Runcie took to sleeping with her head in a bucket to protect her from debris if the house was hit. Kathleen became increasingly anxious about her parents' safety and, within months of their move, persuaded them to sell up again and take lodgings in Wilford where she, from the Otters' vicarage in Lowdham, could keep an eye on them. Robert was left in Crosby as a boarder at his school.

The new arrangement began in September 1940 and was a considerable relief to him. The last few months at home had been a constant strain in which he could do little to help. Almost all his grammar-school years had been overshadowed by his father's ill-health and his mother's distress. He was fond of both his parents, and particularly of his father, but he could not help feeling glad to be free to concentrate on getting his place at university.

The reality of war was making its impact. London, Coventry, and Birmingham had suffered heavy bombing through the late summer and early autumn, and in November the Germans began to concentrate on the destruction of the British ports, particularly Liverpool. Robert took his turn at fire-watching on the school premises two nights a week. Bombs fell very close, though none actually hit the school. Most of the boarders regularly slept in the school basement, and the makeshift informalities of wartime life, together with the long night hours of fire-watching, brought masters and boys together in friendly intimacy. Robert particularly enjoyed the company of his mildly eccentric housemaster, Butler Wright, who was coaching him for his general paper in the forthcoming examinations, and who regaled him in the fire-watching hours with his extraordinarily wide range of off-beat knowledge.

On Sundays, and occasionally on weekday mornings, Robert was still going to St Faith's Church. It had been something of a battle to get his headmaster's permission. Charles Russell was a member of the Modern Churchmen's Union and, as a modernist liberal, did not really approve of the Anglo-Catholic goings-on at St Faith's. The boarders at the school habitually went to St Luke's, where Robert had been prepared for confirmation, and where the worship was 'low church' with nothing extreme that could upset the boys' parents. But Robert's faithfulness to his chosen church was persuasive, and he was allowed to continue as before.

Russell, who was also a member of the Archbishops' Commission on Christian Doctrine, taught divinity to the sixth form, and for the first time formal religious education in school really took hold of Robert's imagination. Years later he could still remember tackling the book of Job. 'He made me see that it wasn't irrelevant – indeed, that it *was* relevant – to wrestle with the problem of doubt; sometimes to shake your fist at God, to face the facts of the suffering world.'

Russell was keen that Robert should try for a place at his own old college, Pembroke, at Cambridge; and in December Robert went there to sit the scholarship examination. He did not win a scholarship. His marks were good enough to earn him a small bursary, but too small to provide him with the financial subsidy he would need. He was interviewed by the Senior Tutor, the Revd Harold Wynn (who was made

Bishop of Ely the following year). Robert was impressed by him, and must himself have made an impression because Wynn remembered him ever afterwards as 'the man who turned down Pembroke in favour of BNC for the sake of a few pounds'.

For it was to Brasenose College, Oxford, that Robert went, after Easter 1941, with the help of a Harrison Foundation scholarship from Merchant Taylors', and a Squire scholarship from the university. It was an obvious choice. The college had a long association with a number of Lancashire schools, including Merchant Taylors', and it particularly welcomed sportsmen. Robert was happy to go to Oxford. He had been taken there for the first time two years before by Angus and Kathleen to look round the colleges and let their spell work on his ambition. Angus had himself been an exhibitioner at St John's and, as a university-educated clergyman, he had brought a new precedent into the Runcie family which had undoubtedly made it easier for Robert to look forward to a similar future at one of the ancient universities and even, perhaps, to ordination. He knew that such an ambition would not find much favour with his father. Mr Runcie's Presbyterian antipathy to the Church of England persisted, and he still referred to Anglican clergy as 'black beetles'. Because of this, Angus's arrival in the family had caused some tensions, but he and Kathleen had consistently encouraged Robert along the path he was now taking. Mr and Mrs Runcie were both delighted that he had got an Oxford place. His two scholarships would not provide enough money to cover all his needs, but they were prepared to borrow some to see him through. They all knew it was uncertain how long he would be there. He was already nineteen, and the age for conscription at that time was twenty. He was not likely to spend more than a year at Oxford before going into one of the Services. It was impossible to predict what might happen after that.

When Robert arrived at Oxford for that Trinity term he found that the Brasenose buildings had been taken over for use as a military school, and the eight new BNC undergraduates were given rooms in Christ Church among the social elite of Oxford students.* Robert's rooms were on the ground floor of Ruskin's Gothic Meadow Buildings, faintly green with damp and overhanging trees. But he had a set of rooms all his own, with a long view through pointed windows, across the Meadow to the river.

Except for his year as a school boarder, he had rarely been away from home before. The family income had allowed only two holidays in his childhood, one when he was very young at Church Stretton in Shropshire, and the other a visit to Prestwick with his parents when Marjorie was there. He had also spent a short holiday with David Molyneux in Colwyn Bay; and that, together with a cadet-force camp, was the sum of his time away from Crosby.

He revelled in his new environment. At first his manners were shy and unobtrusive; but he was soon discovered to be good company and a good cricketer, and he made some noisy and lively friends. He was reading 'Greats', which included classics, philosophy and ancient history, and his tutor was a Greek epigraphical scholar, Marcus Niebuhr Tod. Robert went to his tutorials in Tod's room in Oriel College and found him 'a man of amazing courtesy; a lovely man who gave a touch of really superlative scholarship'. He was also taught by K. J. Spalding of Brasenose who was a philosopher fascinated by Eastern mysticism, hopelessly out of fashion in the Oxford of that time where the philosophical mood had been set by the atheistic Logical Positivism of A. J. Ayer's *Language, Truth and Logic*. K.J.'s tutorials were warm and friendly in front of a hot fire in a room scented by his after-breakfast cigar. It was very easy for his pupils to divert him from the essay in hand to a discussion of the strange horizons of mysticism and the links to be forged between many areas of thought. For Robert it was a greatly enriching experience.

* President of the Christ Church Junior Common Room at that time was Michael Kinchin-Smith, too senior to take more than passing notice of the new undergraduate from Liverpool. Forty years later, after a career in the BBC, Kinchin-Smith, having been appointed Lay Assistant to the Archbishop of Canterbury by Dr Coggan, found himself welcoming his new boss, Archbishop Runcie, to Lambeth Palace.

He still pursued his left-wing politics. The Labour Club at Oxford had been split, and the larger number of members had followed Anthony Crosland and Roy Jenkins into the Democratic Socialist Club, leaving a rump of an extreme socialist Labour Club, which Robert joined. He also went occasionally to Communist Party meetings, even though, since the Russian invasion of Finland, the communists had been in embarrassed disarray.

His church life was rich and varied. The chaplain of Christ Church, Charles Warner, himself a Christian social-ist, quickly recruited Robert as a server at the early services on weekday mornings in Christ Church Cathedral (the college chapel as well as the cathedral of the Oxford diocese). Robert also served regularly in the University Church of St Mary, and in Pusey House, the Oxford centre of Anglo-Catholic faith and practice. For the first time he was brought into touch with some of the distinguished churchmen of the day: the theologian, Oliver Quick; Robert Mortimer, later Bishop of Exeter; and the Bishop of Oxford, Kenneth Kirk.

Among the church-going undergraduates he met Derek Waters, a quiet, shy, and very reserved young man, often the butt of Robert's more extrovert games-playing friends. He was the only child of elderly parents and had never been at ease in the rough and tumble of male adolescence. He was musical, deeply religious, with a wry sense of humour; a better classical scholar than Robert, and reading Greats before going on to theological college to be ordained. As they got to know each other better, Robert found an enjoyment in his company which satisfied that part of his own nature that he kept concealed from the noisy demands of his other friends. Derek asked him home to meet his parents, and Robert received a warm and homely welcome in their small house in Boxgrove Road in Guildford. He discovered that Derek's father, Dr Charles Waters, had a doctorate in music and was both an organist and a composer of church music. As Robert got to know him he found he was a man of surpassing saintliness and devotion, dedicated to his faith, to goodness, and to serving the church as a musician. In his secular life he had worked his way up through the ranks of the Civil Service until he held a senior position in the Ministry of Labour. His wife, Derek's mother, had a personality similar to Robert's own mother, but her romantic sentimentality found its outlet in the religious practices of St Nicholas's Church which was even 'higher' than St Faith's in Crosby.

It soon became clear to Robert just how bound up with their son both Dr and Mrs Waters were. Derek had been born very late in their marriage when they had all but given up hope of children, and since then he had been the focus of their lives, rivalled only by the intensity of their religion. They were touchingly proud of how well he had done at school, and deeply gratified by his call to the priesthood. When he went to Oxford they realised that he was entering a world they could not share, but Robert was a key to it. Robert was part of that world and also their son's friend, and so they made him their friend too. They encouraged him to visit them as often as possible, and made much of him when he went.

In October 1941 Robert celebrated his twentieth birthday and conscription loomed near. During the summer vacation he had learned to drive a tractor and had gone, under a government scheme, to teach the same skill to senior boys at Stockport Grammar School so that they could take part in the wartime agricultural effort. He had rather spoiled his record by failing to get on with the headmaster and driving his tractor across the guy-ropes of the speech-day marquee, but he had managed to win the tennis mixed doubles in Davenport Park. Now he was back at Oxford and, as the term began, he could not be sure that he would be able to complete it, or that he would return for the next one. Though he enjoyed undergraduate life immensely, the uncertainty of how much longer it would last began to lend it an air of unreality.

He had long ago decided that he would go into the army, and he expected to get a commission. Since he had been at Oxford he had been in the Senior Training Corps (where he was taught map-reading by the poet and Fellow of Merton, Edmund Blunden), and gained high marks in the half-written, half-practical test for certificate 'B' which would exempt him from the first weeks of basic army training. Armed with this, he went to the Oxford recruiting office where he was received and interviewed by two Guards officers, a Coldstreamer and a Grenadier, who were obviously used to dealing with promising undergraduates.

Robert knew that he would be expected to have some preference about his regiment and, though his family had no connections with any, he thought his father would be pleased if he chose a Scottish one. As the King's Own Scottish Borderers was virtually the only one he had ever heard of, he mentioned it and asked about the possibility of a commission in it. To his surprise he was immediately asked if he would consider, instead, a commission in the Scots Guards. Embarrassed, he said he did not think he could afford it; he had no money of his own, and he had always understood that it was necessary to have a private income to subsidise one's army pay in a Guards regiment.

The Coldstream adjutant consulted his colleague. Could one live on one's pay in wartime? They discussed mess bills and uniform expenses and, between them, decided that it was not only possible, but quite reasonable. At least, they suggested, Robert could go and try his luck in an interview at the regimental headquarters at Wellington Barracks. The Scots Guards were needing recruits, they told him, because of their recent heavy losses in North Africa.

The interview was arranged for him, and Robert took the train to London and found the barracks in Birdcage Walk close to Buckingham Palace. While he waited he was given the *Daily Telegraph* to read, but he was soon shown into the presence of the commanding officer, Colonel Bill Balfour, DSO, OBE, MC, who had returned from retirement at the outbreak of war to take command of the regiment and to steer it through its necessary wartime expansion. Robert found him unexpectedly and delightfully civilised, and taking it for granted that he had a potential Scots Guards officer in front of him. Robert explained again that he had no money to supplement his army pay, but Colonel Balfour convincingly assured him that it did not matter in the least.

Totally captivated, Robert signed on, having been told he was likely to find himself in an armoured division, in a tank. He returned to Oxford and, that night in college, his friends plied him with beer and jeered at him for his perfidy. His socialist politics were well known, for he had defended their principles strongly. What, his friends wanted to know, would become of those principles once he had joined that most upper-crust echelon of British life: an officers' mess in the Brigade of Guards?

Chapter Six

The Scots Guards

Robert's call-up papers came soon after Easter 1942, allowing him time to complete his fourth university term. It was a hot day in early June when, for the last time, he breakfasted with his friends in hall, and then left Oxford with no idea when he would return. He took a train to London, crossed to Waterloo Station, and took another out to Brookwood in the Surrey heathland, an area traditionally monopolised by the army. His destination was Pirbright Camp, two miles from the station, and despite the heat and his heavy suitcase he decided to walk. Several times he stopped to rest, and found himself thinking dramatically that from that day his life would never again be the same.

He had a rough introduction to his new environment. Three-quarters of his fellow-recruits for the Scots Guards were Etonians who had gone straight from school to the Guards' Depot at Caterham before coming to Pirbright. Robert had been exempt from that preliminary training because of his 'B' certificate gained at Oxford, but it added to his disadvantages in his first meeting with the young men who were to be his companions. Not only had they had some weeks in the real army, but many of them had a family tradition of service with the Scots Guards and believed implicitly in its superior standards. Runcie's different background came as a shock to them, and they were neither sensitive nor good-mannered in concealing their contempt. Surveying him as a tyke from Liverpool, who had arrived on that first day in quite the wrong clothes for the occasion, they made it scathingly clear that they considered that the regiment must indeed be scraping the bottom of the barrel for its new officers. Fortunately there were men at Pirbright who had known Robert at Oxford and came to his defence, but it was still a very difficult first couple of weeks. Robert would have found it hard to believe that several of those young men from Eton, including their ring-leader, Tony Stevenson, were to become life-long friends.

He was glad, on an occasional Sunday, to get away to the Waters's house in Guildford where the pleasure of Derek's parents at seeing him, and their homely comforts, were balm to his social bruises. Derek was also in the army, as a private in the Pioneer Corps, for his many good qualities were not those that the army valued in wartime. His situation was an extreme contrast to Robert's prospects, but to the Waters it made no difference; they were delighted to see Robert, in Derek's absence, almost as a substitute for their beloved son. He relaxed in their domestic Sundays, lunching with them and accompanying them to church. It comforted him and kept alive that quiet religious side of his life that he kept hidden from his army friends.

For he made friends quickly once those early days were over and immediate impressions forgotten. His senior officers saw him as 'a self-effacing, modest, even shy young man in a group who were almost wholly the very opposite'. It was clear from his conversation that he was intelligent and well-read, and it was known that he had had a scholarship to Oxford. But among his contemporaries it was his outstanding gift as a mimic which really broke the ice. His ability to do a perfect rendering of the voice and mannerisms of anyone he observed, whether it was the colonel, the chaplain, or a Glaswegian guardsman, was a source of hilarious delight for his companions.

After the month at Pirbright there followed three months at the Royal Military College into which was compressed the whole special Sandhurst experience that produced the finished army officer and gentleman. He learned about tanks as well as about infantry fighting, radio and guns, and he also learned how to be a 'guardee'. One afternoon a week was spent with Major Charles Fellowes, called back from retirement specially to instruct young officer-cadets in how they should behave, how they should dress, and what language they should use. It was many years before Nancy Mitford was to categorise the differences between 'U' and 'non-U' speech and behaviour, but it was precisely that consciousness of upper-class tradition that Major Fellowes was there to instil. No officer in uniform was ever to be seen carrying a parcel in the street. Whisky was to be called 'whisky' not 'Scotch'. The regimental tie (when they could once again dress in civilian clothes) was to be tied exactly so. On these details depended the peculiar honour of the regiment and, in addition, because it was a Scottish regiment they were joining, the young men must know how to dance Scottish reels and to recognise the wailing tunes of the pipes.

Quick to learn as ever, Robert readily acquired this social gloss on his native good manners. Now that he had proved his worth as good company among his fellows, he was enjoying himself and, as Sandhurst habits took over, he no longer had to watch every word and expression that might remind the old Etonians of his Liverpool origins. Even so, he still occasionally went to the Waters' for a weekend's relaxation in homely company.

On one occasion Derek was there, being his usual quiet, cheerful self with his parents, and delighted to see Robert. But that afternoon as they walked together around Guildford, Derek gave Robert a very different picture of his army life from the one he had shown his parents. Still trying to be amusing about it, he talked wryly of the mockery he underwent in the barrack-room when it was known that he said his prayers and went to church. He endured it, but was sick at heart at the coarseness and brutality with which he was surrounded. He had found no congenial company among the soldiers he was with, and it quickly became clear to Robert that he was desperately unhappy.

Robert did his best to sympathise and give what comfort he could, but he felt guilty and uneasy. His own experience was so different. He himself was now considered a thoroughly good fellow by his contemporaries and, though there was no one with whom he could share the quiet and religious side of his nature as he could with Derek, he had no shortage of intelligent companions. He was also uneasy on another count: the weeks at Sandhurst had made him unpleasantly conscious that he, as an officer-cadet, should not be seen walking with an ordinary private. Glad though he had been to see Derek, it was with a certain relief that he returned to Sandhurst.

At the end of three months the chrysalises turned into butterflies as the cadets went to the prescribed tailors and hatters for their officers' uniforms and appeared for the first time with glossy Sam Browne belts over well-cut jackets. There was the customary passing-out parade, and the senior officer who came to take the salute was a small, spare man with a brisk manner. 'Who's that frightful little squirt?' asked an Etonian Irish Guards officer standing near Robert. Somebody hissed 'Montgomery', but the name meant nothing to them.

Early in November, Second-Lieutenants R. A. K. Runcie and A. R. G. Stevenson were posted together to the Third (Tank) Battalion Scots Guards training on Salisbury Plain. They travelled on a wet Sunday night from Waterloo Station and were met at Salisbury by a truck in which they were driven the twenty-five miles to the village of Codford St Mary on the southern edge of the Plain. There they found the officers' mess, a Nissen hut, under several inches of water. It was their first experience of the quantities of rain and mud that they would learn to live with in the ensuing years.

Serious tank training began. The battalion had just changed from the fast and light Covenanter cruiser tanks to heavy forty-ton Churchills which lumbered along at sixteen miles an hour and were intended to support the infantry in assault. Runcie found that he was to lead a troop of three tanks with Glaswegian crews, one tank commanded by himself, one by his troop sergeant, and one by his troop corporal. Each tank had a crew of five. As well as the commander, whose place was half-standing, half-crouching in the turret, headphones clamped to his ears to keep him in touch with his superior officer and the other tanks in his troop, there was the driver who sat in the front of the hull with a very limited view of where he was going and dependent on the commander for directions; there was a gunner who fired what in the early days seemed a ludicrously small two-pounder, but which was later replaced by a six-pounder and eventually a 75mm gun; a co-driver who was also in charge of the smaller gun mounted in the hull; and with the commander in the turret was the radio-operator who also had the job of loading the main gun.

The battalion was divided into four squadrons, each of which had six troops. Runcie was in Right Flank commanded by Lord Cathcart, who after the war was to command the regiment. Tony Stevenson had gone to 'S' Squadron commanded by the future Home Secretary, Major William Whitelaw. The commander of Left Flank was Major the Hon. Michael Fitzalan Howard, later a Major-General and eventually Marshal of the Diplomatic Corps; and commanding the Headquarters Squadron was the twenty-seventh Chief of Clan Maclean, Major Sir Charles Maclean, who, after being Lord Lieutenant of Argyll and Chief Scout of the British Commonwealth and Empire, became Lord Chamberlain. In the officers' mess there were a considerable number of men who were to have distinguished careers: among those who became Runcie's life-long friends were Hector (subsequently Sir Hector) Laing who became chairman of the United Biscuits conglomerate, and Peter Balfour, chairman of the Scottish whisky distilleries.

After spending the winter months in hard training on Salisbury Plain the battalion moved to Yorkshire in April. Right Flank was stationed at Hawes where battle-training in the Dales became even more intense. Derek was also in Yorkshire, and one Sunday he came with his parents to meet Robert in Hawes; somewhat to Robert's embarrassment, they all went to evensong in the parish church together. It was not that Robert had repudiated his religious life, but he kept it private and unobtrusive. The battalion's church parades, like its chaplain, George Reid, were Church of Scotland, in keeping with the tradition of the regiment, and Reid had accepted that Runcie's high Anglicanism was not compatible with his own tastes. So Robert lay low, as he did throughout the war, and made his communion when a Church of England chaplain (often Tony Tremlett who would later be a colleague in Cambridge) visited the battalion, or a church was readily accessible. His personal religious life he kept very private and, though it was known by his companions, it passed almost without comment. Years later, William Whitelaw said that the mess would have roared with equal laughter had it been suggested that one day Bob Runcie would be Archbishop of Canterbury or that he himself would be Home Secretary.

So it was Robert's good nature, combined with a slight feeling of being put to shame by the Waters family, that took him to evensong with them; and it proved to be a more important gesture than he knew. It was the last time he saw Derek who, shortly afterwards, was drafted overseas to Italy. He had not been there long before he was hit by a shell splinter while on sentry duty, and died a few weeks later.

His parents were completely devastated and they never really recovered. (Thirty years later it was discovered that his father had continued to write a weekly letter to him until a few days before his own death.) They found their comfort in Robert, expending on him much of the love, concern, and prayer that they would have showered on their son, until he came to look upon them almost as substitute parents. He went to stay with them when on leave, and enjoyed being spoiled by them almost as much as they enjoyed spoiling him. He had a growing respect for Derek's father whose dedication to the church and to music was such that in his latter years he twice every Sunday made a difficult journey to London and across to its East End so that he could play the organ in a church that would otherwise have no hope of a skilled musician to lead its choir. In Mrs Waters Robert found motherly warmth and religious understanding and, throughout the years of the war, and when he was in the midst of the fighting, he knew that they both prayed daily for his well-being, and lit innumerable candles in innumerable churches for his safety.

The months in Yorkshire culminated in a ten-day exercise which attempted to simulate real battle conditions as they lived and slept with their tanks. At the end of it the tanks were loaded on to carriers and they moved to Thoresby Park in the Nottinghamshire Dukeries which brought Robert within easy reach of his family. He saw them regularly, dropping in to the Lowdham vicarage with his friends. He found that his father spent most of his time listening to the wireless and having the newspapers read to him by his wife. Mr Runcie followed the progress of the war intently, and demanded complete silence from the family during each news bulletin. Mrs Runcie had become fiercely protective of him and his comfort, but took great pleasure in Kathleen's children. Rosemary, at that time three years old, knew them both as loving, kindly grandparents. She and her baby brother, young Robin (Robert's godson), were allowed to spend only limited time with their grandfather for fear of tiring him, but she remembers that he would often stroke their heads and faces, trying to learn the features of the grandchildren he could never see. Mrs Runcie was a wholly successful grandmother, warm and generous and always ready with little treats and surprises. Robert, too, was a popular uncle who always seemed interested in what the children were doing and made them feel important.

The battalion had its second long and tedious winter of training, and they began to long for action. Tension was mounting and, at the end of April, in complete secrecy, the battalion moved south to join the gathering invasion forces. *En route* they did not know where they were heading for, but they found themselves at Eastwell Park near Charing in Kent, and spent their time there in continual exercises over the high hedges and into the deep ditches of the Kent farmland. The damage that they did was considerable, and kept the army claims department busy; but it was experience that was to prove invaluable soon after they got to France.

On 30 May 1944 the whole brigade attended a 'Service before Battle' in Canterbury Cathedral, the first time Runcie had been in the building. It was conducted by the dean, Dr Hewlett Johnson, known as 'The Red Dean' for his communist sympathies. The sermon was preached by the Archbishop of Canterbury, Dr William Temple, the most distinguished archbishop for many decades in his scholarship, his far-sighted social concern, and his charismatic influence on all who knew him. The band of the Scots Guards played and, after the service, led a march past of the whole brigade.

A week later the first Allied troops landed on the Normandy beaches, but still the Third Battalion was held back. Training went on, and it was more than a month before they moved into the embarkation area, to Bentley in Hampshire. Three days later, on 19 July, they at last drove their tanks on to the Hards at Gosport and began embarking in the Tank Landing Ships.

When they crossed the Channel the following day it was the first time that Runcie had ever left the shores of England. The rough sea did not treat the heavy awkward craft kindly, and he and many others were very sick and thankful beyond measure to land their tanks at Arromanches. All of Right and Left Flanks crossed without serious incident, but part of 'S' Squadron, under Major Whitelaw, boarded a TLS that had already seen long and hard war service, and almost met disaster. As soon as they were at sea, eight tanks broke loose, and the forty-ton Churchills slid from side to side as the ship rolled. For more than three hours their crews struggled to re-chain them, but it proved impossible until they had returned to Gosport. As complete radio silence had been imposed, the rest of the battalion had no idea what had happened to them, and there were many anxious hours of waiting until the missing tanks came safely ashore.

For a further week the squadrons waited among the apple trees of the Normandy orchards, sampling the local cider and calvados, and practising their French on the local people. It was hot July weather and the whole countryside was permeated by the combined smells of thousands of small green apples which rained down on the tanks, and of the very dead and bloated cattle and horses which still lay in the fields as casualties of war. The tank crews spent some time studying with macabre interest the wrecks of Allied tanks from the battles of previous weeks and, taking note of where the hulls of those tanks had proved most vulnerable, welded spare track-plates on to the hulls of their own tanks.

At last, on the evening of 28 July, the order came for them to move to the front line and, within two hours, the battalion was on the march towards the German-held Caumont ridge. So close to the battlefield it was difficult for them to be clear about what was going on but General Montgomery was, at that time, engaging the attention of the German armoured divisions in the Caen area so that the Americans could sweep round to the west with only the German infantry to contend with. The Caumont ridge offered a naturally strong defensive position and, if the Germans continued to hold the southern end, the Allied advance would be at a standstill. So the Scots Guards' tanks, and the infantry of the 15th (Scottish) Division with whom they had trained in Yorkshire, were to make the initial attack southwards from Caumont to the end of the ridge and on to the Bois du Homme. It was Bocage-type country: small fields with high banks and tree-lined hedgerows, alternating with orchards and copses, all intersected by deep, narrow lanes; very like the farmland they had grown used to in Kent. Few military vehicles other than the Churchill tanks could cross such countryside. It was too easy to be trapped in the steep-sided lanes, and the banks were too high for the smaller tanks to negotiate. Only the Churchills with their great length could rear almost vertically over a bank and down the other side. It was an uncomfortable and exhausting journey for the crew.

They travelled all night through this difficult country to the concentration area round the village of Ste Honorine-le-Ducy, three miles from the forward area, and lay up all the next day. The tank crews were able to snatch a few hours' rest, but their leaders had little as they gathered and studied their orders. The next night they moved up the slopes of the ridge just east of Caumont town, and sat listening to a battle being fought by the Grenadiers on the other side of the hill. Then, at seven-thirty in the morning, their orders to move came. As Runcie's tank rumbled to the top of the ridge an

Irish Guards major who happened to be passing cheered them on with the information that it was good hunting country and an Irish hunter would be better than a tank. Runcie waved as Right Flank and 'S' Squadron topped the ridge and went down into the smoke-filled valley where they were met by mortar, shell and machine-gun fire.

Their advance was slow, every hedge and bank a difficult obstacle, and the thick summer leaf of trees and bushes a perfect cover for enemy fire. The battalion was putting into practice the tactics it had learned so well in its training with the infantry. At each hedge the foot-soldiers looked through to see if there were German tanks in the next field. If it was clear, the Churchills crashed over the hedge and spent a quarter of an hour shooting up the next hedgerow and any likely places that might conceal an enemy gun emplacement. Then the rest of the infantry came up and they tackled the next field. It was so like the exercises they had endlessly practised in England that there was no time to absorb the realities either of their own danger or of the fact that they were now in the business of killing the enemy.

Towards midday two Right Flank tanks were blown up in a minefield, but the rest of Right Flank and 'S' Squadron pressed on, leaving the infantry behind, and consolidated their position on the ridge, with Left Flank behind them in support. They kept their tanks' hull down as they waited, for they were dangerously exposed and four miles inside the enemy lines. It was just as they were listening through their headphones to the report of their battle on the six o'clock BBC news that heavy German guns opened fire and twelve of the tanks were destroyed in less than five minutes. Runcie, like all his surviving companions, was stunned by the slaughter. Major Cuthbert, second-in-command of the battalion, was killed, as were Captain Nigel Beeson and Lieutenant Humble of 'S' Squadron, together with twenty-one other ranks. Nearly a score were wounded. 'S' Squadron had suffered the heaviest losses, and Major Whitelaw had quickly to reorganise his remaining tanks. Caring for the wounded as best they could, they had to wait another hour before they were relieved by the Argylls, and the tired tank crews could withdraw to a nearby field for a hot meal – which few could eat – and some sleep.

Messages poured in next day congratulating them on the way they had broken through the German lines, but there was sadness as they buried their friends. In the battle for Caumont the battalion had suffered a third of the fatal casualties it was to know through its whole campaign across Europe. It was valuable experience of real war, but it had been dearly bought.

They had also learned that living in a tank for days on end under battle conditions was very different from spending a few hours in a turret or driving seat on exercise. David Erskine, in his regimental history of the Scots Guards, *The Scots Guards 1919–1955*, persuaded one of the troop commanders to describe it.

To crash straight across the country ignoring the easy route, taking in Churchillian strides small woods, buildings, hills, valleys, sunken roads and, worst of all, those steep high banks which divide the Norman Bocage like ridges on a monstrous waffle; this was something for which we were not prepared by our training in the Dukeries.

There was no luxury and little comfort about the Churchills save when driven slowly along a road: in the small fields of Normandy, among the cider orchards, every move during the hot summer brought down a shower of small, hard, sour apples cascading into the turrets through the commanders' open hatches; after a few days there might be enough to jam the turret.

Five men in close proximity, three in the turret and two below in the driving compartment, all in a thick metal oven, soon produced a foul smell: humanity, apples, cordite and heat. Noise: the perpetual 'mush' through the earphones twenty-four hours each day, and through it the machinery noises, the engine in the background, with the whine of the turret trainer and the thud and rattle of the guns an accompaniment. The surge of power as the tank rose up to the crest of a bank; the pause at the top while the driver, covered with sweat and dust and unable to see, tried to balance his forty tons before the bone jarring crash down into the field beyond, with every loose thing taking life and crashing round inside the turret. Men, boxes of machine-gun ammunition, magazines, shell-cases – and always those small, hard apples.

The skill of the driver, and indeed of all those men in the crew, was remarkable: the operator struggling to keep the wireless on net and the guns loaded; the gunner with eyes always at the telescope however much the turret revolved and crashed around him; the hot stoppages in the machine-guns; the commander, with his head only above his hatches, choked with dust, not quite standing and not quite sitting during all those long Normandy days: always the wireless pounding in his ear-drums.

After dark was the time for maintenance, when the three-ton trucks from the echelon came up with petrol, ammunition and food. Then the guns had to be cleaned and all repairs finished before first light and stand-to. Thanks to the tanks, repairs were not many, but crews could not go on for very long without rest.

After the battle of Caumont Major Whitelaw became second-in-command of the battalion, and the squadrons rested for three days before Right and Left Flanks pushed on, leaving 'S' Squadron to reform. Left Flank headed for the village of Estry while Right Flank spent an unhappy morning sitting at a cross-roads under heavy fire before they could move round Estry to Canteloup. On the way Captain Mathieson, riding in a scout car, was struck by a shell from a German tank and was the first of Right Flank's troop leaders to be killed. The fighting was heavy and difficult all day and Runcie, suffering reaction after Caumont, was depressed and miserable, with none of the exhilaration that had carried him through his first battle. Mathieson's death brought it home to him that his friends were being killed, that they would go on being killed, and that the end to this intolerable fighting was a very long way off. It was some days before he could shake off his depression.

'S' Squadron rejoined them on 11 August and they took

the village of Chênedollé with the relatively light losses of four men killed and fourteen wounded, and then they were left with nothing to do for a month while other Allied divisions advanced at speed across Europe. They spent their time on repairs and maintenance, and on exploring the countryside and what gastronomic delights it still had to offer. Major Fitzalan Howard left for promotion to Brigade Major, and Major John Mann took over the command of Left Flank.

It was the end of September before they could load the tanks on to their transporters and drive through newly-liberated northern France and Belgium until they crossed the border into Holland. Then followed a month of alarms and excursions around Eindhoven, constantly setting off and being ordered back to base until they became known to the local inhabitants as the 'Eindhoven Wanderers'. During this time Runcie had three days' leave in Brussels, and handed his tank over to a replacement officer. When he got back from his leave he was shattered to learn that on the very first morning after he had left, his replacement had received a bullet through his head – a bullet that Runcie could not help feeling had really been meant for him.

By the end of October they were again in the front line, and fighting went on through a cold, wet and snowy winter. If, in the summer, the tanks were stinking ovens, so, in the winter (wrote the troop leader quoted in the regimental history)

they became ice-boxes surrounded by freezing metal, every breeze a draught, and every rainstorm a series of cataracts that poured through the hatches and down the necks of the occupants. Though better than most British tanks at the time, even the Churchill bogged down in the sodden winter fields of Holland; and after a few unbogging operations the inside of the tank became as muddy as an infantryman's trench. In snow and ice the tank behaved like a forty-ton toboggan, sometimes going the way the commander and driver wanted, sometimes not. But, in snow or ice, rain or sunshine, the Churchill tanks, in the idiom of the Guardsmen who fought in them, generally 'got there'.

They fought and they waited and fought again as Holland steadily cleared of German troops. Despite the Ardennes offensive, the battalion celebrated Christmas and Hogmanay at Maastricht in style in a spell of fine frosty weather. Some of them, including Runcie, were invited to a dance at the local castle where they met the five daughters of a Dutch banker and his Belgian wife. Runcie paired off with one of the daughters called Trees, a lively, sparkly girl who was a devout Roman Catholic and insisted, however late a Saturday night party, that Runcie accompanied her to Mass the next morning. Of all his girl-friends during these years, Trees was the most special, and is the one he most probably would have married if marrying had been thinkable at that time. When the battalion moved on into Germany he kept in touch with her, and saw her again in Bonn when the war ended. (The friendship with Trees continued even after she married and, many years later in 1982, after Trees was dead and Runcie was Archbishop, his memories of her were vividly revived when he was visited at Lambeth Palace by her son, very like his mother, who is now a Brother of the Taizé Community.)

The New Year of 1945 brought heavy snow, and it was time to move on. The tanks were white-washed and camouflaged with discarded parachutes as they drove across the German border and helped in the capture of three German villages before returning to Nijmegen. Then came the advance on the Rhine across its marshy plain, with the tanks threading their way through minefields and constantly getting stuck in the mud. Left Flank were the first British tanks through the Siegfried Line, and the whole battalion was involved in the confused capture of Cleve when, at one point in the dark, Right Flank found itself about to do battle with the Grenadiers. All the tanks, and the Canadian infantry with them, were under constant shell-fire, and there were a good many casualties. There was hard fighting round Calbeck castle where the battalion took more than a hundred prisoners and Runcie's troop destroyed an ammunition dump.

In the last week of February they were advancing fast, and on the twenty-seventh Right Flank took over three hundred prisoners on the way to another bridgehead. They pressed on under heavy fire, and one of Runcie's tanks was hit. Most of the crew scrambled out as it started to burn, but the co-driver did not appear. As the four crew dashed for cover, Runcie could see that the turret was stuck in the central position in which it could not be opened. With shells falling all around, he jumped from his own tank and ran to turn the turret and drag the co-driver out. The man was not wounded, only dazed and overcome by smoke, but quite unable to help himself until he had been half-carried to shelter and given time to recover.

Next day they moved on. Left Flank and the Royal Ulster Rifles were to take a strong German defensive position in Berberh Wood near the small town of Winnekendonk, while Right Flank, with infantry from the Lincolnshire Regiment, were to attempt the capture of the town itself. Both the wood and the town were fiercely defended, but Left Flank and the Ulsters established their position at the west end of the wood in the early afternoon while 'S' Squadron and the KOSB cleared the remainder. By four o'clock the decision was made to attempt an assault on the town before dark, and Right Flank and the Lincolns gathered in the north-west corner of the wood about half a mile from the town. They decided to attack at five forty-five, with one troop of tanks and one company of infantry on each side of the main road making their way towards the town while the rest of the squadron, including Runcie's troop, followed behind in support.

As soon as they came within view of the town, and the leading troops were in the open, they met high explosive and armour-piercing shells which knocked out all three tanks on the right of the road and two of the three tanks on the left. But the tanks behind came steadily on. Heavy guns were shelling them, but their attackers were hidden from view by the hedges on either side of the road and between the fields. Runcie's troop was by now in the lead on the right-hand side of the road and, to get a better view of where the shells were coming from, he took his tank into the middle of the field and, taking a rapid sighting, ordered his gunners to open fire. He was in a very exposed position with the enemy guns no more than 500 yards away, and his crew were firing furiously with no thought but to stop the Germans before they were stopped themselves. The effect was almost immediate, and the German guns fell silent. Runcie called up his other tanks and all three rolled on towards the town, shooting up some smaller gun emplacements on the way.

It was an action that earned him the Military Cross, though he was not to know it for some time to come. The official citation read:

During the attack on Winnekendonk on 2 March 1945, Lieutenant Runcie's troop was in support of the leading wave of tanks when they came under heavy and close fire of concealed 88mm and self-propelled guns from the front and both flanks, all three tanks being hit.

Lieutenant Runcie unhesitatingly took his tank out into the open which was the only place from which he could see the enemy weapons, and engaged them so effectively that he knocked out two 75mm SPs and one 88mm, also causing the enemy to abandon a nest of 50mm guns. During this time not only was he shot at with armour-piercing shells from a range of not more than 500 yards, but was also being subjected to very heavy shell and mortar fire. A short time later, while still being fired upon, he personally and successfully directed the fire of our artillery on to an area from which fire was holding up our advance. There is no doubt that Lieutenant Runcie's courageous leadership and the magnificent marksmanship of his troop dealt so effectively with this strong enemy anti-tank screen that our tanks and infantry were able to get on into the town.

Winnekendonk did not fall until late in the evening when

the Germans suddenly gave up after several hours of hand-to-hand fighting in the dark. It was only next day, as the Allied troops surveyed the town and rounded up the prisoners, that they realised with what strength it had been defended. At one point Robert walked over to a German Tiger tank which had almost certainly been knocked out by his own guns. There were four dead men inside it, all about the same age as himself. He quite suddenly felt sick as he realised the significance of killing as never before. It was a bad day as he continued to brood on the human realities of war and what each death meant in terms of life and hope cut short, and in grief and suffering among so many families.

After twenty-four days continually in the line of battle, during which they had advanced twenty-five miles and taken fifteen hundred prisoners, the battalion had three weeks in which to pause and take breath before crossing the Rhine on the night of 25 March and going on to capture Dorsten. In a further hard fight they took Munster on 3 April.

They stayed in Munster for three days while they helped clear the town. Runcie and a fellow troop leader, Archie Fletcher, explored some garages close to where they were billeted, and found a Delage staff-car still flying a German army commander's flag. They were delighted with their prize, but news of their discovery soon reached the brigade headquarters and they were persuaded to present their trophy to Brigadier Greenacre who was magnanimous enough to invite them to help him try it out. With Runcie in the back, they drove round the ruins of the town and then, to try the real paces of the car, they turned on to a main road in the direction of a neighbouring town which the brigadier knew had already been captured by the Grena-diers. They were driving behind an American jeep when it suddenly slewed across the road and burst into flames and four bullets hit the Delage, one of them slightly wounding the brigadier. In less than a moment all three of them were out of the car and into the ditch, crawling back the way they had come as fast as they could, while the German sniper who had shot at them climbed on to the roof of the Delage to take better aim. They crawled, scrambled and ran, and finally got back to brigade headquarters covered in mud and late for dinner, with the brigadier swearing Runcie and Fletcher to secrecy about the whole embarrassing episode. The Delage was recovered next day.

In fine spring weather they continued their advance, meeting on the way thousands of liberated Allied prisoners of war and workers from Germany's slave-labour camps. The Russians were advancing on Berlin, so the British turned north towards the Baltic. The battalion was to be involved in capturing Celle, with Left Flank and 'S' Squadron going in first, and Right Flank bringing up the rear. It fell easily, for the town was full of Allied prisoners and most of the Germans had left, blowing up the bridges as they went. Runcie took his troop into the deserted centre of the town and then realised that in the unexpected quiet he had gone further than planned. As he jumped down into the road from his tank to have a look round, German guns some way ahead opened fire. A reconnaissance party was with his troop, and one of the soldiers volunteered to go forward to see where the guns were. He was a small, neat little man, probably a bank-clerk in peace-time, thought Runcie. For a second he hesitated, wondering if he should go himself, and then let the man go. Almost immediately he knew he had sent the man to his death, and he was again haunted by the belief that someone else had stopped a shot that was meant for him.

The fifty miles to Uelzen were bedevilled by huge craters and tree-trunks that the retreating Germans had left in the road, but the last twenty of those miles were covered at tremendous speed in the dark, taking eight hundred prisoners on the way. The dash was followed by two days and nights of intense fighting until they were relieved by other troops and allowed to take some rest.

On 2 May they were on their last push to the Baltic coast to join up with the Russians. They had set off in the small hours of the morning and at breakfast-time they were in Lüneburg, stuck in a traffic jam in the middle of the town, when the news came over the radio that Hitler was dead. Two days later the battalion celebrated the German surren-

der with an enormous bonfire on the village green at Siebe-
neichen. The celebrations, both official and unofficial, went
on for several days, and then the battalion moved to the
coast at Lütjenburg. There Runcie made history, as a tank
commander, by being responsible for the capture of a German submarine. He saw it lying about three-quarters of a
mile offshore and raced back to the squadron where a
boarding party was quickly organised which drove at speed
to the nearest fishing village. Two ancient fishermen were
ordered to row the party out to the U-boat where they
received the captain's surrender.

It was breakfast-time the next day when Colonel Dunbar,
commander of the battalion, came in to the mess to tell
Runcie he had been awarded the Military Cross for his part
in the battle of Winnekendonk. His time with his tank was
coming to an end. The squadrons spent May helping to sort
out the thousands of refugees who were fleeing from East
Prussia and then on 2 June the tanks, made immaculate
despite their scars, took part in a parade through Kiel in
honour of the King's birthday. It was their last proud drive
before they were taken off to rust away in a tank-park near
Hamburg. Their crews became Foot Guards, and soon had
to give up their tank-men's distinctive black berets. The way
Runcie had worn his had always been a source of amusement
to his fellow-officers. Captain John Mann remembered:

Of all the many officers in my regiment who had come to
some sort of understanding with the tank-man's beret –
and most of us found this quite impossible – Bob's wearing
of his headgear was quite outstandingly the worst and
most laughable. Viewed from the left, his beret managed
to look like half a round black pudding and, from the
right, as though the material had been drenched and was
dripping over his right ear. You have only to look at most
photographs of him at that time to realise what a delight
his particular style with that beret was to all his friends.

They were back in formal caps, and no longer did the
Third Battalion include '(Tank)' in its title. They moved to

Cologne and, in August, Runcie had his first leave at home since he had crossed the Channel on his way to Normandy. He saw his family, but happened to be staying with friends in Bournemouth when V J Day – the end of the war with Japan – was celebrated. Back in Cologne he started, together with Archie Fletcher, taking regular German lessons from an elderly German professor in desperate need of the modest fees they paid him. He also acquired a German girl-friend, just nineteen, very beautiful and sternly anti-Christian. She lived down the road from the officers' mess and, despite the anti-fraternisation rules, they met whenever they could and were even able to make several visits to the opera in Cologne. It was a glorious autumn, and Runcie learned to love the Rhineland countryside in all the richness of its colouring.

They stayed there until the beginning of February when there was a farewell parade for the battalion before it was dispersed. Runcie was one of eight officers and three hundred other ranks who went to join the First Battalion keeping the uneasy peace in Trieste. Duties apart, it was an enjoyable place to be. The British were popular with the Italian-speaking Triestini, and there was sun, sea, and the facilities for all kinds of sport. Runcie was attached to the Italo-Yugoslav Boundary Commission which had the task of drawing the national boundaries between Italy, Yugoslavia and Austria, which meant defining the southern end of the Iron Curtain. Head of the British delegation was Humphrey Waldock (subsequently knighted), who later became president of the European Commission on Human Rights. He was a Fellow of Brasenose College, and after the war became Chichele Professor of International Law at Oxford and had a most distinguished career as an international lawyer. Runcie, who by now had the rank of captain, was so fascinated by this first experience of international diplomacy that, to prolong it, he refused an opportunity of early demobilisation.

Temporarily, however, he acquired another job. The quartermaster, Captain Quinn, an amusing but difficult Irishman, went home on protracted leave, and Runcie was appointed in his place. Peter Balfour described how he filled his temporary post. 'All his powers of mimicry and sharp perception of other people came out with a rush. He became Captain Quinn. With a thick brogue and rolling gait he would come into my office demanding the same outrageous things as his predecessor, well knowing that only a few days before he would have regarded them as outrageous too. He thoroughly enjoyed himself, but I am not sure that I did.'

It was while Runcie was in Trieste that he received the news that his father had died from a heart attack. Since the end of the war his parents had been living with Kathleen and Angus in their new rectory at Cotgrave where Angus, immediately on his demobilisation, had been made rector of All Saints'. Mr Runcie's health had been steadily declining through the years and, though his death was not unexpected, it still came as something of a shock. Robert was saddened and would have gone home had he been able to get there in time for the funeral; but it was still a laborious business crossing Europe and the whole family united in assuring him that there was no need for him to try.

He was finally demobilised in August 1946, leaving – Captain Balfour commented – 'many friendships, but absolutely no inkling that he had ever contemplated taking Orders'. He returned to England to readjust himself, and to pick up his life at Oxford where he had left off.

Chapter Seven

Oxford, Cambridge and Ordination

The army had relinquished Brasenose College, and Runcie was allotted a set of rooms at ground level looking across the grass of the Front Quad. He could see the college gate and the porter's lodge and, rising behind them, the domed roof of the Radcliffe Camera. He moved in at the beginning of the Michaelmas Term, and on 10 November 1946 he wrote to Angus Inglis.

I have settled down here better than I ever imagined possible, although at the moment my power of absorbing any but the simplest truths is very weak and gives me cause for worry. A cheering factor is that on all sides one hears the same lament. The zest for work is there far more than ever it was before, but the machinery is creaking badly. However, in the present state of the world it is comforting beyond all measure to return here where nothing has changed or ever looks likely to change; where the battle of Marathon is still fought over daily, and where a certain amount of consternation has been caused by a man called Gomme of Glasgow University who, since I was last up, has produced a tremendous work of scholarship on Thucydides which has shaken to the foundations the theories of Jowett and Grundy in which Oxford has always taken such pride.

I have very pleasant rooms with a very academic view from the window, of the Camera and St Mary's. The discomforts are not as great as some would have us believe.

No one in BNC shares rooms, but we do two sittings for Hall. The most alarming feature is the shortage of books. The assistants of Blackwell's regard you automatically as a visitor if you ask for a copy of Kant or Descartes. Something resembling a rugger scrum takes place, I am told, in the modern history section of the Radcliffe Camera at 9 o'clock every morning. I am a reader at the Ashmolean so I can get all my history wants supplied there, but a proportion of the vac. will have to be spent in foraging among the second-hand bookshops in London and Nottingham.

I am afraid I have little to report of mutual friends. I have paid one visit to Pusey, but am not following it up so have doubtless fallen from grace in that direction. I serve once a week at St Mary's [the University Church] and have had a long chat with Dick Milford [Vicar of St Mary's] who was interested to hear of your activities. There is the usual course of Sunday night sermons at St Mary's, and the place is as crowded as ever. I am buying a copy of the previous week's sermon each Sunday with the intention of bringing them home and selling them to you at a small profit!

I play hockey occasionally for the college side. BNC has *five* people in the unbeaten varsity rugger side. We last year won the rugger, hockey, soccer and cricket cups. As we also have the President of the Union, the President of the Conservatives, and our Principal is next for Vice-Chancellor, you will see that we are something of a force in the University. Even the mud-slinging *Isis* refers to us as 'that versatile College'.

I take a mild interest in the doings of the Conservatives, and to show my broadmindedness have joined the Socialists so that their card should help to fill up my mantelpiece. But I am restricting all such activities to the absolute minimum this term in order to get into the swing of my work as early as possible. As things are at present I will probably take Schools [final examinations] at the end of Michaelmas Term 1948. I can't be quite certain until we see how things go.

Both my tutors are delightful people but inclined to be a little vague and to develop their pet theories. It is the complaint of all my fellow Greats pupils that one gets a delightful exposition of mysticism for an hour once a week from K. J. Spalding, but that it is not particularly helpful to the study of Descartes and Spinoza. I am becoming more and more entangled in the threads of modern philosophy at which I am making a beginning this term.

He had returned to tutorials in Spalding's cigar-scented rooms, and had found there an extraordinary sense of eternity as 'K. J.' made him feel that his four years in the army, taking part in a war in which the future of Europe was at stake, was so irrelevant to the world of philosophical thought that it might never have happened. His new history tutor was different. Michael Holroyd had spent the war at the intelligence centre at Bletchley. He was a man of wide cultural interests and very knowledgeable about art, not surprisingly since his father had been Keeper of the Tate Gallery and his mother was a portrait painter. He and his wife were both very sociable people and often entertained undergraduates to large luncheon parties at their house. Both the Holroyds became Runcie's friends.

He was four years older, with an entirely new confidence. Since he had last been at Oxford he had learned, like many of his contemporaries, to lead and discipline men and to care for their welfare. He had known fear and exhaustion, and had looked at death many times. All that made surprisingly little difference at Oxford as he and those who had shared such experiences mixed again with undergraduates straight from school. But he had, in those four years, had all the social education that the Brigade of Guards could offer to enhance his natural talent for enjoying friendship, good talk, and amusing company. He could now move easily and confidently in any company.

He had matured in other ways. The naive enthusiasm with which he had responded to the communist theories propounded by his classics master at school, and the extreme socialism of the Labour Club in his first terms at Oxford, had given way to a profound belief in the importance of personal liberty and a horror of any form of totalitarianism. In this he had undoubtedly come under the influence of the friends he had been living and fighting with, many of whom had good minds and a strongly pragmatic view of politics. Most of them were as traditionally Conservative as his parents had been, but were skilful and sophisticated in arguing their case. And the harsh experience of war, with its intensive education in how human beings really behaved, had taken the shine from easy undergraduate idealism about reordering the world for the common good. He was now convinced of the over-riding importance of intellectual and cultural freedom; with the example of Soviet Russia uncomfortably close, and the Cold War coming into being, and with recent memories of the grim, grey face of communism as he had seen it in Trieste, he now believed that Marxism or any of the extreme forms of socialism must inevitably mean – if they were put into practice – a restrictive conformity, the denial of free speech, the manipulation of thought, and the repudiation of most of what made human experience full, various and enriching. He had been fighting for freedom, and freedom was not what the far Left appeared to have on offer. So it was easy for his friends to persuade him that in Britain the Conservative Party stood as the most effective defence against encroaching totalitarianism, and he became a mildly active member of the party. Nevertheless, his social conscience had been awakened, and he abhorred the class prejudices under which he had himself briefly suffered in his first days in the army. He still saw those prejudices among many of his Conservative friends. And he had an abiding hatred of the sort of snobbery that could leave another person feeling small. Justice within society and between nations had become an urgent principle for him. But, for the moment, his first priority was to get his degree, and the easiest way to resolve his conflicting political views until he had more time to sort them out was to join both parties.

For a short while he was college secretary of the Conservative Association, and on the committee. The president at the time was Maurice Chandler whom, thirty years later, he would know again as a leading Anglican layman and member of the General Synod Standing Committee. At the time, Chandler did not think highly of Runcie's dedication to the cause of the party, a view that was shared by the ex-president, Margaret Roberts, now Margaret Thatcher. Before long he was dropped for being too frivolous and not sufficiently single-minded in his allegiance.

His political interests were really international. In his first term back at Oxford he had gone to a packed meeting in Oxford Town Hall (which proved to be the founding of Christian Action) where a speaker had rallied the audience by calling for immediate help for the starving Germans. Everyone who was prepared to send a food parcel to Germany that very week was asked to stand up, and Runcie was among the great number who did so. He had seen enough at first hand of the ruin of Europe to know that its reconstruction and the reconciliation of its peoples was the most immediate and pressing post-war task. Throughout the war, like several thousand other church-minded fighting men, he had been receiving the *Christian Newsletter*, started in 1939 by the ecumenical and missionary-minded layman, J. H. Oldham, as a fortnightly Christian commentary on current events and a forum for discussing the means of bringing about a more just and peaceable world after the war. So it was to the Oxford Bonn Committee that he turned to discuss the reconciliation of Europe and, through it, he went with seven other undergraduates, in the summer vacation of 1947, on an exchange visit to Bonn University, to a seminar organised by Sir Robert Birley as an early move in healing relations with Germany.

His social life was as gay as post-war austerity, strictly-rationed food and scarce alcohol allowed. He was elected president of the Junior Common Room at the beginning of his second academic year and, during his time in office, had the duty of entertaining Princess Elizabeth when she attended a Brasenose garden party. It was his first introduction to the present Queen. He played a lot of cricket and hockey, and went to other clubs and meetings. At the Socratic Club he heard C. S. Lewis aggressively defending the Christian faith against any atheist or agnostic who could be inveigled into coming to the club's meetings. But he was not among the undergraduates who fell under Lewis's spell. He was reading philosophy in the current Oxford climate of logical positivism, and being trained in an attitude of mind which required him to be sceptical of Lewis's dogmatic approach to Christianity. Years later, talking as Archbishop to a younger generation of Oxford undergraduates, he said:

When I gave time to my work, most of my ideas were exposed to the ruthless questioning of logical positivism which was in high fashion in immediately post-war Oxford, and I would certainly testify to its lasting impression on me. You will at least know some of its texts, and perhaps that of Wittgenstein above all. 'Of that about which you cannot be certain, it is better to keep silent.'

I owe much to the teachers of those days for such disciplines as I have acquired in mental agility. I remember Isaiah Berlin exhorting us that we should not spend our lives lying on a bed of unexamined assumptions. I recall how we were taught the principles of empirical verification. In those days a language which professed to treat of truths or realities which are not susceptible of such verification was deeply suspect. It was a reaction to a period when the fluent idealists, or many of them, managed to dovetail their philosophical way of looking at things into their Christian assertions. Thus they would say that Christian assertions were not so much untrue as meaningless. 'OK,' said one of my tutors, 'you can be interested in religion, and I can be interested in billiards, but as a matter of fact I am not interested in either.' It tended to make religion a matter of taste rather than truth.

Nevertheless, the idea of ordination was growing steadily into an assumption with him, prodded along by his brother-in-law, Angus. He felt no real vocation to parish work; he thought rather of ordination followed by a return to an academic career and teaching in a university. It seemed, after his wartime years, a very attractive way of life that would offer him the rigorous intellectual stimulation to which he always responded, while at the same time providing him with the opportunity to live his religion in a congenial but disciplined environment. His call to the priesthood was an intellectual and emotional one, a spiritual need within himself rather than an ardent sense of missionary purpose.

Once he had his degree, ordination would demand two years at a theological college, and Angus was advocating Westcott House in Cambridge, the college at which he had done his own training. It was Angus who wrote to the principal, W. D. L. Greer, early in 1947 to suggest that he might see Runcie. Greer replied that he himself was about to leave Westcott to become Bishop of Manchester, but it so happened that, before he left, he would be coming to Oxford to preach the University Sermon in St Mary's in Eights Week, and he would call on Runcie then to discuss the matter of his vocation.

Eights Week is the week in June that Oxford gives over to eight-oared boat races and innumerable parties. When the day of Greer's visit came, Runcie rushed back from a tremendous all-night party to find Greer already waiting in his rooms which he had left in chaos. Greer surveyed him with amusement, eyeing the peony in Runcie's buttonhole. They sat down while he questioned Runcie about himself, his work, and his wish to be ordained. The conversation went on for some time with Runcie trying hard to remember just why he did want to be ordained. But Greer had a sure touch and knew his young men. 'Oh, well,' he said as he got to his feet, 'I think you would probably do very well for a parish in Manchester.'

The next hurdle was a selection board run by CACTM, the Central Advisory Council for Training for the Ministry. Runcie was required to attend one at St Boniface's College, Warminster, where, with a dozen other candidates, he spent three days being interviewed by assessors who included J. P. Thornton-Duesbery, Principal of Wycliffe Hall, an Evangelical theological college, Henry Lloyd, Dean of Truro

Cathedral, and Canon Duncan Armytage of Windsor who probed anxiously to discover whether he was a member of the Brasenose Hellfire Club that was not only given to the sort of wild parties inappropriate for an aspiring clergyman, but was also reputed to toast the devil.

Back at Oxford his friends tried hard to argue him in other directions: perhaps politics, the Foreign Office, or journalism. Hugo Charteris, later to become a distinguished novelist, already had a job lined up for himself on the *Daily Express* and was sure that he could pull the right strings to get Runcie a similar job on the *Daily Mail*. Runcie was more inclined to listen to Charteris than to anyone. They had been friends since their early days in the Scots Guards when they had met at Codford on Salisbury Plain. Charteris had been with the Third Battalion until they left Yorkshire in 1943 when he was sent out to Italy with a company attached to the Coldstream. He had been twice wounded before winning the Military Cross. It was to their great mutual pleasure that he and Runcie had renewed their friendship at Oxford, and Runcie was fascinated by Charteris's talk of creative writing. But all Charteris's persuasive powers could not now deflect him from the course he now knew he must follow.

He was in his final year and working hard. From his schooldays he had had the facility for long periods of concentration when he settled down to work but, like most normal undergraduates, his social life made heavy inroads into his time. He caught up with reading in the vacations. Since his father's death his mother had gone to share his brother Kenneth's flat in Manchester and, when Robert visited them there, he happily spent long days in the city library. He did the same when he stayed – as he still did – with Mr and Mrs Waters in Guildford. And at Kathleen's he worked in his room so steadily that during the Christmas vacation of 1947 his little niece, Rosemary, and smaller Robin, had to drag him out on Christmas Day to join them round the Christmas tree.

In the weeks before Christmas 1948 he sat his final examinations. Just before they began he had a sudden visit from the new principal of Westcott House, Kenneth Carey, a surprisingly boyish figure who arrived with his coat flying open and a college scarf wound round his neck. 'Are you still on?' he asked Runcie. 'I suppose so,' Runcie replied, preoccupied with his examinations, but also slightly cold round the feet now that his commitment to ordination was so close. His examination results showed how he had worked. He was awarded a First Class Honours degree in *Literae Humaniores*. His first thought was to drop a note to his tutor, Michael Holroyd, saying, 'Congratulations, Michael, on getting a First at last!'

He went to Westcott House in the New Year. It is a pleasantly modest college in Jesus Lane, built of subdued brick round a grass court. Though none of the building is older than the present century, and the larger part honestly and unpretentiously dates from 1926, it has a settled rustic air which has deceived transatlantic visitors into believing it to be medieval. The chapel is plain, the library adequate, and the accommodation spartan.

Westcott House had a distinguished record. It had been founded in 1881 by Professor Westcott (later Bishop of Durham) to provide training in theology and the devotional life for Cambridge graduates who were preparing for ordination. Its special ethos had been created by B. K. Cunningham who had been its principal from 1919 to 1944. Those less well-disposed towards it spoke of Westcott House as 'B.K.'s charm school', for Cunningham, a man of enormous affection and not a little eccentricity, had believed in cherishing and developing each of his student's individual gifts and abilities, while at the same time insisting on a high standard of old-fashioned good manners and formal social behaviour. He had been a gifted teacher of ordinands. He had wanted, said his biographer, J. R. H. Moorman, 'to preserve all that was natural and human in each man, and allow him to develop in his own way according to the will of God'. 'Believe in your best self,' Cunningham would say to his students. 'Know that Christ will help you become it if you will keep yourselves as His disciples in His presence.' But he also liked his young men to dress for dinner.

He was opposed to the idea of a priest as a 'professional', and had been accused by his critics of producing gentlemen amateurs for the Anglican priesthood. It was an appellation his products did not at all deplore, for he had taught them to believe the word 'gentleman' to be a proper description for a Christian in any walk of life, and 'amateur', with its root in the verb 'to love' held no embarrassment for them. The fact remained that, since Cunningham had first put his imprint on Westcott House, the college had consistently produced more bishops and notable clergy for the Church of England than any other.

Cunningham had retired in 1944 at the age of seventy-three, several years later than he should have done. He had hoped to see the war through before handing over to another principal, but increasing deafness and poor health forced him to retire, by which time it was clear that the college needed a new and firm hand to pull it together again. His successor, W. D. L. (Billy) Greer, was a less charismatic figure, but a quiet, humorous Irishman with the strength and sensitivity to recover the college's lost ground without losing any of its special gifts for enhancing the personal qualities of students within its Christian discipline.

There were forty-five ordinands when Runcie went there at the beginning of the Lent Term of 1949, and they were of a higher quality than he had expected. The senior student, or 'Sheriff' in Westcott's accustomed nomenclature, was Patrick Rodger, one day to be bishop first of Manchester and then of Oxford. And there were at least four other future bishops among his fellow-students: Hugh Montefiore (Birmingham), Simon Phipps (Lincoln), Stephen Verney (Repton), and Victor Whitsey (Chester). The most brilliant mind was probably Bill Vanstone who had arrived from Oxford with a First Class degree in Mods and Greats, and added a further First in theology at Cambridge before collecting more academic distinctions in America. His ambition was to be a Lancashire parish priest and, despite his brilliant scholarship, that is what he became.

There were three members of staff. The vice-principal was Alan Webster, later to be dean successively of Norwich and St Paul's Cathedrals. An imaginative and radical thinker, he taught church history, and had shaken the Westcott tradition to its foundations by being the first member of the staff to marry. The students found him an understanding tutor, and it was easy to go to him for sympathetic advice and practical help. The chaplain was Harry Williams, a clever, sensitive priest who had newly arrived from a curacy at All Saints', Margaret Street, the famous bastion of Anglo-Catholicism in London. Years later, as one of the most original theologians and spiritual writers in the Church of England, he was to become a monk of the Community of the Resurrection. At Westcott the students knew him as a fashionable, highly-controlled young clergyman who taught the New Testament, read the lessons in chapel with a sort of passionless beauty, but often gave remarkable addresses at compline which remained memorable for their psychological insight.

Kenneth Carey was boyish, affectionate, and a confirmed bachelor. He lived for his students, both those currently at Westcott, and those who had been ordained and were serving as priests in English parishes or overseas. He had been a friend and disciple of Cunningham and, like him, was a gifted teacher and spiritual director. Academically he fell short of those whom he made his staff, and of many of his students. He could never forget that he had obtained only a Third Class degree in theology, and he constantly compared himself with Winnie-the-Pooh, the bear of very little brain. Yet in this he underestimated himself. It was the opinion of one of his most able vice-principals, John Habgood, later Bishop of Durham, that Carey's frequent reference to his poor academic record was a pastoral ploy intended to bring him closer to those students who shared his own sense of academic inadequacy, and that he actually knew more theology than he let on. He read very widely, said Habgood,

in what one might call middlebrow theology, and was usually able to discuss it very perceptively. He also liked to surround himself with academics, and though he did not say much during the course of a theological discussion,

his remarks were usually to the point . . . A whole generation of future leaders of the church had an enormous
respect for him, not simply as a wise and affectionate
human being, but as a man whose Christian judgment
and grasp of essentials inspired confidence.

According to the prospectus for the Lent Term of 1949,
Carey was teaching prayer and pastoralia, but his influence
permeated the college.

His essential greatness [wrote Denis Shaw, an ex-student]
lay in his power to show others their capacity for being
great. His essential spirituality was his conviction that
spirituality was a common commodity – not a rare gift –
intended to be the property of all God's children. His
essential humanity showed itself in his matter-of-fact
assumption of the worthwhileness of every human life.

The teaching provided by the staff was supplemented by
outside lecturers who, during Runcie's first term, included
Dr A. C. Bouquet on Christian ethics, Professor E. C.
Ratcliff on liturgy, and the Revd E. W. Heaton on the Old
Testament. During the same term visiting lecturers came
to talk on The Church and the Law, Christianity and
Communism, South Africa, and (John Betjeman) on visiting
old churches. It was a pattern which continued, with changing and often distinguished lecturers drawn from the university, and with a wide range of visiting speakers from many
Christian backgrounds.

Peter Coleman, who arrived at Westcott House four years
later, observed that 'there was a sense in which the House
was a kind of annexe and seminary to the University for the
training on site of "gentlemen in Holy Orders", a kind of
in-house joke about ourselves, but based on the vision of the
famous B. K. Cunningham who, in part, Ken Carey tried
to emulate'. He suggested that Cuddesdon, the theological
college close to Oxford of which Runcie was to become
principal in 1960,

was probably the only other theological college of the time

which had that kind of unconscious elitism, and we would probably say now that the training was insufficiently aware of the real changes and challenges of the world of the 'fifties. But the quality of the ordinands, and their width of experience, meant that they could take on board what they needed in their parishes; and much stress was laid on our obligation to remain unmarried, and to go to tough working-class areas in the north for our 'apprenticeship curacy'.

All the ordinands were graduates, and several of those whose first degree was not in theology were taking a theological degree at the university while at Westcott. Runcie decided against it. He would read theology, but not take the degree. He had worked very hard during the previous two years at Oxford, and he decided that at Cambridge he would catch up on his wider education and use the opportunity to explore what the university had to offer in the way of broadening his mind. Carey, with his particular emphasis on the individual growth of each of his students, was in sympathy with this intention.

It was not only the small numbers and intimate size of his new college that made Runcie find it all slightly cosy. The whole atmosphere was intended by Carey to be a family one, though probably with a stronger flavour of the prep school than of a domestic household. All but the newest students had jobs allotted to them with faintly roguish titles. While the senior student was the Sheriff, the one in charge of the chapel music was the 'Minstrel'; there was a 'Bailiff of the Beer' (and even, later, of the light bulbs); and others were called 'Leech', 'Manciple', and 'Masters of the Garbage'. Within two terms Runcie had become, as well as captain of the hockey team, the 'Bishop of St Augustine's'. In other words, he was in charge of a small mission church attached to a primary school along the Huntingdon Road. Though the church belonged to the parish of Chesterton, it had no priest in charge and for some time had been in the regular care of the Westcott ordinands. It had a high-church tradition, and Runcie had the job of organising the weekly evensong and coping with the powerful lady who played the organ and the delightful Miss Norris who ran the Sunday school.

While he never fell as completely under the spell of Carey's charm as many of his fellow-students, Runcie appreciated the freedom that he found at Westcott to develop in new ways. At heart he regarded himself as a historian, and he readily absorbed church history. Biblical studies he enjoyed, and his years of philosophical training had prepared him well for form-criticism. He was attracted to the Catholic modernists and found himself at home with R. H. Lightfoot's *History and the Interpretation of the Gospels* and, in ethics, with R. B. Braithwaite's lectures on moral philosophy. Doctrine was where a good deal of his interest lay; but systematic theology bored him, particularly the German theologians and the current obsession with Barth and Tillich. The scepticism of his philosophical background and his essentially argumentative mind could not be convinced by the building of great superstructures of theological belief on premises which could not be proved. Wherever possible he slid away from those lectures to listen in to what was going on in the English or other schools of the university. He visited art galleries, went to concerts, and read novels.

In many ways it was a light-hearted time, for the college was a very sociable place, much given to its own private jokes. Acting and concert parties were a regular part of its life, and Simon Phipps – who became president of the Cambridge Footlights while he was at Westcott House – produced, acted in, and several times wrote the plays that were put on. Runcie always had a part. He played Caesar ('like an apoplectic colonel' recalled another member of the cast) in *Androcles and the Lion*, and was Saint Peter to Phipps's Judas Iscariot in a play that Phipps wrote. He and Phipps also entertained their fellows with their impromptu mimicry, and Runcie's rendering of the unliturgically-minded Norman Sykes about to preach a sermon passed into Westcott history. However, the first reference in the Westcott House archives to his appearance on the stage suggests that he had a poor aim with a custard pie, even if he had other talents in compensation. Reviewing a concert party the then Sheriff wrote: 'Even if Bob Runcie had to have a second shot at Chris with the custard pie, at least his technique with the female cast had clearly been very well rehearsed.'

In that first end-of-term report there was also mention of a visitor that Simon Phipps had one Sunday afternoon after Runcie had arrived at the college. Ken Carey also told the story in the *Westcott House Chronicle*.

Princess Margaret paid a private visit to the House on Sunday 6th February. At her own request the visit was entirely informal and it turned out to be even more informal than anyone expected. An over-zealous chauffeur brought the royal car to the main gate twenty-five minutes before the time arranged. As a result there was no one to meet her Royal Highness. For a few minutes the Princess, her lady-in-waiting, and the chauffeur stood disconsolately in the porch until a member of the House, who had no idea anything unusual was afoot, appeared with a coal-scuttle which he was on his way to refill. With considerable presence of mind he grasped the situation and saved the honour of the House. After that the visit went well.

Runcie was among those who entertained the Princess to tea.

He still spent most of his vacations with his family and Dr and Mrs Waters. In the summer of 1949 he went on a short walking tour in France with his brother Kenneth. They had seen little of each other for years, and they had to get to know each other again. They crossed to Dieppe and hitched a lift to Rouen where, finding the Tour de France cycling its way through, they had great difficulty in getting accommodation for the night. Next morning they set off with their rucksacks to walk through the Bocage country where Robert had fought. As they passed through the villages, any mention of the Scots Guards' tanks ensured an enthusiastic welcome in the traditional French manner, and it was on a wave of vinous generosity that they went on to discover the place where Robert had all too briefly slept on the night before the battle of Caumont. Their destination was Chartres where they spent the day looking round the cathedral before they parted, and Robert went on to meet some army friends in Paris.

He spent the following Easter with Dr and Mrs Waters who, more than ever as his ordination approached, saw in him the son they had lost. While he was there, late in the evening of Good Friday, a policeman came to the door with the message that his mother was dead. Kenneth had married the previous December, and so she had gone to live with Marjorie whose husband, a civil servant, had been posted to Egypt. They had taken a flat together in Southport, and it was there that Nancy Runcie had a sudden stroke and died almost immediately. Runcie immediately went up to Kathleen and Angus in Nottingham where the funeral was held and Mrs Runcie buried beside her husband in the Cotgrave churchyard. When it was all over, and Runcie returned to Westcott House, he found that one of his mother's last acts had been to send him a small postal order as a present for Easter.

He was to be ordained at Christmas and it was becoming necessary to decide where he would 'serve his title' as a curate. At that time it was taken for granted at Westcott that nearly every self-respecting new clergyman would prove his serious intentions by choosing to go to an industrial parish in the north of England, and Runcie was very willing to look northwards. Kenneth Carey suggested that he might go to Archie Hardy at Hexham Abbey in Northumberland, and arrangements were made for him to visit Hexham and see if he and Hardy took to each other. Meanwhile Hugh Montefiore, who had been a year ahead of Runcie at Westcott, was already in the Newcastle diocese at the parish of St George's, Jesmond, where – most disconcertingly – his vicar left just as he arrived, leaving him to look after the parish during the interregnum. Montefiore was only a deacon, with no experience, and not yet able to celebrate Holy Communion or conduct weddings, so a number of neighbouring clergy had to help out; and he got to know some of them very well. One of them was John Turnbull, vicar of All Saints', Gosforth, who had the reputation of being a first-class vicar, good at training curates, with a lively Anglo-Catholic church in the suburbs of Newcastle. Meeting him one day at a bus-stop, Montefiore suggested to Turnbull that he might like to have Runcie as a curate. Turnbull said he had not previously had one from the prestigious Westcott House, but he agreed to think about it, and to see Runcie.

So Runcie went north to see both Hexham and Gosforth for himself. He fell in love with the Norman abbey, and could imagine himself very happy in the small market town of Hexham. But when he went to see John Turnbull he immediately knew that here was a man who could teach him a good deal. The Gosforth church, All Saints', was a barn of a building after the marvellous abbey. The vicarage was plain, and the Turnbulls' style of life was austere, teetotal, and lacking in the civilised touches that Runcie had grown to like. But he was deeply impressed by John Turnbull himself: a kindly, slightly autocratic man, with a dry sense of humour and a delightful wife. It was obvious that Turnbull was a very good parish priest, caring about his people and clear about his job. It was one of the occasions in Runcie's life when he suddenly knew quite clearly what God wanted him to do. He had no doubt that All Saints', Gosforth, was the parish where he should serve his apprenticeship and learn what being a priest in a parish was all about.

He was Sheriff in the Long Vacation Term of his final year. His immediate predecessor as Sheriff, Stephen Verney, had written in his report at the end of the previous term: 'But at least the moot will be in capable hands. The new Sheriff (Runcie), returned unopposed, enjoys the undivided confidence of the whole house.' Runcie's own report at the end of the Long Vac. Term appears hastily and untidily written. The annual play, which Simon Phipps had written and in which Runcie and Phipps had played leading roles, was a major feature.

Attention was soon concentrated on the House play. We were blessed with two perfect evenings, for a few far-sighted staff had arranged that we should be well grounded in the theology of our position and sermon classes had hotly discussed whether it was right to pray for the weather. 'The Garden of Decision', which was attended by a large number of friends, urged the necessity of making decisions to take decisions. Simon Phipps, author, long-suffering producer and one of the leading actors is to be congratulated and thanked once again for staging a really memorable production with a minimum of fuss.

Not all his report was frivolous. The Bishop of Croydon had conducted what was probably the most helpful retreat they had ever had. A distinguished Roman Catholic layman, Professor Semant, had been to talk about ecumenism. The best outside lecturer had been Mr Colquhoun on the Scout movement. Benjamin Britten, the composer, and Peter Pears, the singer, had been to tea in the college garden. And there had been a happy excursion to Cuddesdon [the theological college near Oxford] where Westcott had apparently shown a greater turn of speed both on the playing fields and in the chapel. 'We were victorious at cricket and tennis and, by a short head, in the Psalms.'

He was to be ordained deacon on Christmas Eve and, as it is the custom of the Church of England that a man should be ordained in the diocese of the bishop who is to appoint him to his first title, Runcie went north to Newcastle a few days before Christmas for his pre-ordination retreat. There were two other ordinands to be made deacon at the same service, and six deacons, including Hugh Montefiore, who were to be ordained priest. They were under a strict rule of silence and spent their time in prayer, reading, and being talked to about their vocation and future life by the Bishop of Newcastle, Noel Hudson, who would ordain them. But Montefiore was in such a difficulty that he had to tell Runcie about it when they went for what should have been a silent walk together. The day after he was priested would be Christmas Day and he would have to celebrate the Holy Communion for the first time. This meant that he would have to sing, solo and unaccompanied, the long Proper Preface for the day, and as he had no singing voice he was very nervous about it. For Runcie the priority was clear: he had to do what he could to help a friend in need. They repaired to some nearby woods where, under his tuition, Montefiore could practise the long chant. They were deep in the middle of this impromptu lesson when the bishop, who had also chosen to take a walk in the woods, suddenly appeared, very startled at the noise being made by two retreatants who were supposed to be keeping a holy silence.

The morning of Christmas Eve was dull and grey when they went into Newcastle to the cathedral. It was packed, not only with the regular Sunday congregation, but with many clergy from the diocese, and with the families and the friends of the men who were being ordained. Of Runcie's family, only his sister Marjorie had been able to come. She had stayed the previous night with Montefiore's wife and family in Jesmond.

The ordinands took their places in the front of the congregation before the bishop. After the litany had been sung the ordination of the new deacons began. The archdeacon solemnly presented them to the bishop and they were asked if they had been inwardly moved by the Holy Ghost to offer themselves for ordination, and whether they would fulfil all the duties laid upon them. The duties were spelt out in the words of the Prayer Book:

to serve, to assist the Priest in Divine Service, and specially when he ministereth Holy Communion, and to help him in the distribution thereof, and to read Holy Scriptures and Homilies in the Church; to instruct the youth in the Catechism; in the absence of the Priest to baptise infants, and to preach if [they] be thereto admitted by the Bishop . . . to search for the sick, poor and impotent people of the Parish, to intimate their estates, names and places where they dwell, unto the [Vicar], that by his exhortation they may be relieved with the alms of the Parishioners, or others.

The bishop asked, 'Will you do this gladly and willingly?' and Runcie and his two fellow-ordinands answered that they would do so by the help of God.

The formal inquisition continued, about the wholesomeness of their lives, their diligence, and their willing obedience to the chief ministers of the church. Then the bishop prayed that they would be filled with the Holy Ghost and would be stable and strong in Christ. As each man individually knelt before him he laid his hands on the ordinand's head and said: 'Take thou authority to execute the office of a Deacon in the Church of God committed unto thee; in the name of the Father, and of the Son, and of the Holy Ghost.' And to each one he gave a New Testament with the authority to read the gospel in church, and to preach it.

The ordination service is set in the order for Holy Communion, and Robert was the new deacon chosen to read the gospel as the liturgy continued to the ordination of the six priests. It was too much for poor Marjorie. Moved by the whole occasion, and remembering how much her mother had looked forward to seeing Robert ordained, she burst into tears and wept through the whole service. She could not control her sobs even over the celebratory cups of coffee in the church hall after the service, and she was still choking them back and unable to talk when Robert took her off to lunch.

Chapter Eight

Back to Cambridge

There followed two of the happiest years of his life. Runcie loved being a curate. Though it was Tyneside, Gosforth itself was a pleasant leafy suburb, and he had comfortable lodgings at 36 Oakfield Road. His landlady was Mrs Tiffin, a Yorkshire widow whose daughter had recently married and left home. She had never had a lodger before, but John Turnbull had suggested to her that she might be the ideal person to take the new curate. She was kind and fussy and Runcie found her cosily religious, full of little sayings from Patience Strong's poems. She was one of Turnbull's most loyal supporters, even though she could never quite get used to the changes he was making in the parish church and tended to get confused between the newly-introduced parish Communion and the parish breakfast which followed it. Her care for Runcie was inordinate and slightly unnerving in its concern. Because her husband had collapsed with a sudden heart attack, she was convinced that her lodger, twenty-seven years old and in the best of athletic health, might suffer the same fate at any time. He had only to drop a book or knock something over in his bedroom for her to rush upstairs expecting to find him lying on the floor. Her constant fears for his health had the disconcerting effect of making him slightly anxious about himself for the first time in his life. All that apart, however, they got on extremely well.

All Saints' Church, though Runcie had found it plain compared with Hexham Abbey, is a large and handsome stone building with a stately tower. It was built at the end of the nineteenth century with locally raised money on land bought from the Gosforth Park Mining Company for 2s. 6d. a square yard. It is Victorian Gothic at its most dignified, with a wide and lofty nave, and the steps to the chancel graced by a finely carved and delicately lace-like oak screen. John Turnbull had been vicar since 1948 and, with Bishop Hudson's encouragement, had from his first year made the parish Communion the central act of worship with a moderate version of the Catholic ritual that Runcie had grown up with in Crosby. It had attracted a fast-growing congregation which, at its peak, numbered a thousand communicants on Easter Day.

A vigorous and disciplined parish life surrounded the thriving church, making it an exemplary parish for new curates to serve their apprenticeship in. John Turnbull as vicar turned out to be all that Runcie had hoped for: strong, kindly, affectionate and godly, with clear ideas about what he was doing. A later curate, Tony Meakin, described him as a man of prayer, caring and compassionate about his people, but a strict disciplinarian. He knew exactly what he wanted and made sure that it happened. He would, however, listen carefully to the opinion of those he respected, and could on occasion be persuaded to alter his ideas. But once his mind was made up, his policy decisions were clear.

Runcie warmed to all these attributes, and in particular appreciated his vicar's strategic thinking about his parish. It was a practical, pragmatic and disciplined approach which he had been used to in the army and which was much in accord with his own instincts. His respect for Turnbull's judgment endured. Though they did not always agree (and sometimes it was his disagreements with Turnbull that shaped Runcie's own thinking) during the whole of Turnbull's life Runcie valued his opinion and would turn to him for his advice.

In this stimulating environment he preached his first sermons and, a month after he arrived, baptized his first babies – three at one service. In the youth club his popularity knew no bounds. Turnbull, highly amused, maintained that it was the business of curates to be popular while it was the business of the vicar to make demands. He gave his curates very much a free hand with the club outings and entertainments, and laughed to see them lionised by the parish maidens. A glimpse of Runcie at this time comes from Neil Dodds, then a boy in the parish. 'There was an "Any Questions?" evening in the church hall with the parish clergy as the panel. A disagreement arose between Robert Runcie and John Turnbull, though on a very amicable basis. I remember John Turnbull trying at least three times to round off the discussion, only to find each time Robert on his feet persisting with his own arguments.'

A year passed quickly and on the day before Christmas Eve 1951 Runcie was back in Newcastle Cathedral to be ordained priest. On this occasion Kathleen and Angus were in the congregation as well as Marjorie. Only two priests and two deacons were being made and, after the simpler ordination of the deacons, Runcie and the curate of another Newcastle parish were formally presented to the bishop, who solemnly warned them of 'how great importance this office is, whereunto ye are called'.

Forasmuch then as your Office is both of so great excellency, and of so great difficulty, [the bishop went on] ye see with how great care and study ye ought to apply yourselves . . . that neither you yourselves offend, nor be the occasion that others offend . . . we have good hope that you have clearly determined, by God's grace, to give yourselves wholly to this Office, whereunto it hath pleased God to call you: so that, as much as lieth in you, you will apply yourselves wholly to this one thing, and draw all your cares and studies this way; and that you will continually pray to God the Father, by the Mediation of our only Saviour Jesus Christ, for the heavenly assistance of the Holy Ghost; that, by daily reading and weighing of the Scriptures, ye may wax riper and stronger in your Ministry; and that ye may so endeavour yourselves, from time to time, to sanctify the lives of you and yours, and to fashion them after the Rule and Doctrine of Christ, that ye may be wholesome and godly examples and patterns for the people to follow.

After that formidable charge he asked them the required questions about their belief, whether they would be diligent in their prayers and Bible-reading, whether they would 'banish and drive away all erroneous doctrine', and whether they and their families would set a good example of wholesome living. Then everyone in the cathedral sang the *Veni Creator*, the thousand-year-old hymn to the Holy Spirit which has been used at every ordination service, in Latin or in English, for at least five centuries: 'Come Holy Ghost, our souls inspire'.

The most solemn moment of ordination had come as Runcie knelt at the bishop's feet and the bishop placed his hands on Runcie's head, and all the other priests who were present crowded round to put a hand on his head also. Then the bishop said: '*Receive the Holy Ghost for the office and work of a Priest in the Church of God, now committed unto thee by the imposition of our hands. Whose sins thou dost forgive, they are forgiven; and whose sins, thou dost retain, they are retained. And be thou a faithful dispenser of the word of God, and of his holy Sacraments.*' And he gave him a Bible with the authority to preach and to minister the holy sacraments. Runcie was now a priest.

On Christmas Day, at seven in the morning, 110 people were in All Saints' Church when he celebrated the Holy Communion for the first time. He had been well trained in the complicated ritual of the service and, as he asked God's blessing on the bread and wine, it was suddenly as though he were experiencing a new conversion. As he remembers it, everything in his life 'seemed to come together' as the elements in his hands became the Body and Blood. It was an experience he was often to know again as he performed the same actions, but never with the same intensity as on that first Christmas morning.

He could now take his full share of weddings, funerals and hearing confessions. He later told one of his army friends, Michael Barne, that one of his first weddings was a fiasco. Barne, remembering the story as it had been told to him, recorded that everything went wrong.

> Few of the congregation had been in church before and some had fortified themselves against the experience. When Bob asked, 'Who giveth this woman?' [a rhetorical question which expects no response] a hand was uncertainly raised from somewhere in the body of the congregation. The service continued. The couple were kneeling at the chancel steps and Bob whispered 'Follow me,' and turned and walked slowly towards the altar. He sensed that something was wrong – and he was right. The couple were indeed following him but still on their knees, struggling. The bride's veil had slipped over one eye, and her dress was ripping. Bob took the opportunity to rasp out of the side of his mouth the well-used Scots Guards' expression – 'Get off your knees! '

His confirmation classes were popular. He had particular success with a group of middle-aged and younger housewives who met for their classes in each other's houses and rapidly became (and remained) faithful members of the congregation. Those were the days when the clergy regularly visited round the parish, and Runcie did his full share. One priest at least, Neil Dodds, who at that time was a boy server in All Saints', says that Runcie was directly instrumental in steering him towards ordination. 'I clearly remember him sitting in my parents' lounge asking if I had ever considered "the ministry". As a boy of fourteen, the only place for that word in my vocabulary at that time was in connection with the Ministry of Food. I recall asking my parents what his interest was in the Civil Service.'

Enjoying himself though he was, Runcie was beginning to feel restless. It was not that he doubted the importance of parish work in the life of the church, but he was missing the intellectual challenge of the university. His energy, abilities, and tremendous capacity for hard work were not being stretched to the full by the daily round of the parish. So when, one evening during the autumn of 1952, Kenneth

Carey suddenly rang him up and asked him if he would be interested in returning to Westcott House as chaplain on the staff, he was immediately attracted to the idea. Hugh Montefiore was already there. The previous year he had gone to take his turn as chaplain at Westcott and now, on Alan Webster's departure from the House for a parish in Durham, Montefiore was going to take over as vice-principal. He and Carey both wanted Runcie to be the new chaplain.

John Turnbull's understanding did not fail his curate even though he thought it a pity he should leave so soon, but it was to Bishop Hudson that Runcie had, with some apprehension, to go for permission. The bishop greeted him kindly enough, but made it clear that he did not consider a job on the staff of a theological college an adequate substitute for three full years' experience as a curate. Yet he relented, possibly in view of Runcie's age, maturity, and obvious ability. He said he would not stand in his way on that occasion, but he hoped that Runcie would very soon return to parish work.

There was general dismay in Gosforth when it was known that young Mr Runcie would be leaving just after Christmas, even though it was in the nature of curates to come and go. He celebrated his last parish Communion at eight o'clock on Christmas morning with 322 communicants, many of whom had made a special effort to come at that early hour because it was his last grand occasion. But the following day, St Stephen's Day, always the anticlimax of the church's year, he celebrated for the very last time at seven in the morning with only seven people. It was goodbye to a way of life he was never fully to know again.

He arrived back at Westcott House in icy January weather when, Kenneth Carey noted, only 'one brave *Iris Stylosa*' in the garden gave any promise of spring. Montefiore and Runcie shared the greater part of the teaching between them. While Montefiore, whose First Class degree had been in theology, taught doctrine and the New Testament, Runcie taught church history and liturgy. Carey mostly kept to those devotional and pastoral subjects on which he could speak with his own brand of spiritual authority and sweetness; but it was his two colleagues who carried the main burden of work. As always, the college drew on the resources of the university to supplement and expand on what the staff could provide, and many of the students were reading for theological degrees. Peter Coleman, a student at the time, found

the opportunity to sit under some marvellous teachers for the best part of my Cambridge time: Owen Chadwick on modern church history, Norman Sykes on the Reformation, David Knowles on monasticism, J. A. T. Robinson and Charlie Moule on the New Testament, Burnaby and H. H. Farmer on doctrine, Ratcliff on liturgy, Bezzant on comparative religion, George Woods on ethics. Hugh Montefiore was splendid on the New Testament. Michael Fisher was running the Franciscans. Michael Ramsey led a university mission for the Student Christian Movement while Billy Graham led one for the Christian Union. Amidst all this, Westcott was a self-confident place. The first batch of really able Oxbridge post-war ordinands had already gone on to their curacies and we were perhaps not quite so good. But several of the students of the time were to prove notable.

He recalls that Carey, Montefiore and Runcie worked together as a harmonious team. 'Ken was the practical man, and Hugh the most intellectually adventurous of the three. Bob, the most Catholic of them, taught both ethics and the Old Testament intelligently, but not with the speculative enthusiasm that Hugh had with the New Testament.'

Tony Meakin, also a student at Westcott when Runcie arrived, says that 'he soon endeared himself to the men with his academic competence, his caring personality, and his ready wit. Indeed, one could almost always be sure that whenever great guffaws of laughter rang round the court, Robert was there in the middle of it.' Peter Coleman adds that he was 'a real friend whom I could do things with without soul-searching, and that was important'.

Even so, those who knew him best at this time still speak of the essential reserve at the centre of his personality. With all his talent for immediate friendship, there seemed to be a private and enigmatic self that even those who worked and lived closely with him felt unable to penetrate. At Westcott House, none of those who would have considered themselves his intimates knew anything of his background or his origins. What his life had been before Oxford and the Scots Guards they could only surmise. It was to be many years before he found it easy to talk freely about Crosby and his early life.

He also had a reluctance, in the last resort, to commit himself theologically. An issue of great importance for the Church of England at that time was its relationship with the Church of South India which had been formed in 1947 by four dioceses in southern India withdrawing from the (Anglican) Church of India, Burma and Ceylon, and uniting with the Methodists and the South India United Church which itself was a union of the Presbyterian, Congregational, and Dutch Reformed churches in that area. Though the Church of South India had taken as its doctrinal basis the four requirements of the Lambeth Quadrilateral,* recognised throughout the Anglican church as essential to reformed Catholic orthodoxy, not all of its ministers had been episcopally ordained and, because of this, the question of full intercommunion between the new church and the Church of England was a vexed one. It was accepted, even by the scheme's critics, that within, say, thirty years, the problem would have ironed itself out because by then the ministry

* These Articles were approved by the Lambeth Conference of 1888.
a. The Holy Scriptures of the Old and New Testaments, as 'containing all things necessary to salvation', and as being the rule and ultimate standard of faith.
b. The Apostles' Creed, as the Baptismal Symbol; and the Nicene Creed, as the sufficient statement of the Christian Faith.
c. The two Sacraments ordained by Christ Himself – Baptism and the Supper of the Lord – ministered with unfailing use of Christ's words of Institution, and of the elements ordained by Him.
d. The Historical Episcopate, locally adapted in the methods of its administration to the varying needs of the nations and peoples called of God into the Unity of His Church.

would be a new generation of clergy who would all have been ordained by bishops within the historic succession. But the matter of the interim relationship was due to be settled by the Convocations, and the church was divided on the issue.

The problem had been exercising the liberal minds of the staff, ex-staff, and students of Westcott House, and the outcome was a book of essays called *The Historic Episcopate* edited by Carey. The contributors were Hugh Montefiore, John Robinson (later to be widely known as the author of *Honest to God*), Barry Till, Bill Vanstone, Alan Webster, and Kenneth Woollcombe (who was to become Bishop of Oxford). Its contention, as Carey described it in the *Westcott House Chronicle*, was that 'a careful study of the evidence of the New Testament and of the traditions of the church pointed to a high doctrine of episcopacy which nevertheless fell short of making episcopacy essential to the life of the church'. If that was the true reading of the evidence, said Carey, it must make a considerable difference in Anglican attitudes towards the Church of South India. 'For the Church of South India is episcopal, and the anomalies therein are not insuperable to any except to those who hold a rigid doctrine of the episcopacy as the *esse* of the church. The question is – is such a doctrine either Anglican or true?'

Runcie was naturally expected to contribute an essay. He had both the scholarship and the appreciation of the issues at stake to do so. But he declined. It was surmised by his colleagues that his enthusiasm for ecumenism was tempered by his strong Catholic feelings of loyalty to the Church of England. Looking back, one of the group suggests that, having found his way into high Anglicanism during his deeply impressionable adolescence, any ambiguities about the historic succession of bishops would have seemed suspiciously like a dilution of the Catholic faith which he was not yet prepared to grapple with. He was also conscious that his fellows were trained primarily as theologians while he himself was basically a classicist and historian, and he might have felt that this was not an enterprise he could enter into on equal terms. He was not theologically adventurous: his originality and venturesomeness lay elsewhere. His outstanding gifts, the complex ones of strategic thinking, a pragmatic grasp of essentials and intuitive judgment, had not yet been revealed; only his skills in friendship, his pastoral understanding, and his capacity for hard work had so far been given full scope.

In October 1954 Montefiore went to be Dean and Fellow of Caius College, and Runcie succeeded him as vice-principal. In that role he stayed at Westcott House for two more years, working just as hard at teaching the same subjects as well as carrying more of the administrative burden in the college. He began to grow weary of it and to think of returning to a parish when, one evening, Owen Chadwick – whom he scarcely knew – called on him in his rooms. Chadwick was the Dean of Trinity Hall, one of the smaller colleges of the university, and he was on the point of leaving to be Master of Selwyn College. His greeting was, 'Some of us think you would make a good Dean of Trinity Hall,' and Runcie was ready to listen.

He was invited to dinner at the college, and then to meet a committee of the Fellows. They were very welcoming, but he hesitantly protested that they wanted a theologian while he was a classicist and historian. That, they said, was unimportant; and it was suggested to him that, in any case, being dean would give him time to read for a theological degree if he wanted to.

In fact he did not, but he moved into Trinity Hall in October 1956. Ken Carey wrote warmly of him in the *Westcott House Chronicle*.

Of course we mutter to ourselves old clichés about our loss being their gain, and like many clichés it is quite true. In our better moments we do wholeheartedly congratulate him and them, but we should be less than human if we did not allow ourselves a little self-pity. During his time here as Chaplain, and then as Vice-Principal, he has made a quite unique contribution to our life. It is not only that he has been an excellent teacher, not only that he has quickened our interest in all sorts of things outside the curriculum, nor that he has ever let us forget the paramount importance of the parishes – all these things he has done supremely well. But I have never known anyone whom one so easily forgave for telling one's own funny stories – and telling them so much better; nor anyone who could enliven a staff meeting by such devastating and entirely unmalicious mimicry. And it goes without saying that we shall miss him most for his friendship.

In the same *Chronicle* Carey announced that the new vice-principal to succeed Runcie would be John Habgood, Etonian, Fellow of King's, trained at Cuddesdon (and who in later years would be the principal of Queen's College, the ecumenical theological college in Birmingham, before becoming Bishop of Durham).

Meanwhile Runcie was settling into his rooms overlooking the quadrangle of Trinity Hall, and taking up his new roles as Fellow, Dean of the college chapel, and assistant tutor. The college had been founded in 1350 for the study of law, and still had a high proportion of law students. It was one of the smaller of the Cambridge colleges, built round two small courts, with a garden – famous for the magnificence of its herbaceous border – stretching down to a terrace on the bank of the Cam: a sunny, peaceful place from which to watch the smooth skill of the expert punters on the river and, at weekends, the shrieking antics of the inexpert as they wove round in circles and tipped each other into the water. Behind a high wall, running parallel to the main garden down to the river bank, was the Fellows' Garden, its privacy strictly preserved from all but the college staff. It was in this garden that Runcie was to propose to his future wife and also celebrate his marriage.

As Dean he was in charge of the services that were daily held in the small panelled chapel with its Jacobean altar table and gilded plaster ceiling. As tutor (a term used differently at Cambridge from Oxford) he had the pastoral care of about a hundred undergraduates, directing and advising on their studies and, when required, taking a fatherly interest in their personal affairs, corresponding with their parents, writing testimonials, and sorting out problems with their grants. (Among these students, for a while, was the future radical theologian, Don Cupitt.) He also lectured on ancient Greek history in the classical faculty, and taught early church history to students reading for the theological Tripos.

Even though he did not read for a theological degree himself, as Chadwick had suggested he might, his time at Trinity Hall contributed significantly to his further education. It was a different atmosphere from the general classical studies at Oxford, or the theological bonhomie of Westcott. He was mixing at the high table with lawyers and with dons from scientific disciplines, and there was a hard-nosed approach to academic discipline that he had not lived with before. His respect for scholarly excellence became even more fixed, and his promotion of it among clergy and laity in the church was to become one of the motivating forces of his subsequent career.

For his work among the undergraduates he had acquired a secretary, a daughter of one of the most distinguished of the Trinity Hall law dons: J. W. Cecil Turner, Reader in Law, and the editor of a number of important textbooks on criminal law. Runcie had known the Turner family since his Oxford days when he had been friendly with one of the older daughters, Jill (herself a future barrister), and had taken her to the May Ball. Since he had been living in Cambridge he had often been invited to the Turners' large house on the outskirts of the town and had met the rest of the uproarious and alarmingly intelligent family of four daughters and two sons. Turner himself was a kindly, witty man, a Fabian; he had fought and been decorated in the 1914–18 war and, as a result of it, had lost his Christian faith and was a declared atheist. His wife, Marjorie, was of equally strong personality, and the family was a well-known part of the Cambridge scene.

It had been the next-to-youngest daughter, Rosalind, known to all as Lindy, who had one day met Runcie in the street and asked, 'By the way, you don't need a secretary, do you?' She was twenty-four years old, lively, pretty, musically gifted, and the one member of the family who did not aspire to academic brilliance. She had inherited her talent for music from her father's father, an opera tenor who sang with the Carl Rosa company under the name of Henri Herbert, and later bought his own theatre to produce operas in Birmingham. She had been born into this intellectually stimulating upper-middle-class family, the sort that before the 1939–45 war had always had a nanny and a cook, and during the war she had been evacuated with her mother, brothers and sisters to Canada. They had moved to America and lived in Massachusetts for two years, and had come back, while the war was still on, across the U-boat-infested Atlantic. Boarding-school in Bedfordshire followed for Lindy, and then the Guildhall School of Music in London. Now she had returned to Cambridge where she was teaching young piano pupils while continuing her own music studies. She was the only member of the Turner family who had some religious faith and was to be seen at the college chapel services. She had become attracted to the amusing Bob Runcie, eleven years older than herself, who so often came to tea; and she also wanted a part-time job to earn some more money. To Runcie, when she asked him, it seemed an excellent arrangement, and it was agreed that she should work for him two mornings a week.

Working together like this, a romance quickly developed between them. Runcie had had girl-friends ever since his adolescence, but there had never been such a strong and ardent personality as Lindy. One of her older sisters warned her – mistakenly – that there was no point in falling in love with him because he was a celibate. But that she did not believe. Before many months had passed, on the night of the May Ball of 1957, or perhaps in the small hours of the following morning, as they walked on the damp grass under the trees in the Fellows' Garden, they decided to be married before the end of the summer's vacation.

Their engagement was announced as soon as the undergraduates had disappeared from Cambridge for the summer; and the speed with which they determined to be married was to thwart the inevitable undergraduate humour (bad for discipline, thought the dean) that they would otherwise have to suffer as an engaged couple. Lindy's father did not altogether welcome the idea of a clergyman in the family (and her mother was less than pleased at such a penniless one), but Cecil Turner and Runcie liked each other personally, and a love of cricket was a bond between them. The wedding was to be in the University Church of Great St Mary's and, like every other young couple planning to take such a step in that parish, they went to receive their formal wedding preparation from the vicar, Mervyn Stockwood. The future and controversial Bishop of Southwark – himself a confirmed bachelor – received them in a dimly-lit sidechapel of the church where he sat in cassock and biretta and talked solemnly to them about the responsibilities of the married state.

The wedding day was Thursday, 5 September, a fine breezy day, and four hundred guests were expected. In the early morning Runcie went with his friend, Dick Hare (subsequently Bishop of Pontefract) who was staying with him in his college rooms, to an early Mass in St Benet's and, on their way back, they were alarmed to see every sign that road works were about to begin in the narrow lane just outside the gates of Trinity Hall. It needed urgent persuasion to get the workmen to agree to keep the gateway clear until after the reception.

The morning was spent greeting friends, and at noon there was a luncheon party at the Blue Boar at which all the Runcie family were present. Kath and Angus had come from Nottinghamshire, Kenneth and his Swiss wife, Ghyslaine, had come from Manchester. Marjorie and her husband were already in Cambridge where they had been living for the past two years, though they had seen relatively little of Robert during that time. Very soon after the wedding they planned to move to Scotland.

The ceremony was at two o'clock and was the straightforward prayer book marriage service. To have put it in the setting of a Eucharist, which Runcie would obviously have preferred, and which would have been according to his own sacramental principles, would have caused embarrassment to the Turner family and many of the guests. Indeed, the guests were quite strongly divided into ecclesiastics and theologians on one side, and lawyers and secularists on the other; many on both sides being distinguished scholars who were, or have since become, well-known names. The service, which began with 'Come down, O Love divine' and finished with 'Now thank we all our God' and the Mozart wedding march, was conducted by Launcelot Scott Fleming, the Bishop of Portsmouth (later, Dean of Windsor), who, until he went to Portsmouth in 1949, had been on and off the staff of Trinity Hall as Dean, Chaplain, and Fellow since 1933. He was a close friend of the Turner family and virtually a Trinity Hall institution, and it had been unthinkable that anyone else should perform the ceremony. He was assisted by the Bishop of Ripon, George Chase, who, as a former Dean of Trinity Hall, had baptized Lindy. Tony Tremlett, the current Trinity Hall Chaplain, also took a part; and Graham Storey, an English don, was Runcie's best man.

The reception was held in the Fellows' garden where Runcie had proposed. By every account, Lindy looked stunning in her long white dress with its big turned-back collar, tiny waist, and long sleeves. The scene was bright and sunny, with skirts and hats fluttering in the wind along with the late summer flowers in the herbaceous borders. Champagne corks popped, and the couple were showered with good wishes.

That same day they flew to Nice for their honeymoon. Runcie, while on the staff at Westcott, had been there twice before to do a holiday relief chaplaincy. The regular chaplain in Nice was a bachelor with indifferent health and a private income, and was able to live in comfort with a Russian manservant. Months before he got engaged, Runcie had promised to go again that summer, but when he knew he was going to be married he had written with his apologies to call off the arrangement. 'How would you like a working honeymoon?' came the reply, with an offer from the chaplain to take his own holiday at a time to suit the newly-weds, and to do up the flat in honour of the bride. It was an offer not to be refused, and when they arrived in Nice they were met by the Russian manservant who took a sentimental delight in treating Lindy like a princess.

They had a marvellous time exploring the Riviera. Runcie's Sunday duties were light, though the British population of Nice started to die off at an alarming rate and he had three funerals in the first week. The church treasurer, a lawyer, was at pains to make sure that Runcie got the full fees for the funerals – enough to take Lindy for a champagne supper which, the lawyer assured them, would have given the three deceased much pleasure had they known. The hospitality of the local British and American residents was overwhelming and occasionally formidable. One splendid lady with a back like a ramrod gave a luncheon party at which Lindy was definitely on trial. She passed with credit, and with the comment, 'Your wife does remind me of the dear archdeacon's wife; so good with the not-quites!'

They returned to their new home in Cambridge in time for the new term. They had inherited from Owen Chadwick a small flat over a shop at 20b King's Parade, the tourist centre of the city, which looked straight across the road to the most famous home of English church music, King's College chapel. The staircase to the flat was so narrow that Lindy's piano had to be hoisted in through an upper window. Robert still kept his rooms in college, and Lindy continued to give music lessons. Among her pupils was Hugh Montefiore's daughter who knew her as 'a marvellous teacher' who could instil enthusiasm even into those who had no particular talent. She also had her effect on Runcie. His friends had always found him fun to be with, but they had noticed a growing 'churchiness'; not that he was either solemn or pompous, but his interests, his conversation, and his humour all tended to have a flavour rather too ecclesiastical. A young and lively wife, not at all churchy herself ('Too much religion makes me go pop' was one of her famous remarks to the press when she found herself destined for Lambeth Palace) nipped this in the bud and, though he continued to work as hard as ever, he opened up to a fresh enjoyment of life.

Their first child, James Robert, was born on Ascension Day, 7 May 1959, in the Mill Road Maternity Hospital while Runcie was celebrating Mass in the college chapel. With a baby they were cramped in their little flat and, during the summer months, James would be put in his carry-cot into one of the window-boxes. The tourists who thronged in King's Parade down below would sometimes be intrigued to see a tiny hand waving from where geraniums might be expected to blow. With a wife and son, and settled in an academic career that he enjoyed, Runcie's future looked certain. All he needed was a larger house for his family to grow in.

Chapter Nine

Cuddesdon – I

Early in 1960 Owen Chadwick again took a hand in Runcie's life. On 3 March Runcie wrote to tell his brother-in-law, Angus Inglis:

> Owen Chadwick came to see me yesterday about the possibility of my becoming Principal of Cuddesdon. Obviously it is a big job to be done for the C of E but I'm not sure that it's my line or that Lindy would enjoy it. But they do want someone who will humanise the place and strengthen the ties with Oxford. It would mean a drop in income but we would get a glorious vicarage and a garden kept up for us. I would certainly prefer to spend a few more years here, and I don't think I would consider any other theological college (including Westcott!), but Cuddesdon is rather different with its parish and church, and a great tradition. Of course it now looks as though we are going to be offered a house in Cambridge which complicates things.
>
> I will keep you informed and welcome any observations. Mind you, I have *not* been offered the job, it's simply that Owen, who is a governor, and the Bishop of Oxford would like to nominate me if I wanted it.

He had once visited the theological college in the small village of Cuddesdon a few miles to the south-east of Oxford when he had been one of a victorious cricket eleven from Westcott House. Cuddesdon College was older than

Westcott. It had been founded in 1854 by Samuel Wilberforce, the gifted Bishop of Oxford (and son of the slave
emancipator) as a diocesan training college for clergy. He
had built it in Cuddesdon, close to the bishop's palace, with
the idea that was current at the time that the bishop should
personally supervise and care for the education of the ordinands. The college had quickly developed a strong Catholic
tradition and had had a stormy history in the first few years,
but it had soon established a reputation for producing some
of the best-trained and dedicated clergy in the Anglican
church. Like Westcott, its primary purpose was to train
graduates but, unlike Westcott, it had a regime that was
almost monastic.

When Owen Chadwick, who had himself been trained
there, knew that the principal, Edward Knapp-Fisher, was
leaving to be Bishop of Pretoria, Runcie's name immediately
occurred to him. He hesitated out of his rival loyalty to
Trinity Hall where he felt that 'Runcie's gifts with the
heathen were so remarkable that I was not sure whether it
could be right that he should go to a place where he would
train none but the committed'. Before approaching Runcie
he had gone to consult Tony Tremlett who had been chaplain at Trinity Hall during both Chadwick's and Runcie's
time, and was also a Cuddesdon man. The two of them had
considered the claims of their shared and divided loyalties
and had agreed that Runcie should be persuaded – provided
the governors of Cuddesdon agreed to elect him – to go to
Cuddesdon. It was at that point that Chadwick went to see
Runcie.

Runcie's own doubts were on the same grounds as Chadwick's: he was finding a ministry among lay people and the
unconverted as well as among committed Christians; but he
was sufficiently attracted to the idea to allow Chadwick to
go to his fellow-governors. Meanwhile another suggestion
had been hinted at by W. C. Costin, President of St John's,
Oxford, who wanted him to be dean there. On 3 April
Runcie again wrote to Inglis.

My affairs have been a little disturbed by 'possibilities'

recently. Costin wrote to me about St John's. There were some advantages, a bit more money and possibly academic security; but in the end I didn't go to see them. A move to a similar sort of job in Oxford would not have been too popular here, and in the end of the day my ambitions are not − because I haven't the gifts − book writing and professorial chairs. Anyway I might not have been offered it even if I had submitted to interview, and that would have been a blow to my pride! Owen Chadwick was *slightly* against it because he said I was established at the Hall, and it would take a few years to get established in the same way at another college.

Meanwhile Cuddesdon is now v. much on the map. I am seeing Harry Oxon [Harry Carpenter, Bishop of Oxford] on Thursday so that I ought then to have some details. So far I've heard nothing, although such is security that I'm constantly being asked whether I've accepted! I wish things didn t move quite so slowly because it makes other work difficult when the future is unsettled.

He added at the end of his letter that from Palm Sunday to Easter Day he, with Lindy and James, would be staying with Tony Tremlett, now vicar of St Stephen's, Rochester Row, in Westminster, 'where I will be preaching my heart out during Holy Week; but I hope it will be a break for Lindy because Tony Tremlett has a really cosy vicarage in Vincent Square with a housekeeper who used to be a nanny!'

It was while they were staying with Tremlett that the formal offer came and it provided Tremlett with the opportunity to give his advice. He was blunt and to the point. Much as Runcie enjoyed university life, he must know himself that he was never likely to write the large and significant books that would make his academic reputation and, if he stayed at Trinity Hall, or took a similar job at another college, he ran the risk, said Tremlett, of 'finishing up as a failed don'. Cuddesdon, on the other hand, offered him a chance to use his real gifts for teaching, organisation, and even more important, bringing a fresh mind and his very special talents to what had become a hidebound college.

It was within his ability to tune it to meet the church's need for high-calibre Catholic clergy trained to cope with the opportunities and complexities of contemporary life.

Runcie accepted what he said and knew that it was probably true. A major attraction for him was that the job at Cuddesdon included the incumbency of a country parish, with all the down-to-earth pastoral responsibilities among the local people that that involved. It looked like the best of all worlds: the responsibility for training fifty or more bright young men to be caring, intelligent, and faithful priests; the proximity of Oxford University which he could exploit to the full by drawing on its resources to widen the teaching in the college; and a parish which he knew he would enjoy and which would anchor all that he was doing in the daily realities of church life. All that remained was that Lindy should be persuaded. She did not want to leave Cambridge where she had lived nearly all her life, where she had her friends and her pupils; but at least she could look forward to a large house and garden in the country. With her reluctant agreement, Runcie had made his decision by Easter Day.

He was to move to Cuddesdon at the beginning of the academic year, but his career at Trinity Hall had a fillip to its ending. He wrote to Inglis on 2 July:

I am having a slight break between terms, so to speak, but with a lot of Cuddesdon and Trinity Hall correspondence. The Long Vac. term begins on Thursday and I'm hanging on to my job and even doing some teaching. Furthermore you will be astonished to learn that I am about to become Junior Proctor! By an ancient statute, Trinity Hall must provide a Proctor if one of those in office dies or resigns. The Junior Proctor has just resigned, and the Master is presenting me to the Vice-Chancellor tomorrow. There will have to be a special Congregation of the Senate to elect me, but I don't expect I will be opposed. The net result is that I will be Proctor until the end of the academic year, i.e. October 1st. We do not walk in the Long Vac. [a reference to the disciplinary duties of the Proctors] and my quarter's salary should be about £120 which may even pay the removal van.

I don't think I have ever been more touched by the thoughtfulness of the secular dons. The Master said 'I thought you might like the money and it won't do you any harm in the future to have been a proctor – if only for three months.' From Sept 1st until October 1st I will be a pluralist on an eighteenth-century scale, still holding all my jobs at TH plus the proctorship *and* being Vicar of Cuddesdon and Principal of the Theological College. But the move is going to be frightfully expensive. We have already spent a good deal on furniture and curtain material *and* ordered a car. We decided we should get a new one, and have chosen a Mini-Minor – they are so economical to run, and we thought it would be just the thing for Oxford traffic and parking problems. We should get it by August.

I don't know whether we shall get much in the way of a holiday. An idea struck me and I wonder whether it would commend itself to you. Would you and Kath like to come and live in our flat for a few days in August and look after James? He is no trouble and it's such an easy flat to run. I could then take Lindy away for three days or so, and I think it would be just what we need about then.

Quite apart from that, would you like to come over for a night? You could dine [in the college], which you have never done, and if you come on July 25th there is a special Congregation to give Honorary Degrees and you might be amused to see the Junior Proctor!

Money was something of a problem, and continued to be. All his life he had had no more than just enough to live on. It was the situation in which he had been brought up, and since then he had lived on army pay, university grants, a curate's stipend, and the relatively meagre salaries paid to theological college and university staff. He had never been particularly thrifty, and yet he and his wife had entered into a way of life where they would probably always find themselves in larger-than-average houses, and expected to give as well as to receive hospitality, often on a substantial scale.

The vicarage at Cuddesdon, built in 1852, has twenty-six rooms and is the oldest part of the complex of college buildings. It stands sideways to the road, its front door facing the door of the college 30 yards away, across a gravel sweep. The college architect was George Edmund Street, later famous for his Law Courts in the Strand, and Cuddesdon was his first important commission. Writing about him in a history of the founding of Cuddesdon, Owen Chadwick says:

> He reverenced the thirteenth century and regarded the pointed arch as the most beautiful as well as 'incomparably the most convenient' of all forms of building . . . Like Ruskin and Morris he believed that the architect should also be a craftsman, able to paint on the walls he built, able to shape the ironwork as well as the stone. He believed that true art must spring from religion; that the artist needed a religious earnestness and self-sacrifice in pursuit of his art.

But, with all this religious principle and dedication, he was restricted in the building of Cuddesdon by the shortage of money and by Wilberforce's plan to build a college that would accommodate only twenty-one students to begin with, but be capable of later expansion. Even this did not really explain the inconveniences of the building, the narrowness of the passages, and the chapel on the top floor which could only be reached by a turret stone staircase. An early critic commented: 'The very picturesquesness of the external outline has resulted in more ups and downs than convenience would have dictated. If (absit omen) a decease were to occur, we are puzzled to trace the course of the coffin . . .'

The Gothic buildings of the college, with the vicarage, stood a little apart from the village, across the road from the bishop's palace whose garden adjoined the church. The surrounding land was green and pleasant, and there were only about five hundred people in the parish. In social terms it was quite unlike the two parishes that Runcie had known intimately: the rising middle class of Crosby, and the comfortable suburb of Gosforth. Apart from a few farmers, half the village were farm-workers and their families, and most of the rest were employed at the Cowley motor works. About three-quarters of them (partly in compliment to the excellence of the bingo club) were paid-up members of the Labour Party. Few of them went to church, but with so many parsons and potential parsons thronging the village they had high expectations of the clergy and their ministrations. The college was regarded, said Peter Cornwell who knew Cuddesdon both as a student and as a member of staff, 'as a sort of corporate lord of the manor'.

With the multitude of bedrooms in the vicarage, and a constant demand for places in the college, several students slept in the Runcies' house and became Lindy's friends, drinking coffee with her in the kitchen. Runcie also had his large study in the house, near the front door. Even so, there was not much overlap between college and family life. Every morning he went across to the college at seven o'clock for Mattins followed by meditation, and the Eucharist was celebrated at eight. Then came breakfast – in college – the morning's work, intercessions said at midday, lunch, the afternoon work period, Evensong at four thirty, more work and supper, and the day officially finished with Compline at nine thirty after which the students kept silence until breakfast while Runcie returned to his family. Mattins, meditation and Compline were obligatory every day; attendance at the other services was optional but expected. Compline on Saturday nights, though half an hour later than on other days, was an especial hardship, particularly for married men who had to rush back from their rare few hours with their families (not to mention the unmarried men who rushed back from parties in Oxford and occasionally crept out again).

Not only was the regime stricter in many respects than the one Runcie had known at Westcott, it was also monastic in its almost total denial of the existence of the female sex.

Westcott had been very much a male establishment as Kenneth Carey, in spite of having a number of women friends, did not always find it easy to get on with women in general. But wives and girl-friends had been made welcome as guests, and the involvement with the surrounding university had meant an open social life for the ordinands. In contrast the Cuddesdon that Runcie inherited hardly ever allowed women on the premises, and the basic rule, which applied to staff and students alike, was that no wives or fiancées must live within two miles of the college, and that all meals, with the exception of lunch on Saturdays, were to be eaten in college. The nearest a wife ever got to sharing anything of her husband's way of life was being allowed to accompany him to the parish Communion in the parish church on Sunday mornings and afterwards, by special arrangement, being entertained to coffee in the vicarage by the then principal's mother. It was a state of affairs which put extraordinary strains on family life, and it says much for the commitment of the ordinands (and the support of their wives) that they were prepared to put up with it, for this was only a few years before enlightenment came to the theological colleges and they began to recognise an ordinand's wife as a partner in her husband's ministry, and to accept that she, too, would need support and preparation for the demanding way of life which lay before them both.

For the first few months Runcie submitted himself and his family to all the disciplines of the college timetable, sharing the life of his students, going to all the services and every meal as well as taking a heavy load of teaching and administration. His free afternoons and college vacations he devoted to the parish. Inevitably his family life suffered, and Lindy was often very lonely. It was not easy on a young wife with a small child and – quite soon – another child on the way. It was clear, however, that her personality made its own impact on the college. Not only did she make friends of those students who lodged in the vicarage, she began having tea in the college on Saturdays, and to make other wives welcome. She also had a series of *au pairs* and occasional girl-friends to stay with her, and in the course of time provided wives for at least two members of staff by doing so. Runcie was by no means the first married principal of Cuddesdon, but it was he and Lindy between them who first – but gradually – made women an accepted and normal part of college life.

He had gone to Cuddesdon conscious of its great tradition and its century-old reputation for producing devoted priests of high calibre. His task was to ease the college out of its strait-jacket and widen its horizons, but he is not and never has been an iconoclast. He was sensitive about alarming those who placed much value on the strict spiritual discipline which had always been Cuddesdon's hallmark, and there was much about it which appealed to his own instincts. However intellectually open-minded he might be, emotionally he was both Catholic and conservative, and tradition was important to him. There were many changes that he was determined to make, but among his most loyal colleagues on the staff there were some who thought he did not move fast enough.

The four staff in the first few months were Runcie himself, John Brooks the vice-principal, Anthony Bird, recently arrived as chaplain, and John Ruston who was curate of the parish as well as tutor in the college. Between them they did nearly all the teaching; and though there were academic lecturers, notably Professor H. F. D. Sparks on the New Testament, and Wilfrid Browning on doctrine, the involvement with the university was on nothing like the scale that Runcie hoped for. It was an exception for an ordinand with a degree in some other discipline to be reading for a theological degree while at Cuddesdon, though some of the students already had such a degree before coming to the college.

It was the strengthening of Cuddesdon's academic life that Runcie tackled first. By the beginning of Lent 1961 when he wrote his first Lent Letter – the principal's annual communication to all Cuddesdon men, and in which he always stuck to the opening address, 'My dear Sir' – he was able to say what he had already achieved:

However modest we may be about the equipment of the resident staff, I don't think Cuddesdon could be regarded as a theological waste land in a term when Professor Henry Chadwick is conducting a seminar on Ideas of Sin and Guilt, Dr Mascall has been lecturing on Christian Initiation, and David Jenkins, the Chaplain of Queen's, is lecturing once a week on the Atonement. Professor Sparks still finds time to visit us, and his seminar on The Liturgical Use of the Psalms is by no means restricted to an Old Testament analysis. The Rector of Garsington (A. J. W. Pritchard) is caring for our Christian Morals. The energetic Chaplain of Littlemore, one of the country's most progressive mental hospitals, has arranged a course of lectures and practical classes under the direct supervision of the Medical Superintendent.

This sample of stimulus regularly supplied from outside is recorded not only to express gratitude, but also to challenge some of the wilder generalisations about 'country colleges' current in a recent spate of books, articles, and pamphlets on theological education. There are compelling arguments in favour of establishing a new theological college in a modern university – the undergraduate population is expanding rapidly, and it is highly desirable that a man studying for a degree in any subject should be aware of the existence of theology as a serious intellectual discipline. The established colleges in Oxford, Cambridge, and Durham have made notable contributions to the intellectual exchange of these universities – but it is a pity some of the promoters of [the idea of] the new college have wrapped up their project in rhetoric which is contemptuous of existing methods.

We are told we need a new college 'wide open to the world', and it is suggested that such an institution would at last be 'a sign to the nation' that the church means business. Naturally I am not complacent enough to imagine that we don't need constantly to examine our methods in the light of the kind of world and ministry which lie ahead of a man. Recent experience has taught me that there is far too little 'conversation' between theology and other disciplines studied in a university, and there is a desperate need for more undergraduates of *first-class calibre* to undertake this task and fill our teaching posts; but we also need to remind ourselves that the primary concern of a place like Cuddesdon is not with post-graduate research, but with pre-ordination training.

He then went on to quote some words of Charles Smyth: 'Given a man who has attained a decent academic standard, especially a man who has very properly read theology for an Honours degree, it is infinitely more important that he should be set to learn the life of discipline and devotion in the wilds of rural England than that he should hang about in a theological college on the periphery of a university, acquiring a little additional or general culture . . .'

That was certainly repudiating what had been his own view of his theological training when he was doing it at Westcott House. Twelve years before, he had treated Westcott as something of a relaxation after his hard work for his degree at Oxford. He had now totally changed his idea of training for the priesthood and, as the years went on, increasingly put his emphasis on the need for intellectual rigour to produce clergy who could talk with intelligent confidence of the things of God in the sceptical modern world.

In September 1961 John Brooks left the staff to go to a parish in Zambia and, at Christmas, John Ruston went to join Bishop Knapp-Fisher in Pretoria leaving, remarked Runcie in his next Lent Letter, Anthony Bird as 'the only member of the old staff who has not so far fled to Africa'. It was now that he began to show his exceptional gift for picking the unexpectedly right person for the right job; often he selected people very different from himself, but whose talents he had noted and was prepared to trust. It was a flair which only rarely let him down.

His first appointment was Lionel Wickham whom he had known as a student at Westcott, and whom he invited from a curacy in Lincolnshire to teach philosophical theology. Wickham has since become lecturer in theology at the University of Southampton. To replace Ruston, Runcie summoned Peter Cornwell, a former Cuddesdon student, also with a degree in theology, from his curacy in a difficult housing estate in Hull. Cornwell had been recommended by Anthony Bird and was at first reluctant to leave his industrial parish, but Runcie inveigled him back to Cuddesdon and the curacy of the parish church by describing Cuddesdon village as a suburb of Cowley and its motor works 'full of sociological problems'. With Bird, himself a theologian (and hitherto the only one on the staff), they made a strong resident team; and to them was added, as a regular non-resident lecturer, A. M. Allchin, at that time Librarian of Pusey House and making his reputation as a writer and ecumenist. In addition, Runcie wrote, 'We have invited a University theologian to give one course of lectures each term, and we continue to benefit from the regular teaching supplied by the Archdeacon of Oxford in Hebrew, and the Rector of Garsington in Morals.' He went on to say that the year-long course at the Littlemore Mental Hospital which had been arranged by the chaplain, Andrew Mepham, with the co-operation of the medical and nursing staff, had proved a very valuable addition to the curriculum.

Through hard work, assigned reading, lectures and seminars, men are trained for the pastoral ministry by clinical experience under supervision. Whilst emphatically not an attempt to produce amateur psychologists, such experience does equip a student to recognise the limitations as well as the opportunities of pastoral care, and I am convinced that the traditional teaching of pastoralia and ethics in a theological college must be supplemented by some such clinical case-work if it is to be at all related to a modern understanding of behaviour patterns.

His own experience was widened in 1962 when he had his first taste of the missionary church overseas. He was invited to deliver the Teape lectures at St Stephen's College in Delhi. He had had a long association with the Cambridge Mission to Delhi which was founded in Cambridge University in 1877, largely at the instigation of Professor Westcott (after whom Westcott House was named). It aimed to provide Cambridge-trained men to work in Delhi backed by the resources of both the university and the Society for the Propagation of the Gospel, the older of the church's two great missionary societies, which provided an office in its own building in Westminster. When Runcie had arrived on the staff of Westcott following the departure of Alan Webster, he had taken over from Webster the secretaryship of the Mission with the job of ensuring the continuation of the university's support in cash and recruits. He had to find and encourage representatives in each college, to foster the vocations of any men who felt that they might be called to work with the Cambridge Brotherhood in the city of Delhi, or in St Stephen's College which had become part of the Punjab university, and to seek out and entertain students who came to Cambridge from the Delhi areas. He had put his usual energy into this work and, though he had passed on the secretaryship when he left Cambridge, the invitation to give the six Teape lectures was a recognition of what he had done for the Mission.

It was his first long trip abroad and he was determined to make the most of it. With the help of a friendly travel agent he arranged a tour that would include a few days in Rome and Jerusalem on his way out to India, and as much of India as time and money would allow. At the beginning of November Lindy drove him to the airport and he said goodbye, promising to be home for Christmas. Cuddesdon was left in the care of Anthony Bird, and staff, students and friends alike promised to look after Lindy, James, and three-month-old Rebecca who had been born on the first of August.

It was his second visit to Rome. He had gone there for a week in 1954 with Dr and Mrs Waters mainly with the purpose of making a pilgrimage to find Derek's grave near Salerno. This second visit coincided with the meeting of the Second Vatican Council and, during the four days he spent there, he saw in and around St Peter's Square many of the leading Roman Catholic figures taking part in that momentous conference which was to shake the monolithic structure of the Roman Catholic Church so that it would never be the same again. At that time Runcie was an anonymous and only mildly distinguished Anglican tourist observing a great event from its periphery. Yet it was preparing the way for one of the greatest occasions of his own future when, twenty years later, he led the Pope up the aisle of Canterbury Cathedral at a historic moment for Western Christendom.

Meanwhile he was an English clergyman, by no means flush with money, travelling alone in foreign parts, and to get to Jerusalem he had first to go to Beirut. It was there, as he stayed overnight in a hotel, that his entire stock of travellers' cheques – not quite a hundred pounds – was stolen while he slept. It was a disaster. He had taken nearly all the money that he and Lindy possessed, and he had to send a frantic cable home to get Lindy to go to the bank and stop the cheques. Even though most of the money was eventually recovered, and in the meanwhile he was able to borrow a little in Jerusalem, it left him almost entirely dependent on the hospitality and generosity of his hosts for the rest of his travels.

In Jerusalem he stayed in St George's Hostel, part of the complex of pleasant buildings which surround the unimaginative nineteenth-century Anglican cathedral dedicated to England's patron saint (who would have been much more at home in that landscape than in the green and pleasant land which adopted him). While he was there Runcie was able to see the new St George's College which was to be a study and training centre for Anglican clergy from all over the world. It had just been completed, its first principal installed, and it was waiting to receive its first students.

He visited the holy places where Jesus of Nazareth walked, taught, and suffered. Chief among them is the Church of the Holy Sepulchre which encompasses the traditional sites of both the Crucifixion and Christ's tomb. The sacredness of these shrines in Christian belief is almost too much to comprehend, hidden as they are beneath all the accretions of seventeen hundred years of Eastern Christian worship. When in the ornate and over-decorated Chapel of Golgotha, or when contemplating the elaborately-carved marble which surrounds the last resting place of our Lord's earthly body, it requires a heroic effort of the imaginative will, on a first visit, to perceive those two sites as the sordid places of torture and execution, and the simple rock tomb which Joseph of Arimathea had bought for himself, but in which he laid the dead Jesus.

Runcie felt unprepared for what he had come to see. The great church was girded about with scaffolding in preparation for its massive restoration which had been argued about for years by the different Christian churches who controlled different parts of the building, and which was at last about to begin. It was full of holy clutter. It had none of the simplicity, tidiness and restrained English good taste that Anglicans have come to take for granted in their own great churches. Orthodox Christianity – and the Eastern Orthodox Churches are the dominant influence in the Holy Sepulchre – expresses its piety with ikons, images, lamps, candles, jewels and glitter of all kinds which can present an almost insurmountable barrier to the Western imagination until one begins (as Runcie came to in the years which followed) to love and understand it.

Bethlehem was quite different. He went there on his own in an Arab bus noisy with local life and a prolonged altercation over the presence on board of a full-grown sheep. It was late in the afternoon, and the light was beginning to fail as he entered the huge and ancient basilica through its tiny doorway, the 'eye of the needle' through which no camel, ox, or horse can pass. He found himself alone as he wandered among the rose-coloured columns of the oldest great church in Christendom, and descended the steps past the bronze Crusader doors to the cave where Christians believe that Jesus was born. It is now covered with marble and hung with votive lamps like the holy sites in Jerusalem; but on Runcie, alone in the near darkness of that November afternoon, it had a powerful effect. It had always been Christmas, the great feast of the Incarnation, of God becoming Man in the form of a defenceless baby, which had meant most to him of all the festivals of the Christian year; and this was the very place, cherished from the earliest Christian traditions, where it had happened. The holy magic of that moment was enhanced by the sudden quiet arrival of a group of local schoolchildren who trooped into the shrine for their evening prayers, sang a hymn, and left with as little fuss as they had arrived. It was unforgettable.

He travelled on to Delhi where he gave his six lectures on 'Christianity and Culture' in St Stephen's College. His work for the Mission in Cambridge had given him many friends and connections in the city, and there was also Ernest John, an Indian priest who had been for a time his fellow-curate in Gosforth. Runcie was entertained by them all. He was taken to see the local church life and to visit the tourist sites. The snapshots that he brought home with him show him in front of the Taj Mahal as well as in many a church compound with welcoming garlands of flowers hung round his neck.

Calcutta was his next stop where he gave the same six lectures, suitably adapted, at Bishop's College, a theological college founded in 1820 for training Indian clergy. He spent some days with the Oxford Mission to Calcutta (a society comparable to the Cambridge Mission to Delhi) and saw for himself the appalling Calcutta slums. He stayed for a few days with Murray Rogers in his *ashram*, living in the style of the simplest Indian people, sitting on a cow-dung floor meditating for two hours at a time on the eternal truths common to Christianity and the Eastern mystics, and living on fruit and chappatis – an experience which he felt nearly killed him! From there he went to Bangalore and gave his lectures for a third time in the United Theological College. He had there a chance to see something of the Church of South India which had been the cause of so much contro- versy during his student days at Westcott.

Back in Cuddesdon he told his students of what he had found in India.

I was surprised by the number of Christian institutions in North India in relation to the tiny Christian population.

Colleges, schools, hospitals, orphanages, mostly created by Europeans, now increasingly run by Indian Christians, and admitting people of any faith or none. Relics of the days of British rule, were they simply the products of Victorian sentiment – 'Sugaring the pill of the British Raj'? I don't believe it, and neither by and large do thoughtful Indians. They seem to me to have been the attempt by dedicated men and women to see in the opening up of India to European trade and commerce an opportunity to take the love and compassion of Christ along too, and their work has made a difference to India here and now. Small if judged by baptisms, but considerable in the perspective of the Kingdom of God.

Christian schools and colleges never recognised the caste system. From the start they sat down Muslim and Hindu together, and what they pioneered has now become official policy; but the Christian school or college is still uniquely free from divisive regional, linguistic, or state prejudices. The care for the weak and under-privileged – the Red Cross element in our faith – has played a significant part in creating a network of hospitals, while the nursing *profession* is almost wholly Christian in origin.

From time to time I met missionaries of the old school: the Girtonian of ninety, living in one room on the outskirts of Delhi, still teaching in a primary school, but the founder and first headmistress of one of India's leading girls' high schools; or the old lady of eighty-six to whom perhaps more than anyone India owes the idea of strict professional training for nurses, content to live out her days in the country to which she has given her life; or the Cuddesdon priest in his eighties, ministering still in the Kolar gold field because there is just no one to take his place.

Cuddesdon men had a long tradition of serving overseas and Runcie was throwing out a challenge to his current students.

But there are fresh tasks, and for these India needs far more people of the calibre of those old warrior missionaries who were ready to give their lives and not simply 'short service'. The Victorian trappings easily raise a smile: the Gothic churches, the Arnold school mottoes about playing the game, the Urdu versions of bad *Ancient and Modern* hymns, and the pitch-pine pews for worshippers with a native genius for sitting cross-legged for hours in silent adoration; but I believe, paradoxically enough, that the Christian witness in India would be less dated and less odd if, alongside the Indian Christians whose families were often lifted out of their old social and economic background, and were provided with a new mission compound background to which they tenaciously cling, there were more European teachers, doctors, and clergy to share with them our own experiences, to warn them of our own failures, and to adapt the church's life and structure to a technical and industrial society.

Drawing on his brief experience of overseas theological training, he suggested in his Lent Letter of 1963 that the essential question was not how to train priests who had the answers, but rather, 'How can we organise theological training so that ordinands are en route to becoming priests who can face the questions?' It was an attitude which was to see him through the theologically explosive year of the publication of *Honest to God*.

The book came out in March and on the Sunday before it appeared its author, John Robinson, at that time Bishop of Woolwich, had summed it up in an article in the *Observer* with the title 'Our image of God must go!' Nothing that he said was new to the theological world of the universities, and Runcie had known Robinson for most of his time in Cambridge where such interpretations of Christian theology had been current for years. Only twelve months earlier a collection of essays by ten theologians – nine of them from Cambridge including Hugh Montefiore, Harry Williams, and John Habgood – had been published under the title of *Soundings*, foreshadowing much of what *Honest to God* was to proclaim in a more popular form. It was edited by Dr Alec Vidler who wrote in his Introduction: 'We believe that there are very important questions which theologians are now being called upon to face, and which are not yet being faced with the necessary seriousness and determination. We do not profess yet to see our way through them . . . Our task is to try to see what the questions are that we ought to be facing in the 1960s . . .' *Soundings* included the first public airing of the so-called New Morality. It was revolutionary in 1962 for Harry Williams to write that 'a great deal of what Christians call virtue, on closer inspection turns out to be cowardice – a refusal to give myself away because I am too frightened to do it. This is most obviously true in the sphere of sexual ethics, because here more than anywhere there seems to be an enormous amount of double-think.'

'*Soundings* produced a rather muffled explosion,' wrote Roger Lloyd in his history of *The Church of England 1900-1965*, whereas *Honest to God* had

> loosed the long pent-up thunders of the gathering storm which exploded in a great and sudden roar . . . It immediately set in motion a tremendous public debate, and for a long time the air was full of violent charges and denunciations and the defences made against them. The former were as intemperate as they were noisy, and the defenders from time to time adopted a tone which was both injured and shrill. *Honest to God* in fact caused a great controversy. Just as no previous theological book had sold so quickly, so none had caused so much excitement or given rise to so much quarrelling.

Runcie had had warning in the previous December that the book was coming out. He, Owen Chadwick and Hugh Montefiore had decided to give Bishop Noel Hudson, who had ordained Runcie and Montefiore, a dinner on his seventieth birthday. During the course of that evening Montefiore told Runcie that John Robinson had written a book that he personally thought it would be a mistake to publish. Soon after that Runcie saw a proof copy, and his surprise was that Robinson, not usually the easiest of theological writers, had produced something so readily accessible to the general public.

The outcry was enormous, and Bishop Robinson received over a thousand letters in the first three months after the book's publication, many of them accusing him of having destroyed the faith of the faithful. But for huge numbers of other Christians it was a liberating experience. David Jenkins, who was at that time coming from Oxford every week to lecture at Cuddesdon, summed it up at the start of a critical contribution he wrote for *The Honest to God Debate*, a paperback that David Edwards of the SCM Press thought it worth while to publish as a follow-up to the original book.

The evidence of my own contacts and those of many of my friends is sufficient to convince me that the approach of the book has encouraged many people to feel able to look again, with a very real feeling of discovery, at questions concerning God, the meaning and context of life, and the practice and possibility of religion. Persons who have felt encouraged and set free by the example of the book to renew their quest into these matters include some who have hitherto 'written off' all talk of God and all practice of religion, and some who have succeeded in clinging with more or less difficulty and desperation to a 'Faith' and the practices of a Faith which they have not dared to investigate deeply because they have more than half suspected that under investigation the 'Faith' will collapse. Thus the book constitutes an occasion of liberation and advance, whatever occasions of stumbling it may also be in danger of offering.

Through all the furore, with even the Archbishop of Canterbury, Michael Ramsey, at first speaking against the book (a reaction he later regretted), Runcie remained calm. Peter Cornwell commented that his constitutional conservatism in the *practice* of Christianity, together with his sensitivity to atmosphere, meant that 'the theological kicking around among students and staff was against a secure background . . . he knew when to put the boot in and when to let it ride'. Runcie had faith in the theologians on his staff, together with Jenkins and Henry Chadwick, to provide the *gravitas* of theological debate. Looking back, he says he had a team capable of encouraging the students to believe that theological education in its radical form could be a liberating experience.

The church needed to go through the process of realising that Christians did not need to hold by impossible beliefs; for in any congregation there were Christians often filled with guilt because they thought they were supposed to believe literally all that they were told, like Jesus suddenly reappearing in clouds in the sky, and they couldn't actually believe it, but dared not admit it. You needed to communicate to such people something that they could *feel* to be true as a deeply spiritual expression of the incarnational experience. The staff at Cuddesdon at that time were excellent because they helped to send people out from the college who had the fundamental integrity and coherence of character to face the questions that were being asked.

He gave the whole affair only a passing reference in his Lent Letter of 1964. 'While not unscathed by *Honest to God* ... and much else, it may be reassuring to some of our readers to know that the old firm is still very much in business'; and he went on to pay more critical attention to Leslie Paul's report on *The Deployment and Payment of the Clergy* which had also been recently published. It was proposing radical reforms in the distribution of the clergy among the parishes, an end to the parson's freehold, the reorganisation and amalgamation of parishes and their boundaries, and the deployment of new curates, not where they wanted to go, or where their theological college principals thought they would get the best training, but where, in the church's judgment, they were most needed. 'Those who are under training are unlikely to be dazzled by or optimistic about the results of pastoral reorganisation,' he wrote. 'Modern unbelief and moral confusion are too close to them for that; but only on the far side of these reforms do they see any new pattern of ministry emerging in recognisable shape.' And he went on to consider what has become known as the non-stipendiary ministry, the training and ordination of men who will remain in their secular jobs while exercising their ministry, a practice that was already widespread in other parts of the Anglican Communion.

It is time that kites flown in periodicals and paperbacks about 'supplementary ministry' were grounded in some general strategy, for it is becoming increasingly difficult to believe that the 'general purposes' incumbent should be the only end-product of all our training schemes. Whenever attention is drawn to the need for specialised training and a diversified ministry, it is interpreted as an attack upon, or an underestimation of, the parochial ministry; but the object of such controlled experiment is surely to bring the parish priest's fundamental role within manageable proportions. Parish priests fall down on their jobs not simply through overwork, but also from the knowledge of work which can never be done . . . If in any large town parish, in addition to the vicar and one or two curates, there might be four or five men in priest's orders (but still in ordinary secular employment) celebrating the sacraments, preaching the Word, and sharing the priestly responsibility for the whole parish, the effect might be tremendous. Similarly in the country, where the situation is rapidly demanding an even larger grouping of parishes, it would still be possible in many cases, if the vicar had the assistance of such men, to keep a priest within the community life of the village, but at the same time linking the village with the larger grouping of villages which is slowly being accepted as the norm for country life in educational and social matters.

For those who sit on recruitment committees and CACTM selection boards, such a way forward seems simplicity itself beside Mr Paul's demand for a vastly increased army of professional clergymen all pushed through the general purposes training. That could only lead to a lowering of standards in our colleges. I am inclined to believe that we need to produce less men earmarked for the exacting work of a parish priest, but they would need to be surrounded and supported by other kinds of ministry. Which should be called 'supplementary' would remain an academic question. The shortage of clergy is not so serious as their misuse.

That year the students had a different sort of parish experience. Instead of the usual fortnight spent in some urban deanery, taking part in parish life and having a foretaste of some of the cosier aspects of being a curate, the whole college involved itself in a sociological survey in the diocese of Portsmouth. The students carried it out under the direction of the Social Sciences department of South-ampton University. For the whole of the Michaelmas Term they had been having a preliminary course of sociology lectures by Maurice Broady who had come up from South-ampton each week. He helped the staff and students to compile a questionnaire to be put to a sample of nearly four hundred regular worshippers from seven churches, and to two hundred 'marginal adherents' who had recently had children baptized but did not regularly go to church. Each one of the sample was interviewed about his or her religious and social background, belief, and relationships with the church. The clergy and leading laity were also interviewed, and a geographical analysis made by mapping the addresses of people listed on the church electoral rolls. Two years later the experiment was repeated in Birmingham with interviews of every tenth person on the secular electoral registers, giving a real cross-section of the community regardless of any church connection. The sociological value of the studies might have been questionable, said Runcie, but there was no doubt that the ordinands learned a great deal about the attitudes of the ordinary people among whom they would later work.

As the scope of the teaching widened and deepened, and the academic requirements grew tougher, so other parts of the college regime relaxed. In Runcie's third Lent Letter one change was made dramatically apparent to Cuddesdon's ex-students when they learned that not only had the vice-principal and the chaplain both married in the previous year, but they were actually living with their wives in the village. It was Lindy who had indirectly brought this revolution about. Anthony Bird's wife had been Lindy's German *au pair*, working in England in order to learn English; and Peter Cornwell's wife was a friend of Lindy's who had come to stay at the vicarage to look after James while Lindy gave birth to Rebecca. With marriages and babies practically on the premises, Cuddesdon was no longer the semi-monastic establishment it had so recently been, and wives, families, and girl-friends were now welcomed at the college at weekends, and some of the wives, as time went on, were invited to attend some of the lectures given by outside lecturers.

However, even this progress was not enough to satisfy Mark Santer when he arrived with his Dutch wife, a psychologist, to replace Lionel Wickham in September 1963. Both the Santers were appalled when they found how much of a bachelor establishment the college still was. Though women were seen in the college precincts more frequently, it was still only at carefully designated times. Staff and students were still expected to have all their week-day meals, including breakfast, in college, as well as lunch on Sundays – a particular hardship for married men. They were also obliged to return for Compline each night. It was not the rules that had changed so much as the atmosphere. Runcie was warm and delightful when he met the wives and girl-friends, and made them welcome when they were invited, but women were still emphatically not part of the college life.

The addition of Santer to the staff was an example of Runcie's instinct for picking exceptional men, for he had not actually met Santer when the idea of inviting him to Cuddesdon occurred to him. While at Trinity Hall he had marked the examination papers of some of the undergraduates reading classics, and the papers submitted by one of the students had so impressed him that he had made a point of finding out who was this bright lad who wrote all his papers in purple ink. He learned that it was Mark Santer, who not only got the best First Class degree that year, but was thinking of taking orders, and was going to Westcott House. While at Westcott, Santer obtained another First in theology, and then received a World Council of Churches scholarship for a year's ecumenical studies in Holland, where he met his wife. When Runcie needed to replace his curate and tutor he remembered Santer, got in touch with him through Westcott, and discovered he was on the point of ordination. He persuaded him to serve his title as curate of Cuddesdon at the same time as teaching in the college.

Runcie had not mistaken his ability. After four years at Cuddesdon Santer returned to Cambridge as a don and then, in 1973, started seven years as a distinguished principal of Westcott House before being consecrated Suffragan Bishop of Kensington in 1980.

Chapter Ten

Cuddesdon – II

Runcie's demand for intellectual respectability for his college was constant. Cuddesdon, like Westcott House, catered mainly for intelligent graduates and could therefore afford to give its students time and space to grow in other ways without too tight an academic programme. But he saw to it that they continued to have the highest quality teachers available; nor would he let his students off the academic hook. When a young lawyer, Nicholas Coulton, who was about to come to Cuddesdon as an ordinand, asked if he could be excused Greek, Runcie replied: 'I am afraid you have struck a principal who is a believer in the subject! In these days, when so much is loose and free in the study of theology, it seems to me an important discipline to undergo a more precise and accurate study within the main field.'

Standards were not so high elsewhere. He was concerned that among the two dozen Anglican theological colleges, each with its own distinct character, there were a number that concentrated on devotional and pastoral studies, but lacked the theological rigour and sound learning which Runcie quite passionately believed to be the true hallmark of the Church of England. As time went on, particularly as more and more of the traditional landmarks of Christian faith and practice seemed to be undermined by the explosion of radical theology often misunderstood, or only half understood, by those who most deplored it, he believed it essential for a priest to have a really sound grasp of theology if he was to be equipped to maintain his faith in the modern, sceptical world. In an article in the *Church Times* on 4 March 1966 he summarised what he saw as the intellectual task of the colleges:

> . . . to think through a theological problem, relating it to the documents of the Christian faith and to the coherent totality of Christian doctrine, and thus aiming at some relevant formulation in modern terms. The procedure in our study of ethics is first to awaken an awareness of the moral problems of men and women today and the situations which give rise to them; then to consider the tools which the Christian tradition has made available for handling ethical problems; and finally to use the tools in such a way that a piece of teaching or counselling or direction can be given which has not only been assimilated as 'the truth', but as the truth for the teacher or counsellor as part of the basis of his own personal life.

'Solemnly intoning "the Bible says" or "the church teaches" is no substitute for hard thinking,' he said. He himself lectured on church history and prayer. He had always regarded history as 'his' subject, and he had taken on the teaching of prayer because he believed it right that the principal who was ultimately responsible for the training of the men in his care should teach what was at the very centre of the Christian life. 'Clergy must be teachers of prayer' his students copied into their notebooks, as he talked about the need for 'ruthless simplicity and sincerity'. Those who knew him well suspected that his own prayer life was one of perpetual intellectual wrestling in an activity of the will which did not come easily to him. Ten years later, in an address in St Albans Abbey, he said, 'I confess there will be many here for whom prayer comes more naturally than it does for me. I am a teeth-grinding sort of person, of nervous fits and starts, a walking zoo of conflicting emotions; but unless I let go from time to time and discover that I am given a sort of unity by God, I know that I will not preserve my sanity, let alone my efficiency.' Without it he could not have survived the pace he set himself, and in his attempt to relate his prayer to the demands of his daily life his students would sometimes see him at prayer with his diary open in front of him.

What few people knew was that, since the summer of 1963, he had been a member of 'the Cell', a tiny group of Christians who supported each other in prayer and had an unseen influence on the theological colleges. The Cell had first been gathered in 1937 by Reginald Somerset Ward, one of the unsung saints among spiritual directors, who had invited Leslie Owen, Lumsden Barkway, and E. R. Morgan (all future bishops), together with the Provost of Newcastle, J. N. Bateman-Champain, to join him in two days of prayer and discussion. At the next meeting they added the Bishop of Knaresborough, P. F. D. Labilliere, and in 1942 they were joined by Eric Abbott (subsequently Dean of Westminster) who, as Somerset Ward aged, became the pivot of the group.

In the early years there were never more than six members, and new ones joined only when the older ones died or became too elderly to attend the meetings regularly. Michael Gresford Jones, Bishop of St Albans, replaced Owen, and Mark Hodson, the future Bishop of Hereford, replaced Bateman-Champain. Christopher Pepys, Bishop of Buckingham, and Adrian Somerset Ward, son of the founder, also joined.

The Cell met (and continues to meet) approximately every nine months, usually from a Friday afternoon to a Sunday morning. The strictly disciplined programme was divided between prayer and discussion, the daily offices, civilised meals, and silence. Attendance at the meetings was obligatory, and that attendance, together with praying for each other every day, were the only rules they all had to keep. The subject of each meeting was selected after a period of prayer, followed by discussion and more prayer, on the first evening; and that of the thirty-fifth meeting of the Cell, the first that Runcie went to, was typical: 'How is the contemporary crisis in Western society affecting the young priest in his prayers and his affections? And what does the Holy Spirit of discipline teach both him and his advisers?'

That meeting was held in the Deanery at Westminster on

17–19 June 1963. At first sight Runcie seems to have been a surprising choice to be invited to join that very exclusive group of deeply prayerful men. Several of the rest of them were well-known spiritual directors: Runcie, for all his theological intelligence and pastoral understanding, did not have that sort of spiritual reputation. One member of the Cell at that time suggests that perhaps the group felt it was getting a little precious and needed a fresh and sharp mind to contribute to its thinking. And as principal of Cuddesdon he would be seen by the group, which had always tended to be Catholic in its churchmanship, as a key person in the church, responsible for the largest and most prestigious of the Catholic theological colleges. Whatever their reasons, the choice was a most successful one, and Runcie has himself become the pivot of the group, while the spiritual support of the Cell to him personally grows more important through the years.

After each meeting it was customary for the chairman, chosen for the occasion, to write both an official record and a personal impression of the proceedings. At that first meeting that Runcie went to in 1963 the group was inevitably preoccupied with *Honest to God* and the New Morality. The chairman, probably Christopher Pepys, wrote:

We took colour from our new member (for our discussions gained in liveliness) and we were delighted to be re-inforced by the principal of a theological college. Principals, we heard, were battered men, they carry the burdens . . . but this principal, en route for his holiday at Nice, seemed the stronger for his encounters . . . Ideas flowed freely and interesting phrases were in good supply . . . Harry Williams [on the New Morality] occupied as much time as we could afford him, and his influence on young ordinands is something to which I suspect we must return. For some, Harry Williams is marvellous, for others he is more of a pathological problem. '*Honest to God* is the secret antagonist in every sermon' . . . The old father/son relationship in theological colleges has given way to something less paternal. Principals are both loved and respected and are objects of attack. 'Here is authority, and authority must not get us into its grasp.' But there is spirituality, and the new spirituality is more respectful of the Holy Spirit than the old. Repeatedly we came back to the truth that the Holy Spirit is in the ferment of these days, always glorifying Jesus and centralising him.

The chairman's more formal record speaks of the diminished power of the old spiritual authorities among the younger generation of clergy and society at large, and a heightened longing for personal significance. 'Meditation upon a historical Jesus becomes more and more difficult for many, but they have not yet been taught a new way of prayer in contemplation and simplicity and faith, and that the Holy Spirit can teach and give them a new spirituality.' The practical conclusions in the report all concern the need for a more disciplined prayer life for the Cell and to 'sound God's call to our ordinands to become such priests as will reveal the Holy Spirit of discipline in the constraint and restraint of love, Godwards and manwards'.

By his third meeting, at St Albans in February 1965, Runcie was himself in the chair. In his record and personal impression his style cut through the spiritual prolixity of some of his fellow-members. His formal record is sharply clear about what constituted 'the young priest's burden of failure'. In the climate of the time, the Cell concluded, everything seemed to be intellectually in a state of flux, with a loss of absolute standards. 'The world's cult of success,' wrote Runcie, 'makes the Cross-Resurrection look silly, and prevents the young priests from embracing the whole paradox of Christian life.' Neither the *Book of Common Prayer* nor the ecclesiastical machine corresponded with the realities of contemporary life. What was needed was coherence: the coherence between a priest's prayer life and his grappling with contemporary problems; also needed was wise spiritual direction.

His impression was written with his characteristic humour:

Greeted by a gracious Sister [in the Retreat House] with a choice between a quiet waterless bedroom or all mod. cons. plus the pulsating throb of the A5 might have been a sign for the sensitive that the desert and the metropolis, withdrawal and involvement, provided our agenda; but we had already brought our concerns with us, and after our prayer of offering we settled down to share them . . . The 'massive irrelevance' of the Ordinal, the Offices, visiting and the parochial mission were all passed under review as we tried to give some shape to the fightings without and the fears within which depressed the young priest, deprived him of joy, and discouraged the ordinand . . . Lumsden dropped in for lunch and Christopher dropped out for the evening to negotiate the country lanes of three dioceses, an institution and a squirearchal bun fight. Meanwhile the rest of us turned to Part II. The TV screen and Sunday papers had taken the place of synagogues and street corners for public self-examination and confession . . . The inside and the outside truth about Our Lord has to be known in the bones of the young priest if his confidence is to be properly grounded and his defeats seen as victories. If resentment and denigration double the suffering, insensitivity and conservatism shoulder a false Cross. We cannot choose the ground on which to fight the Lord's battles, but it is possible to fight on the wrong ground if there is no unitive prayer and wise, experienced direction at a time when a man's devotional vocabulary needs to be purged of so many words in the great manuals . . . Metaphors always mark the Cell's most moving moments. (Have we not been told in *Soundings* that artists in touch with the springs of creative imagination are more reliable guides than second-hand theological treatises!) Anyway, a homing pigeon wheeling and wheeling under the skies and suddenly getting a course seemed to say something about the vitality and spontaneity of rules and discipline, and 'the ocean of God's love' about the stillness which we enter 'as the ocean pacific', in contemplative prayer.

Eucharistia never seems easier than on the last morning

of the Cell ... As we talked and laughed and prayed together it became increasingly difficult to hear the bell which seemed to be tolling as for a doomed system throughout our opening session.

The Cell continued to wrestle with the problems and the meaning of the priesthood in the contemporary world, and Runcie contributed to it his practical working knowledge of young ordinands and their training, and took from the Cell back to Cuddesdon the pooled insights that were the product of the tough and rigorous prayer.

During his years at Cuddesdon he gained steadily in authority in all that he undertook. It was as if the principal-ship, by putting him in command, gave him the space to spread his wings. He still had a lot in reserve. It was not until he reached Canterbury that he showed the full range of his abilities, but it was at Cuddesdon that he came into his own, and the church began to recognise his potential as a leader.

Among the students he was 'the boss', though he was familiarly known as Princeps, and that was how he signed his letters to them. While always friendly, to some of them he appeared slightly distant, a bit remote, 'the whisk of a cassock going past in the corridor'. Yet no one could be more caring in sympathy and practical help when a man, or a wife, was in trouble. 'When the news was brought me that my father had died, you, Robert, were the first priest and friend to comfort me. Thank you!' wrote an ordinand's wife some years later; and when he was appointed to Canter-bury, among the five thousand letters he received, scores were from old Cuddesdon students remembering instances of his kindness. All of them remembered his humour. 'Please go on telling us,' wrote Tim Surtees, 'to enjoy our religion, and to show us that you do, too. I know that you have lots of other gifts for the church, but I think this is perhaps one that no one else has in quite the same way.'

What many of them remembered with delight was how, at the end of each term, there was always a sherry party for the leavers and, in bidding them farewell, Runcie would always manage to say something really funny about each man. It sounded quite spontaneous, but those who knew how he worked were sure that he took a great deal of trouble over it. His sense of humour was never very far away. Even in chapel when reading the lessons the inflection in his voice as he came to such passages as 'I may go up and down upon the mountains and bewail my virginity' was enough to send a ripple of laughter among the ordinands. 'For the first time,' said one, 'I learned that holy scripture could have its funny side. It was very healthy.'

His responsibilities for the college did not end with the education of the men who came to it. He was in charge of extensive buildings of historic interest and expensive to maintain. Much of the money needed for decoration and repairs came from the donations of old Cuddesdon students and friends, and Runcie's Lent Letters always included a paragraph or two about what was being done, and the encouraging generosity that made it possible. By his second year the annual donations had risen from £848 to £1,438, and the trend continued, one year reaching over £7,000. The bad winter of 1962–3 added to the problems with a burst pipe under the marble floor of the chapel causing water to cascade into the dining-room below. It happened just before the students were due back for the spring term. 'I believe Ezekiel prophesied floods from the sanctuary,' wrote Runcie. 'The domestic staff certainly began to look apocalyptic, or perhaps eschatological is the right word; but thanks to plumbing miracles wrought by Mr Townsend and the part loyally played by the rest of the staff, we opened our doors on the right day with warmth and hot water and the usual high quality food from the kitchen.'

During his first two years the college was rewired and the fire precautions brought up to standard with help from central church funds. With the donation money, the common-room was refurbished, new mattresses bought, and he was able to move on to the more ambitious plan of redecorating the chapel. His ally was John Betjeman whom Runcie, remembering Betjeman's popularity when he lectured at Westcott, had invited to Cuddesdon to speak to the students about the historic parish churches they might one day be called upon to care for. As was expected, the poet toured the Victorian Gothic buildings of the college with a knowledgeable eye. 'Oh dear,' he said. 'What a lot of damage has been done to this place.' He looked sadly at the windows which had been stripped of their leading, and at the chapel where the once lavishly decorated walls were plain white, the multi-coloured tiled floor covered with plain carpet, and the ornate Victorian triptych which had dominated the sanctuary removed in favour of a simple English altar with plain curtain hung between its angel-topped riddel posts. 'We must send for John Piper,' said Betjeman.

The distinguished painter and window designer came and looked and, that same afternoon, made his recommendations. The Pre-Raphaelite paintings on the walls of the chapel could not be recovered, but at least some richness of colour could be contrived, and he sat down there and then with a bucket and pots of paint and mixed a shade of Venetian red that he thought would do. He also suggested that the carpets should be taken up and thrown out, the English altar removed elsewhere, and the triptych restored in all its exuberant glory. The chapel was transformed, and Runcie was soon able to write: 'By a skilful use of colour, particularly a new shade to be known henceforth as "Cuddesdon red", a restoration of the original proportions of the altar and the building, the removal of deadening curtains and carpets, and the provision of simple Victorian hoop lighting, Mr John Piper has given us once again a chapel with warmth and colour, a depth which sends you to your knees, and a basilican resonance which tests our plainsong.' He added, 'John Piper and his colleague, Patrick Reyntiens, took a little time off their major work for the new Roman Catholic cathedral in Liverpool to produce a window for the chapel, modest but distinguished, as was the kind of advice we were given so freely in planning this operation.'

Further improvements were under discussion, he reported. They included a westward extension of the chapel as a memorial to Eric Graham, a former principal of the college. The response was forthcoming, and by the next

Lent Runcie was writing about the 'marvellous generosity' of his correspondents who had already given £3,400 towards the target of £5,000; and that there were 'curtain fabrics to be fingered, prototype chairs to be sat upon, spongy tiles to be converted by imagination into suspended ceilings, and electrical specification language to impose new problems of communication'. A refashioning of the dining-room followed, and an extra bathroom and improvements to the library. Most revolutionary, however, was the amount of accommodation for married staff that he now provided. Two wooden bungalows were erected in part of the vicarage garden, and two bungalows purchased in the village.

As vicar of the parish, Runcie was also responsible for the parish church. He was grateful that his predecessor had not left him with an empty purse, for on his arrival at Cuddesdon he was faced with the need for expensive repairs on the church tower which he carried through. He enjoyed being vicar with all its local involvement, and gave as much time to it as he could, to the extent that some of his parishioners appeared to regard him as a vicar who ran a theological college as a hobby on the side. He was persuaded into a number of local roles, and was elected chairman of the parish council (the local unit of secular local government) with its worries about street-lighting and bus-stops. He was chairman of the managers of the village school where Lindy was teaching music, of the youth committee, and of the Angling Association. He did not fish himself, but the anglers were going through a politically delicate period as the genuine locals protested about the encroachment of rich 'foreigners' from Oxford and London on their fishing rights, and Runcie's natural gift for diplomacy was called upon to resolve the situation. He was also chairman of the village sports club, and each year played cricket for the village side in their annual match against the college.

Soon after he arrived in the village, work began to replace the burned-out bishop's palace across the road from the college. (The result was not a good house, and it has since been put to another use.) Runcie was extremely pleased when Harry Carpenter, the Bishop of Oxford, moved in;

and it was a happy relationship with Runcie often turning to the bishop for advice and support. However, there was far more land attached to the palace than any bishop could want for a garden, and the Church Commissioners were very slow in deciding what should be done with it. Runcie took the matter in hand and, in the course of an afternoon stroll through the encroaching undergrowth with Sir Hubert Ashton, the first Church Estates Commissioner, developed a plan for twenty-five houses of the sort that would bring some much-needed middle-class residents to the village to bridge the social gap between the local land-owners and the farm-hands and factory-workers who constituted most of the residents. The houses were built three years later and had the effect on the village community that he hoped for.

Over the wider area the Runcies found a variety of interesting neighbours. Among them, living in the nearby village of Great Milton, was the Cretan archaeologist, Sinclair Hood, and it was through him that the Runcies came to take their most enjoyable holidays for the next ten years or more. Hood suggested to the well-known archaeologist, Sir Mortimer Wheeler, that Runcie should be asked to lecture on some of the cruises to the classical sites in the eastern Mediterranean run by Swan Tours who offered cultural as well as the more usual holiday pleasures.

The suggestion was taken up, and their first cruise was in 1968. Runcie wrote to tell his sister, Kath, that it was a great success:

. . . hardly a rest, but a fascinating experience crammed into fifteen days. We sailed through the Bosphorus just as the Czech crisis burst and there was much hesitation as to whether we should continue to Bulgaria and the USSR, particularly as we had characters like Lord Carrington on board caught between wishing to make a gesture against the Soviet Union and anxious to send a telegram to London stating that it was *extremely* difficult for him to return for the emergency session of Parliament! However, it seemed to me, though not to the capitalist clientele of Messrs Swan, that it was as undesirable to be hobnobbing with the near Fascist regime in Greece as to be touring the seaside resorts of the Crimea. Part of the company was academic, part distinguished people out for a cultured rest, and part keen on living it up with dancing and midnight bathing. So you can imagine the temptation to candle-burning at both ends.

At first he had found some of his fellow-lecturers intimidating. 'They all seemed so learned and such professional classics. In the event they turned out to be very good company with three extremely nice wives, and I've even been asked to marry the daughter of the Deputy Keeper of the British Museum next summer!'

As usual he put a lot of work into the lectures, and not only because he knew he would have a number of critical academics in his audience. The research he did for the cruises he enjoyed for its own sake, and it became the nearest thing to a real hobby and relaxation, apart from his cricket and tennis, that he had ever had. He was a very popular lecturer. Peter Balfour, who had been the Adjutant of Runcie's battalion in the Scots Guards during the war, received an advertising brochure for a Swan's cruise through his letterbox and immediately spotted Runcie's name on the programme.

I felt I had to go on this cruise because of Bob, and persuaded my wife to go. This was a new Bob, married, and our wives became firm friends: a prince of the church, with all the authority that goes with it, but still with the same twinkle, power of mimicry, and sharp eye for the ridiculous. Because he had been a soldier he was asked to lecture on the various occasions where military history had collided with culture, as well as the more obvious places of biblical and religious significance. Three episodes in particular I remember vividly. The first a thumbnail sketch of the whole Dardanelles campaign as we were steaming off Suvla Bay. It was brilliantly done. You could see and feel the desperation and courage; but what brought tears to the eyes was the scenes he described of reconciliation years later when contestants from both sides came together, and the whole thing – at least spiritually – was not in vain.

Two other contrasting moments. First, Bob Runcie standing where St Paul stood at Ephesus, beseeching the Ephesians to listen to him; and the second in the amphitheatre at Delphi when the hopes and fears of all religions were made apparent to us. These made it easier for me to bridge the gap that I had found between the high-spirited and highly competent young officer I had known with his experience of war and people, and the deeply-thinking cleric.

As well as renewing old friendships, both the Runcies were to make many new and lasting friends on the Swan cruises in the ensuing years.

At the end of 1968 he became chairman of the Conference of Theological College Principals which meant that he chaired the annual meeting of the conference immediately after Christmas, and then acted on its behalf for the following year. It was a stressful time to be in office. Because of a long period of rising costs and a declining number of ordinands there had been a recent report by an archbishops' working party which recommended that the number of colleges should be reduced from twenty-five to fourteen. Cuddesdon was safe from threatened closure or merger into another college as it was bursting at the seams and had the highest quota of graduate ordinands among all the colleges, but Runcie was in favour of some national plan, even though he could not go along with the report's fixation on large colleges located in universities. It was just his luck, he wrote to Kath, that it should be his turn to be chairman at a time when the whole future of the colleges seemed to be in the melting pot. 'I can now look forward to a year of journeys to London and interminable meetings, and I have now to represent the theological colleges on all the ACCM and a good many other central committees.'

By now he was the most senior of the college principals, and had been at Cuddesdon almost the whole decade of the

Top left: Robert
Alexander Kennedy,
aged two.

Above: Lieutenant
R. A. K. Runcie, 1943.

Left: Wedding Day, 5
September 1957.

The newly-consecrated Bishop of St Albans with
Archbishop Michael Ramsey and (*right*) Bishop Frank
Cocks who was consecrated Suffragan Bishop of
Shrewsbury at the same ceremony on 24 February 1970.

Captain of the Bishop of St Albans' XI.

Anglican-Orthodox conversation during a meeting of the
sub-commission at St Albans in 1975.

Archbishop-designate, with Lindy, James and Rebecca in 1979.

Enthronement at Canterbury on 25 March 1980.

With Cardinal Basil Hume, Roman Catholic Archbishop of Westminster, and the Bishop of Bedford.

Meeting the Pope for the first time in Accra on 9 May 1980.

On a visit to Northern Ireland accompanied by Richard Chartres and Terry Waite.

Top left: On the first visit an Archbishop of Canterbury has ever made to China.

Top right: Greeting HRH the Duchess of Kent (and the Duke of Kent) in St Paul's Cathedral after the Falklands service.

With a patient at St Joseph's Hospice for the dying.

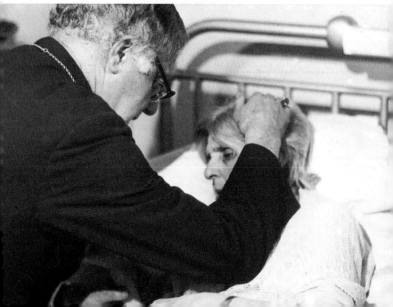

Silver Wedding Anniversary in 1982.

sixties. Lindy was settled in the local community as a music teacher, both privately and at the local school, and she had gone a long way to resigning herself to a largely absentee husband, though Runcie had been persuaded to take a regular afternoon off each week to spend with her and the family. James was going to the Dragon preparatory school in Oxford, and Rebecca had started in the junior department of the Oxford High School. They were all well established. Lindy had her friends among the students, who would come and drink coffee with her in the vicarage kitchen and play bridge with her on Saturday evenings. James, a football enthusiast, regularly inveigled other students into playing football with him. All of them had tea in college on Saturday afternoons, took part in the entertainments there, and had a social life in and around the village.

But the time was coming for Runcie to make a move. Ten years was a long time in one place for a man of his quality. The unseen powers in church and state who were responsible for senior appointments must have had their eyes on him for some time. He had recently accepted one minor recognition by being made a canon of Lincoln Cathedral which always kept two prebendal stalls for theologians from outside the diocese, and it was not unexpected that, with the Bishop of Lincoln, Kenneth Riches, being himself a former principal of Cuddesdon, Runcie should be chosen to fill one of them. He had been installed early in 1969, the archaic ceremony witnessed by a posse of mocking students from Cuddesdon, but had not so far had the opportunity to fulfil what was to be his duty of preaching once each year in the cathedral.

In the past three years he had also turned down two jobs. He had been invited to stand for election to a bishopric in Western Australia with the strong likelihood that he would succeed to the archbishopric of the province. Full of misgivings about whether God was really calling him to serve on the other side of the world, a prospect which his family hated, he took the letter across the road to ask the bishop's advice and was relieved when Harry Carpenter roared with laughter at the idea, particularly at that part of the letter which asked that Runcie's (affirmative) reply should be accompanied by a sample of urine. He had also been offered the deanery of Guildford, a much more attractive proposition, but it had come too soon when he still felt he had a job to complete at Cuddesdon.

However, his feelings were different when, on 10 October 1969, as he was having breakfast in college with the students, he opened an innocuous-looking envelope and found inside it another that was addressed to him in the outsize type always used by the Prime Minister's office in Downing Street. He kept it carefully hidden from the curious eyes of the ordinands and went to open it in his office. It was a letter from Harold Wilson formally telling him that there would be a vacancy in the bishopric of St Albans when Dr Gresford Jones retired, and asking him to allow his name to be submitted to the Queen for the appointment.

Almost as soon as he had read it and shown it to Lindy, there was a telephone call from the Archbishop's Appointments Secretary, Bill Saumarez Smith, saying he would call later in the day. When he came he was quite convinced that Runcie should accept the appointment. St Albans, he said, was a flourishing young diocese but had become rather cosy and could do with some of the slightly more astringent qualities of learning and leadership that Runcie could bring to it. Besides, he declared as though clinching the argument, the diocese was exactly midway between Oxford and Cambridge: what could be more appropriate!

It had not been a total surprise, for Runcie knew St Albans quite well, and it had come to his ears that he was being tipped for the job. Nevertheless, he took a week to make up his mind and to gain Lindy's willing agreement, for she was now so well settled in Cuddesdon that she was reluctant to move again. He wrote to the Prime Minister with his acceptance, and on 22 October he received his reply. 'The Queen has been graciously pleased to approve your nomination as Bishop of St Albans in succession to Dr Gresford Jones. I am confident that you will justify the choice that Her Majesty has made.' The die was cast and that evening he told the Cuddesdon students that he would be leaving and ordered them to pray for the diocese of St Albans.

They observed that he did not do it without drama, for he announced it at Compline just as they were obliged to observe the night's silence and – officially anyway – could not talk about it even among themselves until breakfast-time the following morning. The news was made public at noon that day and, by the evening, was in the newspapers.

All the local Hertfordshire and Bedfordshire papers which covered the St Albans diocese carried the announcement with enthusiasm and immediately homed in on the fact that the new bishop had a distinguished war record and was a sportsman. The *Herts Advertiser* summed it up with the headline, 'Wartime Hero and Spurs Fan is the New Bishop'. As well as spelling out his academic and ecclesiastical career, and giving an account of how he had won the Military Cross, they made much of the fact that he still played cricket and tennis and that, whenever he could, he took ten-year-old James to watch football – not only the Oxford United football team, but also Tottenham Hotspur whose practice ground was in the St Albans diocese. On the strength of that, James, a cheerful, bespectacled redhead, nearly upstaged his father by getting a feature all to himself, talking knowledgeably about the Spurs' current form and the prospects for Watford in the Second Division. He told the reporters that he played hockey, football, and rugby at the Dragon School, and had doubts about his parents' plans to send him to Marlborough because that was a rugger school and he preferred soccer.

The local news coverage was extensive. At forty-eight Runcie was among the youngest of the diocesan bishops, with an attractive wife who was obviously a person in her own right, a pianist, a music teacher, and a notable housewife (it was not long before the Hertfordshire papers were asking her for cookery tips and domestic advice as well as asking her to write a music column), and with two young happy children. All of them had strong outgoing personalities, with a range of interests which identified them with ordinary families everywhere, and the reporters loved them.

The letters of congratulation began to flood in from ex-Cuddesdon students and staff, from Cambridge (Hugh

Montefiore, who had succeeded Mervyn Stockwood as Vicar of Great St Mary's, wrote, 'I always thought you were a natural diocesan as you have a great gift for the Ministry of Encouragement'), from parishioners in Gosforth, from friends and acquaintances all over the country, and from Delhi and Calcutta where they still remembered his visit with pleasure. There were also letters of welcome from most of the bishops and from his new diocese: the clergy and people in public life, the Lord Lieutenant, and ordinary lay people, all looking forward to his coming, and many offering their help and suggestions for his future work among them.

There was much to be arranged and it so happened that within a very few days of the announcement the Archbishop of Canterbury, Michael Ramsey, was due to visit Cuddesdon and stay at the vicarage. Cuddesdon had been his own theological college and he retained a great affection for it, making periodic visits whenever it was possible, and talking to the students about prayer and holiness. This visit gave him the opportunity to discuss Runcie's consecration with him, which was planned to take place in Westminster Abbey on St Matthias's Day, 24 February, and also to write his appreciation of Runcie's work at Cuddesdon.

Thank you for the hospitality of Cuddesdon to us last Monday. It was the last of my visits in your regime, and I look back on the series of them with great thankfulness, for what they have meant to me personally, and for all that I believe God has done in Cuddesdon in your time in conserving things that are old and applying them in very new ways for the church of today. *That* will last.

He finished with an invitation to all the family to stay, as was customary, at Lambeth Palace for the night before the consecration.

Before that there had to be the formal election by the Chapter of St Albans Abbey, followed by its confirmation; but, to general embarrassment and dismay, it did not look as though those formalities would run as smoothly as normal. Among the honorary canons were a number who were prepared to be ecclesiastical revolutionaries (of a very orderly kind) and resist the traditional farce of the election with its *congé d'élire* and foregone conclusion. However, at the beginning of January, a compromise with honour appeared to be reached when five of them declared that they would take their stand at the next annual general meeting of the Chapter and refuse to take part in any future episcopal elections, but meanwhile, in the case of Robert Runcie, the Prime Minister and his colleagues had obviously taken great care and made a very good choice, and they therefore felt able to vote 'Yes' (*placet*) on this occasion, but they still considered the procedure itself to be quite outmoded. There was no personal animosity against Runcie, and nobody seemed seriously worried that history would be made by a modern chapter refusing to accept the royal nomination.

Meanwhile Runcie's immediate concern was the winding up of his present job at Cuddesdon, and of his chairmanship of the Principals' Conference which had met in full session, including the assistant staff of the colleges, immediately after Christmas. On 4 January 1970 he wrote to Kath:

I have been wholly committed to the Conference of Principals and Staffs during the past week. It was a strenuous swan song as I have been chairman for the past year and this is always the occasion for lively debate and a certain amount of in-fighting. It went far better than I dared to hope, and I returned to Cuddesdon yesterday slightly demob-happy and ready to burn about 40 files. We met at the College of St Mark and St John in Chelsea. We took time off to see the New Year in at a pub in the King's Road. Quite an experience!

I am now hoping to disengage a little and intend that Jan. 24–25th will be my last active weekend at Cuddesdon in charge of college and parish. This gives me a month to the Consecration and I hope, among other things, to take a gentle northern tour and stay at least a night with you.

Arrangements are going fairly smoothly and I am much moved by the people who want to give me things. I am beginning to be short of things to suggest! I would of course be very pleased if you and Myf [Marjorie] and Ken could give me my pectoral cross: but I think it may cost too much. The situation is as follows. The jeweller in Hampstead who produced Lindy's wedding and engagement rings is making my ring. He has found a lovely stone and is taking great trouble about it. He was brought up in St Albans and went to St Albans School, so it is all very appropriate. The ring will be a present from all who have served on the staff here.

He introduced me to a young man who is just starting out and getting his first commissions, e.g. a silver key for the Queen Mother to open an extension to the Fishmongers' Hall. He produced some designs for a pectoral cross but we didn't like them, so he is trying again. If what he produced this week still seems on the wrong lines I may need to send you an SOS . . . but at the moment we are rather taken with the idea of helping a young artist.

Meanwhile there are cassocks in Cambridge, copes and mitres in London, evening dress in Oxford, all for fitting. It's quite a game.

Don't worry about Lindy. Her mixture of extreme honesty and extreme domestic efficiency can often be explosive and difficult to live with, but it enables her to communicate with and win the respect of people with whom the church is seldom in touch. She already has the Church Commissioners' architect eating out of her hand because she understands which way plumbing systems work and can get really animated about eliminating a step in the hall. Anyway, they are not only doing everything she has asked for, but adding some improvements. The wheel has come full circle in fashionable colours and my study is to be done in chocolate brown which is, according to our friend John Piper, the *in* colour at the moment!

The Gresford Joneses had left Abbey Gate House, the bishop's residence facing the west end of the Abbey in St Albans Close, in the middle of December, and Lindy was deep in consultation and correspondence with the Commissioners over carpets and curtains and kitchen fittings. The Commissioners were responsible for the basic furnishing of the public rooms, including the reception rooms, the bishop's study, and the principal guest bedroom. In the rest of the house some things were to be bought from the Gresford Joneses, and there were curtains and carpets to be altered and brought from Cuddesdon. Alterations were also to be made to the kitchen. Whether the work would be finished in time for the family to move into their new home before Runcie was enthroned in the cathedral on 14 March was uncertain, but they hoped to be in by Easter.

There was a farewell party in the college with 120 students, former students and staff, and the governors. Runcie and his family were overwhelmed with parting presents. Among them were furnishings for the private chapel in Abbey Gate House: a pair of candlesticks from the governors, and a modern crucifix, a copy of the one in the college dining hall, carved by the same nun of the Community of St Clare who had done the original. Former and present students gave a cope and mitre, and Mark Santer presented the specially-made episcopal ring on behalf of all the staff who had served with Runcie. The parish and village of Cuddesdon also gave him a cope and mitre.

The time for his consecration was now getting very close, and Runcie went to spend a few days in a private retreat with the contemplative nuns at the Priory of Our Lady at Burford in the Cotswolds. After all the bustle of practical details in handing over his work in the college, the farewell engagements and parties in Cuddesdon, the planning of guest lists and the enthronement service, and answering the hundreds of people who wrote to congratulate him and who wanted to come to both his consecration and enthronement, he needed a few days alone and in silence to prepare himself spiritually for what was in front of him. From Burford he wrote again to Kath:

It is good to be here for a few days' quiet with the sun shining on the snow, and a holy sister occasionally coming in to make up the fire, fill a hot water bottle, or produce food on a tray. I will be returning to Cuddesdon on Thursday night. Thank you both for all your support and help which means so much to me. Between the Consecration and the Enthronement I am still hoping to pay you a visit.

I trust the arrangement for next week will suit you. The Confirmation of the Election will be in St Margaret's, Westminster, at 4.30 p.m. on Monday night. A congregation is *not* expected, but I would be delighted if Angus or both of you turned up. I shall have my barrister sister-in-law, Jill, to act as my Advocate. I think it is the first time in history it has been done by a woman! We will be staying at Lambeth for the night. Lindy will be bringing the children up straight from school and so will miss St Margaret's. Rebecca has been presented with a mini-suitcase by the college for this night away.

Despite the fierce rubric in the service sheet, you are all expected to make your communion at the Consecration Service if you wish. I think all my students will too! The party afterwards may be a bit of a scrum, but you will know plenty of the guests, though there will be some, like the Mayor and Town Clerk of St Albans, whom I have never met.

The confirmation of his election was on 23 February. Runcie arrived with Lindy's sister at St Margaret's, the parish church of the House of Commons which stands under the shadow of Westminster Abbey. It was the first time that he experienced that extraordinary ritual in which, with a group of solemn lawyers arrayed in wigs and gowns, he was declared to be who everybody said he was: 'Robert Alexander Kennedy . . . being a man provident and discreet, deservedly well esteemed for his learning, good life, and morals, of liberal condition, born of lawful marriage, of fit and lawful age . . .' and to have been properly elected by the Dean and Chapter of St Albans being capitularly assembled.

The ceremony was a throw-back to medieval times when, without the benefits of modern communications, photography, and transport, there could be grounds for doubt that the person elected by the chapter of a far-flung diocese was indeed the same as the one presented for legal and national recognition as the rightful bishop of that diocese. After innumerable declarations that all was in order, Runcie made his oath of allegiance to the Queen and of obedience to the Archbishop of Canterbury, assented to the Thirty-nine Articles, and swore that he would not abuse his power by accepting bribes or selling benefices or preferments in the church. Only then was he declared to be Bishop-elect of St Albans, entitled to exercise jurisdiction in that diocese.

Runcie was one of two bishops to be consecrated the following day: the other was Frank Cocks being made the Suffragan Bishop of Shrewsbury, who, like Runcie, was staying the night with his family at Lambeth Palace. It was therefore a large dinner party that Archbishop and Mrs Ramsey held for them, and it included the Provincial Registrar, David Carey, the chaplains, and the preacher for the next day's service, Harry Williams, whom Runcie had not seen for some time.

Since their days together in Cambridge, Williams had had a serious breakdown (as he described in his autobiography, *Some Day I'll Find You*) and had recently become a monk of the Community of the Resurrection in Mirfield; his reputation as a spiritual writer was enhanced by his working out of his own interior crises. In his first months in Mirfield he had been reading more widely than his previous academic career had ever allowed, and this had a brilliant but nerve-racking result for, at the beginning of the consecration service, he worked all his recent thinking into his sermon which lasted the sadistic length (his own phrase) of forty minutes, about three times as long as expected. It was a very fine discourse, and later published, but it disorganised everybody's timetable for the rest of the day.

The abbey was full and forty-one bishops had come to take part. The pattern of the service was like that of the ordination services, set into a Eucharist. The two bishops were presented to the archbishop in turn, each by two bishops, and were formally examined about their life, faith, and intentions. 'Are you ready, with all faithful diligence, to banish and drive away all erroneous and strange doctrine contrary to God's word? . . . Will you maintain and set forward, as much as shall lie in you, quietness, love, and peace among all men; and such as be unquiet, disobedient and criminous within your Diocese, correct and punish, according to such authority as you have by God's Word, and as to you shall be committed by the Ordinance of this Realm? . . . Will you show yourself gentle, and be merciful for Christ's sake to poor and needy people, and to all strangers destitute of help?'

After the singing of the *Veni Creator Spiritus* and a prayer by the archbishop, each of the new bishops knelt in turn while the archbishop laid his hands on his head and all of the forty-one bishops crowded round and did likewise, the new bishop completely hidden by the great crowd of his episcopal brothers praying that he should receive the Holy Spirit for the office and work of a bishop. Then the archbishop gave him a Bible, exhorting him to read it and think upon the things in it; to be a shepherd to the flock of Christ; to 'hold up the weak, heal the sick, bind up the broken, bring again the outcasts, seek the lost'. And to 'be so merciful that you be not too remiss; so minister discipline that you forget not mercy: that when the chief Shepherd shall appear, you may receive the never-fading crown of glory . . .'

The service came to an end and the archbishop presented the two new bishops to the people, and there were congratulations and photographs. It was traditional that immediately after the service each new bishop should hold a party for his family and friends, and Runcie had his in the precincts of the abbey. It had been organised by Lindy with the Cuddesdon students as waiters, and a great crowd of friends were there.

The following day he had to go to Buckingham Palace to do homage to the Queen. He arrived, as bidden, shortly after noon, and feeling rather nervous. He was taken to an ante-room and immediately felt better when he discovered that the Equerry, Patrick Plunkett, recognised him from his army days, and introduced him to George Thomas, Secretary of State for Wales (and later Speaker of the House of Commons) who was standing in for the Home Secretary,

James Callaghan, who was in Ireland. Also there, as Clerk of the Closet, was the Bishop of Chester, Roger Wilson.

It was the first time that George Thomas had taken part in one of these ceremonies, and he and Runcie were both nervous as they were shown in to the Queen who was standing in the middle of one of the drawing rooms. As Runcie knelt on a faldstool before her, his hands between hers to repeat the oath of allegiance, Thomas read it aloud with all the drama of which a Welsh Methodist lay preacher is capable. 'He did it very well, didn't he?' said the Queen with a twinkle after it was over, and showed how well she had done her own homework by asking Runcie knowledgeable questions about his new diocese.

The organisation of his enthronement three weeks later had been a matter of continual correspondence with the St Albans Cathedral authorities almost ever since the appointment had been announced. The details of the service, which included the formal reception of the new bishop into his cathedral, the reading of the archbishop's mandate, and the taking of yet another oath, as well as the placing of the bishop in his throne, and the greetings from other churches and local authorities, had been discussed and drafted with minute care. The guest lists had been a huge task, making sure that every parish, every area of life in the diocese – local government, hospitals, schools, industry, trade unions, commerce, police, and innumerable voluntary organisations – was represented, together with all Runcie's personal guests, family, friends, students and parishioners from Cuddesdon. Seating had to be meticulously planned for over two thousand people in the abbey, not to mention the parking arrangements.

At three o'clock on the afternoon of Saturday, 14 March, Runcie, arrayed in cope and mitre, approached the closed doors of his cathedral, raised his crozier and, in the centuries-old tradition, struck the doors three times. He was admitted and welcomed into the crowded abbey by the dean and, after the required legal ceremonies, was led to his throne to a fanfare of trumpets by the trumpeters of the Royal Horse Guards and 1st Dragoons (his old friend from the Scots Guards, Archie Fletcher, had helped to arrange that) and the singing of the *Te Deum* by the choir.

He preached for the first time as bishop on the need of the Christian in the modern world to listen and to learn and to explore new styles of leadership:

> Have we not noticed that Jesus's idea of a leader is of a man who is above all there to serve – to help other people do things for themselves, to enable others to lead their community and transform it and renew it, not from outside, but within? That's really what the church exists to be – the agent to free people and communities to discover in themselves the transforming power of God . . . The church is a servant, not a rival to society. If it is able to inspire enterprises and then watch them break away and sail off under other auspices, it should rejoice to support and back them, not seek to dominate them. It is the power to inspire which matters.

After his first episcopal blessing the representatives of the Roman Catholic and Free Churches brought their greetings, as did the mayor of St Albans and the chairmen of the two county councils in the diocese. Slowly the processions gathered and moved through the abbey as choir and congregation roared out the final hymn, and Runcie stepped out through the west doors to greet the crowd waiting there, having been duly and finally inducted, installed and enthroned as Bishop of St Albans.

Chapter Eleven

St Albans – I

Though there is a whole industry devoted to training new clergy to be parish curates and eventually vicars, nobody trains a new bishop to be a bishop. As soon as a man is consecrated he goes straight to his new job, gathering information where he can, and plunging directly into his very considerable management and pastoral responsibilities. A diocesan bishop has great autonomy within his territory except where he is subject to the complexities of ecclesiastical and civil law. But clergy and laity have high – sometimes unreal – expectations of him, and he is constantly called upon to exercise his judgment in matters of church order and discipline and to express his views on wide areas of social concern. He finds himself *ex officio* chairman of committees dealing with a range of matters for which he may have had virtually no experience. He is responsible for many appointments. He is at the centre of much church ceremony, and civil ceremony too, and is expected to speak pertinently and memorably on all manner of occasions. If his diocese is to advance the cause of Jesus Christ he must be able to think and plan strategically. And he must make himself widely available to those of his clergy and laity who need him, as a loving and just Father-in-God.

Until recently the most help a new bishop could hope for, other than advice from his colleagues, was a few days in-service training at St George's House, Windsor, which has pioneered short courses for senior clergy already in post. But Robert Runcie, since he has become archbishop, has recognised the urgent need that new bishops have for practical down-to-earth advice about how to do their job, and has taken action. Under the editorship of Mrs Ruth Hook, wife of the former Bishop of Bradford, a kit of practical information has been compiled, giving the new bishop a good idea of what will be expected of him, what his closest colleagues in the diocese – the archdeacons, registrar, chancellor, and diocesan secretary – do, and the pitfalls to avoid. There is also a section to help his wife to cope with what will be expected of her.

In 1970, however, when Runcie was a new bishop himself, he like others before him had to plunge in at the deep end. The very morning after his enthronement, which happened to be Passion Sunday, he went to Hoddesdon to hold his first confirmation, trusting that his episcopal robes would hide his nervousness. He reminded himself that whatever he did would be accepted as correct simply because he was the bishop, provided he did it with assurance. All went well that morning, but later in the day his ability to carry off an unrehearsed situation with assured grace was tested in a different way. While he was preaching at a packed festival Evensong in a parish church in Hitchin a woman wandered up from the back of the church to the front of the congregation, her arms held above her head, repeatedly proclaiming 'Jesus is here!' Runcie had gently to agree with her and to ask her to sit down until he had finished his sermon.

From now on his life was to be full of preaching engagements, and he regarded them as an opportunity to talk to his people and to teach. He prepared each sermon with great care, always taking trouble, even if using a theme he had used before, to relate it to the place and people where he was preaching. One of the real challenges to his ability to hold a congregation was at the Easter Monday Youth Pilgrimage which followed just two weeks after his enthronement. Every year up to six thousand young people came from all over the diocese, most of them on foot, to gather in Verulamium Park, and to process up the road past Abbey Gate House to fill the cathedral nave (the longest in England), sitting on the floor, crammed tightly together. It was always a happy event, but the crowd had to be handled skilfully to ensure that the occasion, though joyous, was not merely hilarious. Runcie took particular care over these addresses, determined that, though they should have their amusing moments, they should also include some solid Christian teaching.

On the Monday morning of his first week he took the chair at his first staff meeting with the senior clergy of the diocese: the two suffragan bishops, John Trillo, Bishop of Hertford (soon to be Bishop of Chelmsford) and John Hare, Bishop of Bedford, together with the dean and the two archdeacons. The Diocesan Secretary, Dennis Yates, came to part of the meeting. Between them they had charge of a well-run diocese with many active and intelligent Christians, and less financial problems than most. The diocese was a young one, having been created in 1877 to incorporate the two counties of Hertfordshire and Essex. Then, in 1914, Essex had become the new diocese of Chelmsford, and Bedfordshire had been carved from the Ely diocese and given to St Albans. Hertfordshire, close to London, was affluent commuter-land, while Bedfordshire, north of industrial Luton, was largely agricultural.

Before Runcie's arrival, Michael Gresford Jones had been bishop for nineteen years, and had presided over an enormous increase of population in the diocese as the new towns of Hatfield, Hemel Hempstead, and Stevenage expanded rapidly. Gresford-Jones, a quiet pastoral, much-loved bishop, had ruled his diocese on highly centralised lines through his staff meeting though, somewhat ahead of his time, had also had regular larger meetings involving representatives of several areas of diocesan life. However, the fortnightly staff meetings were where the regular business of the diocese was done.

Runcie readily admitted that his first job was to learn. He is the first to say that he does not enjoy the details of administration and finance, and the only gift he claims in that direction is the ability to pick and appoint good administrators (a gift which is sometimes brilliant, and only rarely lets him down). Nevertheless, he is a first-class chairman, and the more high-powered and challenging a committee, the more he enjoys it; he often gets more interested in complexities than he expected when reading the agenda.

This was quickly apparent in St Albans. 'As Bishop Runcie settled in,' remembers John Trillo, 'we all became aware of his star quality. He had to learn the job of bishoping and was manifestly impatient until he had managed, by dint of extremely hard work, to master the various aspects of the job. He worked immensely hard at this, and I can remember an intricate Pastoral Committee meeting in which problems were discussed concerning fourteen or fifteen parishes, and in every case he said at the end, "Well, I will have a look at it myself," which of course he did.'

It was a time of changes in the church. The year 1970 was to see the institution of three-tier synodical government throughout the Church of England, with the laity playing a full part in decision-making. Clergy and laity would be meeting regularly and on equal terms in deanery synods (representing a score or so of parishes), in diocesan synods, and with all the bishops at the General Synod which was to be inaugurated by the Queen in Westminster in November that year. Part of the structure in each diocese would be a bishop's council, a much larger body than the staff meeting, incorporating elected clergy and lay representatives, and functioning both as adviser to the bishop, and as standing committee to the diocesan synod. This new form of ecclesiastical government could be seen as natural evolution in a church which was at last recognising that an intelligent and educated laity had its own contribution to make, and its own ministry in partnership with that of the clergy. The organisation of the Church of England was about to get off to a fresh start, and there could be no better time for a bishop with Runcie's particular gifts for strategy, communication, delegation, and readiness for controlled experiment, to pick up the reins of a bishopric which had almost more than its fair share of committed and enthusiastic church members.

He had many good pastoral clergy. He met nearly every one of them that September at the diocese's triennial clergy conference held at Keble College, Oxford. The residential four-day conference had been a tradition in the diocese for some years, and the turn-out of clergy was almost a hundred per cent. For Runcie it was stepping back into the familiar Oxford world of orderly morning liturgy, lectures, and leisurely afternoons. He had agreed that the conference on this occasion should conform to its traditional pattern, and he gave three devotional lectures and spent as much time as he could in talking to and getting to know those clergy he had not yet been able to visit. But he recognised even while he was there that in three years' time he would have to make changes. The day of the formal Oxbridge and entirely masculine and priestly gathering had passed; the next time the clergy met there would be lay men and women among them, and they would be expected to settle to a short burst of rigorous training.

By the time the clergy conference was over he felt ready to start mapping out a strategy for the future. He had been in the diocese six months, had learned rapidly and consulted widely, and now had some idea where he wanted to start. In his presidential address to the diocesan synod which met for the first time on the last day of October he gave some hints about his priorities.

Top of his list was 'Christian education in the widest sense'. The provision of in-service training for the clergy and a variety of training schemes for the laity was to be one of the first matters to be studied by the synod. This, it soon became clear, was his own great personal interest and, while he was prepared to delegate the chairmanship of many other diocesan concerns to the suffragan bishops and others, education he kept for himself.

In his address to the synod he also raised the huge questions of pastoral reorganisation (the rationalisation and up-dating of parish boundaries and groupings), the payment and deployment of the clergy, and ecumenical co-operation with other churches. All these were matters that would keep the synods throughout the church busy for years to come. 'If the church is to realise its constitutional life synodically,' he said, 'it must take a greater responsibility for the care and deployment of those engaged in its ministry. And when I say the church I mean the church, the whole body; neither fatherly bishops acting benevolently, nor chapters of clergy acting traditionally, nor single-minded laity in bondage to trust deeds; but the whole body: bishops, clergy, and laity, acting together for the good of all.'

He encouraged the diocese to take seriously the ethical problems facing the world at large. Nor did he overlook the importance of the church's inner life:

I welcome the growth of informal caring, praying, Bible studying groups. We will need these resource points. We will need sheltered beds where seed thoughts can grow secretly before they are put out to see if they will grow vigorously in the life of the church. More people than we may realise need help with their prayers, with the religious upbringing of their children. There are many who have doubts and difficulties to voice, ideas and experiences to offer, if only they can find someone who will listen and care. To ensure that this inner feeding of our life blood in the Body of Christ is not forgotten, it might be that deaneries should consider having schools of prayer or a retreat conference during their first year. If that were to happen we should have our synods both praying and planning.

A week later he was in London at the inauguration of the General Synod which began with a splendid Eucharist in Westminster Abbey attended by the Queen, with the abbey packed with synod members who had processed to their places under their diocesan banners. After the service the Synod gathered for the first time in its normal meeting place, the circular assembly hall of Church House, where the Queen addressed it and wished it well before it got down to business.

It was at the following session in February 1971 that Runcie played his first major role in the General Synod. All through his first year as bishop a major preoccupation had been his chairmanship of an archbishops' commission which had the task of producing an acceptable scheme for reorganising the theological colleges. Inflation and falling numbers of ordinands (problems common to all the mainstream churches in Europe) had made it essential, but none of the reports and schemes so far produced had met with anything but resistance as the colleges fought for individual survival. The three-member commission – the others were Kenneth Woollcombe, later Bishop of Oxford but at that time the principal of the theological college in Edinburgh, and D. R. Wigram, former headmaster of Monkton Combe School – had been set up in February 1970 to produce a scheme based on reducing the total number of ordinands' places in the colleges to 850. Each college that would survive intact must be economically viable, and the balanced variety of theological training that the colleges between them offered was to be maintained.

The commission worked fast. Woollcombe first visited all the colleges and then Runcie and Wigram made further visits. They talked with staff and students, with governing bodies, with the faculties of theology in the universities with which many of the colleges were linked, and with the department of ACCM in Church House. Their confidential report to the House of Bishops was written by mid-September, and it was a concise and succinct document with clear recommendations about all the colleges under review. Some were to be increased in size, some to be merged or closed. Of the two colleges that Runcie knew intimately, Cuddesdon, which had never suffered from empty places, was to continue with sixty ordinands, and Westcott House was already moving into a federation with an Evangelical and a Methodist college in Cambridge, not losing its identity, but sharing facilities.

The bishops consulted the theological college principals and amended some of the recommendations. Most controversial among the changes they made was their decision to close Kelham, the college run by the Society of the Sacred Mission, to which the Runcie Commission had allotted fifty places and, in its place, to reprieve Chichester which the commission had wanted to close. News of the proposed closure of Kelham leaked out and provoked great protest in the church. Kelham had long had the reputation for taking non-graduates, often at an early age, and, after training them within a monastic regime, producing some very fine parish priests. It seemed extraordinary that a college that had made such an outstanding and unique contribution to the Anglican clergy should be brought to an end.

However, most people were unaware that the college of Kelham had fallen on bad days. In August the vice-principal left, a move planned for some time; but his departure was almost immediately followed by that of the principal who left both the college and the order very suddenly in a blaze of publicity to get married. The community, badly shaken, was questioning the future of the college, and this inevitably undermined the confidence of the bishops, especially in view of the battle that Chichester was putting up for survival.

The bishops produced their own report, Runcie collating the amendments, and it was introduced to the General Synod by the Archbishop of Canterbury, Michael Ramsey, with the words: 'Many times in the past I have heard people describe their job as unenviable, and I can now say that for the first time in my happy life I know what the adjective means.' He referred to the anxiety that had hung over the colleges for the past five years and had increased intolerably in recent months. All the colleges felt insecure, knowing that the axe might fall on any one of them; and, since the Runcie report, they had continued to live with insecurity, knowing that it was still possible for decisions to be reversed – as several already had been. The House of Bishops, said Ramsey, was still prepared to listen to pleas on behalf of individual colleges, but only on the understanding that if one college was spared another on the list would have to go. What was essential was that hard decisions should be made as quickly as possible to bring the anxiety to an end.

Runcie got to his feet and defended the report. He spoke of the immense variety that the commission had found among the colleges, not only of churchmanship and tradition, but of situation. They had seen colleges that were full and flourishing, and those that were half empty and insecure; those that were giving a high standard of theological education, and those that were struggling with inadequate resources. All, however, had a contribution to make. 'We tried to avoid straight closures,' he said, 'and we envisaged some future for all college traditions. It [the report] is a delicately balanced structure. Do not be deceived by its simplicity ... it is a working document for decisions.'

It was the start of a very long debate. On the whole the need for such a scheme was accepted; the arguments were over the fate of individual colleges, Kelham in particular. So many of the speeches appealed for Kelham's reprieve that the House of Bishops was asked to think again. They did so overnight, coming back to the Synod the following morning with the suggestion that Kelham should, for the time being, continue with twenty-five students which, with its regular quota of overseas students, should make it viable. The Runcie Commission was asked to revise the figures among the other colleges to maintain the total of 850.

In due course most of the recommendations were adopted and there was a general reshuffle among the colleges. Even Cuddesdon was affected for it combined with another Oxford theological college, Ripon Hall, which moved on to the Cuddesdon site: the combined college was henceforth known as Ripon College, Cuddesdon, with seventy students. But there was no happy ending for Kelham. The community had lost the will to keep it as a going concern, and the college was run down over three years, the property at Kelham sold, and the monks changed their style of living and dispersed themselves in small houses working in urban areas.

Meanwhile, changes were progressing in the diocese. A great advance from Runcie's point of view was his acquisition of a full-time domestic chaplain. His predecessor had not found one necessary, but Runcie felt the need of a personal assistant with whom he could share his thoughts, to whom he could delegate a good deal of administration, and who could have enough of a roving commission to keep in touch with the clergy and what they were thinking. Runcie had had this appointment in mind soon after his arrival in the diocese and, having sought the agreement of his suffragan bishops and the senior staff, had been considering who among his ex-students might be the right person.

One such student he had already been trying to persuade to come to the St Albans diocese to work in Welwyn Garden City. Nicholas Coulton was at that time a curate in the Worcestershire market town of Pershore and before ordination had been a lawyer (he was the man whom Runcie had refused to let off Greek). He liked Pershore and was not keen to go to Welwyn, but in any case he was being considered for a university chaplaincy in Oxford.

By chance he happened to be walking along Broad Street in Oxford when the door of a parked car swung open and Lindy called to him. She had dropped Robert off at Blackwell's bookshop before a meeting, and she had just discovered that he had left his briefcase in the car. Would Nicholas take it to him if he was going that way? Coulton responded willingly and found Runcie in the bookshop, and after a few minutes' conversation the bishop got out his diary and asked Coulton if he would visit him in St Albans to talk about the possibility of becoming his chaplain.

They met in December, and the conversation was so much to their mutual satisfaction that Runcie wrote to Coulton on Boxing Day making him a firm offer. The job had many creative possibilities, he wrote, but no precise definition. There were six areas in which Coulton would be expected to function. He was to be a companion to the bishop, 'a sounding-board for wild ideas and a feeder-in of better ideas'. He was to be a liaison officer, particularly with the rural deans, keeping the bishop in touch as closely as possible with the diocese; and, so that Coulton would himself know what was going on, he was to be secretary of the staff meeting. In this area he was also to improve the integration between the bishop's secretariat and the diocesan administration. He would have a special responsibility for communications in the diocese and would take over the editorship of the diocesan leaflet, a small monthly publication of diocesan news which always included a letter from the diocesan or one of the suffragan bishops. He would have some role in the care and training of ordinands in the diocese. He would be domestic chaplain in the narrow sense of looking after the bishop's private chapel and services. And, so that he would have some roots in parish life in St Albans, he would be an honorary member of staff at the church of St Saviour's.

Put in those terms, the job offered plenty that was stimulating, and Coulton arrived to take up his duties on the first of May. The intention was that he should eventually live in a small cottage in the cathedral precincts, but as this was not yet vacant he moved into Abbey Gate House, sharing the domestic life of the Runcies on a temporary basis which became permanent when it proved to be a congenial and convenient arrangement.

Coulton's legal background and methodical habits were invaluable when it came to organising the bishop's office and administration. Runcie, though not always tidy-minded himself, demanded high standards in secretarial work, and made it a rule that every letter should have a reply – perfectly typed and presented – by return of post if at all possible. For the first few months he inherited his predecessor's secretary who when she retired was replaced by Jill Jackson. She was shortly joined by Inez Luckraft, a clergy widow with four children and twenty-five years' parish experience, who came at first as a part-time assistant, but eventually took over as the bishop's full-time personal secretary. She was to stay with Runcie for eleven years and to accompany him to Lambeth.

Once the office was running smoothly Coulton could turn to his wider brief and spend much of his time out and about in the diocese. He spent comparatively little time in the customary role of a domestic chaplain, carrying a crozier three paces behind the heels of the bishop on ceremonial occasions. He did not usually accompany Runcie to confirmations (of which there could be up to two dozen a month shared between the three bishops) or on many other routine episcopal visits, though he always went to institutions of new clergy and to the pre-ordination retreats, the occasions on which he could get to know the new clergy of the diocese. He also set about planning a new, larger and better diocesan leaflet quickly enough for the diocesan synod to give its approval at its October session.

That synod was the occasion for setting in motion more changes. John Trillo had left to be bishop of the diocese of Chelmsford, and Runcie's old friend from Westcott days, Victor Whitsey, was coming to be the new Suffragan Bishop of Hertford. Runcie lost no time in making use of Whitsey's blunt Lancashire sense, and the synod debated and resolved to set up a working party under the newly-arrived Whitsey to review the work of all the diocesan boards and councils and to recommend new and more effective structures.

In his presidential address Runcie touched on the issue which, more than anything else at that time, was perplexing and dividing the church: the scheme for reunion with the Methodists. He had been a late convert to the scheme, but now made it clear that he was strongly in support of it. When, the following February, the diocese's readiness to unite with the Methodists was put to the vote, Runcie voted for it, as did the houses of clergy and laity, though with majorities just on the borderline of the 75 per cent that would be needed in the General Synod if the scheme was to go through.

He voted the same way on the fateful day, 3 May 1972, when the General Synod held its special meeting and all Methodists and Anglicans held their breath. The scheme, initiated by the Church of England, had already been accepted by the Methodists, but increasingly acrimonious argument among the Anglicans caused the early enthusiasm for it to wane. After a long debate, and a powerful and passionate plea on behalf of the scheme by Archbishop Michael Ramsey who dominated the day, a majority of General Synod members voted for it, but not a sufficiently large majority to reach the percentage required.

Later that year Runcie issued an *ad clerum* letter to all the clergy of the diocese outlining the relationship he hoped they would have with Methodist churches in their areas. 'It is necessary for us to respond to this situation with more generosity locally than *appears* to have been shown by the debate and voting in the General Synod,' he said. 'I urge all Anglicans in the diocese to consider again the principle that we shall never do separately what in conscience we can do together.' He spelt out his guidelines. Free Church ministers, e.g. Methodists, Baptists, or United Reformed, could be invited to preach in Anglican churches and, if it was a Eucharistic service, to assist in the distribution of Holy Communion. The Anglican clergy could accept reciprocal invitations. There could also be joint ecumenical services of a non-sacramental character, but joint Eucharists only by special permission. Under recent synodical legislation, all communicant members of other churches could be invited to share communion at Anglican altars; for Anglicans to receive communion in the Free Churches was a matter for individual conscience. The sharing of buildings, after a period of two congregations growing together, would be welcomed; and joint baptisms and confirmations would be encouraged where they were appropriate.

Also in the *ad clerum* he gave his guidelines on marriage discipline. While he himself wanted to see a relaxation of the church's rules brought about by legislation, he was not prepared to have those rules broken. 'The marriage in church of any person whose former marriage has been dissolved otherwise than by death cannot at present be permitted. There are no exceptions to this rule, and clergy are asked not to encourage applications to the bishop for special consideration.' He did, however, readily give his approval to local services of thanksgiving, dedication and prayer for those who had been remarried by a civil ceremony. Other problems, for example where one partner was not baptized, he was content to leave to the discretion of the parish priest.

He felt strongly about the need for a reform that would allow remarriage in church for those people whose first marriage had been an acknowledged mistake and failure and who genuinely wished their second attempt to be blessed by God. He tried to force the issue in the General Synod of November 1974. A report, *Marriage, Divorce, and the Church*, had been produced by an archbishops' commission, and had been debated inconclusively in 1972 and referred to the dioceses for discussion without any clear questions being put. The result was that not all dioceses had discussed it, and few of them had reported back with definite views. When the report was debated again Runcie brought an amendment asking that a clear mandate should be sought. His amendment was defeated by a tie in the House of Clergy, and in 1974 he brought back his amendment as a main motion. He was again defeated, this time by the laity, and the debate within the church was still inconclusive.

Writing about it in the now enlarged and lively *See Round*, he said:

Christians are called both to witness to the ideals of Christ and to share his sensitive compassion for individual cases. I believe that indissolubility, life-long commitment to the marriage relationship, is not only an ideal, it is of the very nature of marriage. But it is not something automatic, nor is it the creation of law. Divorce is unnatural. It is surgery, not re-arrangement, but we are involved in the 'cure of souls'. That is the background from which I am trying to help the church make its contribution in a field where we have no monopoly of understanding and love.

We are faced with the fact that some who come for marriage after a previous failure appear to be more seriously desirous of constructing a life-long relationship and seeking God's blessing for it than some who are technically qualified for the ceremony in church. Ought we to be shifting our emphasis away from technical qualifications and to concentrate more on the human relationships which confront us?

We are still responsible for conducting the majority of weddings in this country. The numbers are falling and some think this is a more healthy and realistic state of affairs. I respect the heart-searchings of priests who are asked to conduct weddings in the parish church for those who seldom if ever set foot there; but I believe it is not always weak or hypocritical to set such anxieties aside and offer such people God's grace and blessing with wholehearted rejoicing. The church is not going through the motions, making people mouth what they do not believe. To take each other as man or wife is a human act. If people still want to do this solemn act in church, however inarticulate they may be about what it means to them, it sounds mean or possessive to try to withhold God's blessing. Even when the desire is mainly social, is it not worth showing that Christians can rejoice in human happiness? If encouragement and enthusiasm are what people find when they approach the church about their real human concerns, they are far more likely to recognise the grace and blessing of God when it is offered, and to seek his mercy and help when things go awry.

So I am not ashamed of our broad traditions of welcome, although I recognise the heavy responsibility of the welcomers. It seems to follow that we cannot stand aside from what is happening to marriage and the family at large and simply cater for an easily definable group of church members. A new law has made for easier divorce. The temptation is to screw up our rules tighter. Otherwise, it is said, there is no incentive to persevere when you strike a bad patch – or 'we need to help people to accept the imperfect marriage out of which God may bring good in completely unforeseen ways' – or 'Christians are to witness to the Cross and to the possibility of renewal and redemption, and not simply the happiness of neat harmonies'.

All these things are true, but will they be really shared and understood if they are uttered in a Canute-like way and based on law rather than on the Gospel? I believe the truth will be heard when it is matched with sympathy about the real world in which people find themselves – a world in which the options open are greatly increased with the new biological possibilities, a fresh status for women, the prolongation of life; and these internal changes in the marriage relationship coincide with external changes in which many of the traditional tasks of the family such as education, care for the ill and elderly, are taken over by the state.

*

He had long believed in the theological validity of this compassionate approach to divorce and remarriage. While at Cuddesdon he had written a paper on marriage discipline in the Early Church showing that the rigid attitude on the indissolubility of the marriage bond had come comparatively late in church history. These views of his were strengthened by his growing familiarity with the Eastern Orthodox Churches and their theology which holds that, while marriages are in principle indissoluble, some marriage relationships do in fact die and when that happens, even though it is the result of human sin, men and women ought to be helped to start again.

This Orthodox principle of Economy (*Oikonomia*) has always particularly appealed to him with its recognition that God continues to work for the salvation of man, sometimes by means that do not conform to the church's laws. He finds it right that the church should have enough confidence in the presence within it of the Spirit of Christ, and of the Christian truth in its norms of belief and morals, to be able to be flexible and compassionate with individual exceptions that occur and need special attention. It is a difficult theology to define, and has often been the cause of castigations of the Orthodox Church for time-serving, for it enables them to deal with such matters as guest communicants and church and state relations. But it is a clear, if pragmatic, principle that divine common sense can discern the reality of sacramental grace bestowed by God outside the normal canonical boundaries of the church.

Runcie's interest in the Orthodox Churches was fuelled by his lecture cruises in the eastern Mediterranean, which gave him the opportunity to see more of their life and worship, particularly in Greece, and in Russia where he had stayed in Odessa and Yalta. He also had friends in Romania where he and Lindy had been on holiday a number of times, staying with a widowed Romanian Orthodox bishop whose son had come as a student to Cuddesdon. Runcie, always a traditionalist where worship was concerned, was increasingly drawn to the timeless ceremonies and music of the Orthodox liturgy, and fascinated by Christians whose thinking was shaped by traditions so different from his own.

Then, in 1973, his old friend Bishop Harry Carpenter of Oxford urged him to join the Commission for Anglican–Orthodox Joint Doctrinal Discussions, due to meet that July at Hertford College, Oxford. Runcie protested that the commission needed a better theologian than himself, but Carpenter, with an eye to the future when he would soon be retiring from the Anglican chairmanship and would need another bishop to succeed him, insisted that Runcie's knowledge of Greek and Greece, of Romania and Russia, and his friendship and sympathy for the Orthodox Churches, were more important in holding the conversations together.

The theological discussions had started in 1931 after a decade of gradual approach between the Anglican and Orthodox churches, and the meetings had steadily become more frequent as mutual confidence grew. The aim was to explore the common ground between the two communions in the hope of eventual unity between them; but there were deep differences. The historic split between Eastern and Western Christendom took place in the eleventh century over doctrinal quarrels principally about the Pope's claims to supremacy and the Western addition of the *filioque* clause to the Creed. Constantinople and Rome grew apart, and the Roman church was further split and fragmented by the reformers of the sixteenth century while the Orthodox church, made up of many self-governing local or national churches, maintained a firm and unwavering tradition while adapting to changing political boundaries and systems. For centuries East and West knew little about each other, and an English traveller in the mid-nineteenth century was shocked to discover that the Patriarch of Constantinople, senior among the Orthodox church leaders, had never even heard of the Archbishop of Canterbury. But since the time of the First World War there had been a growing desire between Orthodox and Anglicans to increase their mutual understanding, even though the Orthodox were fundamentally doubtful about Anglican comprehensiveness and radical theology, and Anglicans tended to be impatient with what they saw as extreme Orthodox conservatism.

Runcie went as a member to the Oxford meeting of the commission where the participants, recorded Colin Davey who edited the published account, *Anglican–Orthodox Dialogue*, 'represented the whole Orthodox Church and the Anglican Communion. Among the subjects discussed frankly but cordially was that of comprehensiveness, and although not all Orthodox difficulties with this concept were resolved there was a deeper Orthodox appreciation of its more positive aspects. The work of the Holy Spirit was discussed, and the Anglicans stressed the possibility of discerning the work of the Spirit outside the boundaries of the institutional church . . .' They also considered a number of other matters including relations with the Church of South India, and the position of the Thirty-Nine Articles in the Anglican tradition.

It was Carpenter's last meeting, and Runcie became the Anglican co-chairman when a sub-commission met in Romania the following year as guests of His Beatitude Justinian, the Romanian Patriarch. There they discussed the authority of the Ecumenical Councils and in 1975, when Runcie returned the Romanian hospitality and the commission met in St Albans, they agreed a statement on that ancient authority. They met again that month in London, and in 1976 they were invited to Moscow where the work of the commission in the previous three years was scrutinised and approved for publication as the Moscow Agreed Statement which mapped out the common ground held by both communions. It had not been an easy achievement. In *Anglican–Orthodox Dialogue* Colin Davey records several samples of the dialogue that took place in Moscow among which the following exchange of views is both typical and revealing.

Archbishop Basil (Orthodox): We must not make concessions to the modernistic and liberal interpretation of the Bible.

Bishop Hanson (Anglican) expressed anxiety about the remarks of Bishop Basil. Surely, he said, the Orthodox do not wish to reject wholesale all the findings of the critical study of the Bible in Europe and America over the last 200 years. As Anglicans we are not ashamed to share in this movement of the intellect, and we are confident that such sharing can be combined with orthodoxy of belief.

Archbishop Stylianos (Orthodox): The critical study of the Bible has not occurred only in the last 200 years, nor only in Europe and America. As our discussions in Crete made clear, contemporary Orthodox do not reject all critical study of the Bible. But in the critical study of the Bible over the last 200 years there have been tendencies which are indeed liberal and modernistic.

Archbishop Basil: Certainly, we Orthodox do not reject all historical study of the Bible; but we do not endorse that particular tendency which treats the Bible purely as a human document . . .

Nor, of course, did the Anglicans, but the criteria of orthodoxy were markedly different on both sides. It was Runcie's task to hold them together at a personal level in friendship and amity while they attempted to thrash out the theological minutiae, a task he continued to manage successfully for the next four years.

Meanwhile another major task had come his way. On 6 October 1972 the then Bishop of Durham, Ian Ramsey, collapsed and died at the end of a meeting in Broadcasting House. It was a great shock, though not wholly surprising, because it had been his first journey to London on his own since a severe heart attack the previous Easter. But the church was shaken. The small, tubby Lancastrian, born in a terraced house in Bolton, combined great theological scholarship with a loving personality and a passionate concern for the underdog. Nobody wrote more penetratingly about Christian ethics, and nobody found it harder to say 'no' to anything that was asked of him. It was believed by many that he should follow the other Ramsey – Michael – to Canterbury; but he worked himself to death before that assumption could be put to the test, leaving those who knew him best unconvinced that he would ever have had the discipline of discrimination, the ability to plan and stick to priorities, that was essential to the archbishopric.

The meeting he had chaired just before he died was of the Central Religious Advisory Committee, familiarly known as CRAC. It is a unique body in that it serves both the BBC and the Independent Broadcasting Authority, two fiercely competitive organisations. Each keeps the other under close scrutiny, and when brought face to face they are apt to wag tails and growl at the same time. No other advisory committee has such a task as CRAC. Its members are nominated by the separate authorities, though expected to deal impartially with both, and to keep strict confidentiality to the extent that, at meetings, BBC papers must be hastily stuffed out of sight before IBA personnel come into the room, and *vice versa*. The members broadly represent the mainstream churches in the British Isles and tend to be high-powered, including bishops, theologians, academics, and experienced 'media persons'. They gather twice a year for a two-day session, and have virtually four meetings in one as they meet with each authority in turn as well as having a joint meeting (requiring delicate footwork) and a meeting on their own. Their discussions are concerned primarily not so much with individual programmes but with formulating the policies and strategy of religious broadcasting.

A successor to Ian Ramsey had to be found. 'Though the chairmanship of CRAC does not take up much time,' wrote John Lang then the BBC's Head of Religious Broadcasting (later Dean of Lichfield), 'it does require substantial skill. The committee includes members of all the main churches in the country and represents many different opinions within them. Further, it advises both the broadcasting authorities and has to walk delicately between them. Finally, it deals directly with senior professional broadcasters who know their jobs thoroughly. They are friendly but also formidable.'

Senior members of the religious departments of the two authorities consulted together. By tradition the CRAC chairman was a bishop of the established church, and they needed someone with diplomatic skills, authority, and with a personality that would mix well with the governors and senior professionals. Those most concerned, Penry Jones, Kenneth Lamb, Christopher Martin and John Lang, already knew Bishop Runcie. He seemed to have the attributes required, he was conveniently close to London, and he was a fairly new bishop who, with luck, was not too heavily committed elsewhere. The only disadvantage was that he was not yet in the House of Lords, but seniority would solve that within a year or two. They consulted Archbishop Ramsey, the first of the Archbishops of Canterbury to recognise the mass media as important in the thinking of the church. He approved their choice, and Runcie accepted.

He took over CRAC at a demanding time. The committee had been worrying at two major issues: whether the 'closed period' was still desirable; and whether religious broadcasting, hitherto always Christian in its assumptions, should be widened to take account of the other faiths now represented by growing numbers in the United Kingdom.

The 'closed period' was an inheritance from the earliest days of broadcasting when no programmes at all were allowed on the air on Sunday evenings during the hours when people 'ought' (according to Lord Reith) to be in church. When in the 1930s it was found that, far from attending evening service, would-be listeners merely tuned into Radio Luxembourg and other commercial stations, the BBC accepted the principle that broadcasting should be allowed on Sunday evenings provided those hours were devoted to church services or suitable religious programmes.

In due course this convention spread to the television channels with a closed period from six fifteen to seven twenty-five p.m. But this protectionism had its drawbacks, in particular that because religious programmes were assured of a safe place in the schedules and did not have to compete with other programmes for air time, they were regarded among the professionals as a soft option not meriting the attention of first-class producers. Broadcasting staff like John Lang, anxious to improve the quality of the programmes, saw a break-out from the closed period, exposing their departments to the competitive world where they would have to fight for air time on their merits, as the healthy way to better and more effective religious programmes. Many – but not all – CRAC members agreed.

The other worry was that Britain had become a pluralistic society, with Muslims, for example, outnumbering Methodists. The original aim of religious broadcasting at the BBC (adopted by the independent television companies) was to 'reflect the worship, thought and action of those churches which represent the mainstream of the Christian tradition in this country, to stress what is most relevant in the Christian faith for the modern world, and to try to reach those outside it'. But could Britain still be called a Christian country? And were the Christians who were responsible for religious broadcasting being either fair or charitable to the Jews, Muslims, Sikhs, Hindus, Buddhists, and people of other faiths now citizens in this country?

Just after Runcie assumed the chair at CRAC, the need for answers to these questions was dramatically sharpened by the setting up of yet another government commission, under Lord Annan, to consider the future of broadcasting, together with the implications of all the new technology. It was suspected that the Annan commission would probe unfavourably at the privilege of the closed period, and would let in a cold draught on religious broadcasting generally. CRAC would be expected to give evidence, and the wise course would be for it to come up with its own recommendations in these sensitive areas.

So the twice-yearly CRAC meetings concentrated on these issues on which the members were by no means agreed. The key meeting was in March 1975 when, breaking with precedent, the committee met for a residential meeting at Addington Palace, the former country home of the Archbishops of Canterbury near Croydon. There the evidence was drafted, and new 'aims of religious broadcasting' agreed, widening them beyond the exclusive Christian monopoly to reflect 'the worship, thought, and action of the principal religious traditions represented in Britain, recognising that these traditions are mainly though not exclusively Christian'.

The argument over the closed period proved more difficult to resolve, and it was Runcie himself who produced a compromise at the following meeting in October when the evidence had to be finalised. The closed period should neither be fully retained nor discarded, but should shrink to thirty-five minutes on the understanding that a slot for further religious programming should be made available later (but not too late) on a Sunday evening.

Both proposals commended themselves to the Annan commission, and the next few years saw a noticeable rise in the quality of religious programmes as some excellent producers were attracted to making programmes with a religious theme (though 'religious' came to be interpreted rather too widely for some people's taste). Runcie served for six years as chairman of CRAC, winning the respect of the broadcasting authorities, and gaining a knowledge of how the media professionals worked and a sympathy for their problems that was to prove invaluable when he became a sought-after national figure at the centre of their attentions.

Chapter Twelve

St Albans – II

Every diocesan bishop is Visitor to his cathedral, holding
the final authority in all matters to do with its ministry and
discipline, but he is not involved in its daily governance,
which is usually exclusively a matter for the dean and
chapter. At St Albans, however, the relationship of the
bishop to the abbey is closer than at most other cathedrals.
St Albans Abbey is also a parish church, the dean its rector,
and the abbey is governed by a cathedral council – a grander
version of a parochial church council – in which the bishop
has a direct voice through two lay representatives. More
informally, he also lives in a house in its precincts and,
Abbey Gate House chapel being no more than a small
oratory, usually uses the cathedral for his daily worship
when he is at home.

Runcie would not let this major centre of ministry in his
diocese escape his detailed attention for long. Half-way
through his second year at St Albans he made a formal
Visitation to the abbey and, as usual, he had done his
homework and taken great pains over it. His Charge to
the dean and chapter, while couched in courteous and
appreciative language, was tough and well-informed. He
emphasised the need for well co-ordinated administration
and properly thought-out job briefs for all the cathedral
staff. In formal words he asked for their co-operation in his
educational plans for the diocese, integrating the work of
the Diocesan Educational Council with that of the cathedral
in a way that would 'illustrate the unity of the diocese

focused in the person of the bishop who holds the supreme teaching office and, by virtue of his order, gives the cathedral its unique character'. He linked this with his desire to establish a theological library within the cathedral precincts, putting together the library of the now-closed Cheshunt Theological College which had been made over to the diocese, with the Hudson Memorial and the cathedral libraries, to make one good comprehensive library attractive to both scholarly and general readers. He made pertinent comments on the furnishings of the abbey, and the standard of its public notices. He hinted at the need for possible new buildings to provide meeting rooms and a refectory for the public. While he was able to praise the high standards of the abbey's music, worship, and daily life, he saw scope for many creative possibilities.

His old friend the dean, Noel Kennaby, who had been Provost of Newcastle Cathedral when Runcie was ordained, was due to retire. Runcie wanted someone to replace him who could bring a fresh imagination to the abbey, and he was determined to have his own way. Though the appointment of the dean was a matter for the Crown, the appointment to the rectory, which provided the larger part of the dean's stipend, was in his own hands. He got the man he wanted.

Peter Moore had been a childhood friend and contemporary of the long-dead Derek Waters, and it was through Derek that Runcie had made friends with Moore at Oxford. Since then Moore had spent ten years at Pershore Abbey where, with great flair, he had transformed what had been a drearily used and neglected church; and Runcie considered that he had 'the dash and determination' to do as much for the abbey. (Any recent visitor to the abbey, seeing the new chapter house, refectory, the cathedral shop, and the atmosphere of humming community life which permeates the great church will consider Runcie's judgment justified.)

Moore was installed as rector and dean on 3 November 1973, and Runcie preached at his installation.

We live in an age of cathedrals, and I say to your dean, 'Don't be afraid to serve a cathedral', for the truth is that, in a day of diminishing Christian interest, and a day when all are speaking of finding vital Christian life in small groups, the cathedral seems to be more secure than the place of many a parish church. The multitudes, and not just the privileged few, are on the move today, and one of the centres they move towards – as iron filings to a magnet – is a great cathedral. Never have greater numbers flocked to our cathedrals; and even if some of them look, when trapped by a service, as if they were witnessing a waxworks show, it would be a bold and arrogant person who suggested that there was no Christian impact, no sense of being in a place hallowed by generations of worship, no expression of wonder at the mystery – and no blame attaching to the waxworks!

Let them find here, I plead, a welcoming church – a meeting place for men and women, for young and old, for citizen and foreigner, for Church and State, black and white, intellectual and mechanic, scientist and artist, antiquarian and space-minded, saint and sinner. Does that sound exaggerated? It will if by welcome we mean only the guided tour, the smile with the hymn-book, and the suggestion that if you try hard you will get used to our little ways.

We must create conditions for meeting which go deeper in terms of answering that search for meaning which characterises an age where the majority of our people are divided, half believing, half disbelieving. Nicodemus today is more likely to be found around the book-stall of a cathedral than visiting the vicar by night or a parish church by day. We must create conditions for meeting which go deeper than conventional kindness, which take account of new kinds of deprivation in our society – the deprivation of those who are judged inadequate or to have offended by the norms of our society: and their numbers increase as standards and the pace rise – the slow-witted, physically handicapped, those who dare not to admit to their loneliness because somewhere loneliness has been regarded as a sign of failure, a failure to adapt, a failure to be popular, a failure to succeed in our kind of society.

'I pray that your eyes may be opened that you may see the hope that is set before you' – in a place of welcome, a place to discover faith, a place of meeting and healing.

Early the following year Archbishop Ramsey announced that he would retire the day after his seventieth birthday in November. Speculation about his successor began, and Ladbroke's, the bookmakers, suddenly took notice of the often-quoted fact that 'more people go to church on Sundays than go to football matches on Saturday afternoons' and concluded that the appointment of an Archbishop of Canterbury must therefore be of sufficient public interest to open a book on the 'Cantuar stakes'. With the amused help of the staff of the *Church Times*, they drew up a list of runners. As soon as the bets started to come in it was clear that the Archbishop of York, Dr Donald Coggan, was the favourite.

He continued to be the favourite throughout the time of speculation. Other bishops were mentioned, including Kenneth Woollcombe and Runcie, but it was generally agreed that they were probably too young. 'Not this time round' was the common verdict. Even so, Abbey Gate House was rung up by a tabloid newspaper wanting Runcie's views on his possible promotion and the telephone was answered by Nick Coulton with such sceptical amazement that the paper's Trollopian report next day – ' "Good Heavens!" cried the chaplain' – led an irritated Runcie to say that he would deal with any further such enquiries himself. Not for a moment did he expect that the offer would be made to him.

Nobody was kept in suspense for long. The short odds on Dr Coggan were an accurate forecast of the views of the Prime Minister and the Queen, and in the middle of May it was announced that he would be enthroned at Canterbury early in 1975. That left a vacancy at York, and it proved difficult to fill. In church circles it became known that it had been offered to Bishop John Howe, the Executive Officer of the Anglican Consultative Council, and also to the Bishop of Manchester, Patrick Rodger (later Bishop of Oxford), who had been at Manchester the same length of time as

Runcie had been at St Albans. Both had turned it down. It was with mixed feelings that Runcie found in his post the familiar-looking letter from Downing Street offering the archbishopric to him.

An offer of promotion (even when one is third on the list) is always flattering, and this one had the temptation that it would take him back to his native north, for which he had a romantic attachment. Born in Lancashire of Scottish ancestry, his parochial experience shaped in Newcastle at a time when every self-respecting young clergyman felt in honour bound to dedicate himself to the industrial northern counties, Runcie had always felt that one day he must go back there. But, even with the Prime Minister's letter in his hand, he knew that this was not the time to do so. After five years all his plans for St Albans were just beginning to come to the boil. The diocesan administration and its boards and councils were being restructured. The needs and resources of the diocese were being assessed. In June he had ordained the largest number of new priests and deacons the diocese had ever known at one ordination. And, to bring all this together, a three-year plan for ministry and mission was being formulated. He could not contemplate leaving St Albans just as all this was taking shape. Nor would it be fair to his wife and children who had just had time to re-establish themselves and to build up their lives in new surroundings. Lindy had a horror of the huge archbishop's palace at York. She had acquired a fresh set of pupils and friends in St Albans and, though James and Rebecca were at boarding school most of the time, they too had their new friends. Runcie had no real doubts about saying 'no' to York and it was soon announced that Stuart Blanch, the Bishop of Liverpool, had accepted it.

In October the whole diocesan synod had a residential meeting at a conference centre in Cardington where the three-year plan was agreed. By the following April, such was the financial good health of the diocese (financial solvency is always considered an indication of vigorous church life) that Runcie felt compelled in *See Round* to thank the parishes for their 'magnificent response to the quota' (the parishes' contribution to diocesan and central church funds, assessed according to their population and financial resources), and added that 'the figures requested might have astonished and depressed us five years ago. Yet in 1974 we received over 99.5 per cent of the money, and an emergency request for a further £80 per clergyman in each parish yielded £27,000 which is again almost 100 per cent.'

In a later *See Round* he gave some idea of a typical week in his diary.

Monday: our fortnightly staff meeting. The three bishops share their pastoral confidences, recording cases of illness or emergency and the action that has to be taken. There is a chance for us to pray together. We invite a rural dean to lunch and he brings us up to date in his area. There is a little gamesmanship as we attempt to show how 'in touch' we are. In a larger group in the afternoon we review some general appointments and questions such as the new chaplaincies at Hatfield Polytechnic and the Cranfield Institute.

Tuesday: a day of interviews in which major issues such as the future of colleges of education, pastoral reorganisation, retirement of the clergy, and remarriage, are seen as they affect individuals. In the evening I institute David Elliott as vicar of All Saints', Borehamwood, and welcome him back to the diocese after several years in Africa. A mixture of visitors from his parish in Africa and from the diocese and locality provide an encouraging springboard for his new ministry.

Wednesday: I see members of the education team individually before a meeting of the Education Committee. That standard of discussion is high as we talk through their part in the diocesan centenary (due in 1977) which will not simply be a commemoration of the past.

Thursday: I address the annual meeting of the Council of Churches and suggest that their role is to be a focus for

Christian honesty in the community. Here, if anywhere, at a time when individual churches are bothered about their domestic budgets and strengthening the loyalty of the local congregations, they should be reminding us of the critical issues which face the churches – the gap between Christians in the West, or between theologian and preacher, the major moral issues of which we should be reminding the nation, the future shape of the local community, and the obstacles created by duplicating the resources. I can't promise them a peaceful year if they do their stuff, but one of creative discomfort. They seem to take it on the chin.

Friday: a London day. I take the chair for the steering committee for the Anglican–Orthodox Conversations, and we lay plans for our next meeting in Moscow. I slip into the House of Lords and try to understand the implications of the Community Land Bill for the redeployment of church property, especially in city centres. Among the commuting strap-hangers on the way home I fail to recognise a notable Reader from the diocese. How different people look in vestries! Another travelling companion tries to put me right on the ordination of women.

Saturday: the Diocesan Synod. I try to comment on the Archbishops' Call to the Nation [a pastoral letter issued the previous month by the Archbishops of Canterbury and York asking Christian people to think seriously about the state of society and its needs]. I believe that we should be positive in our response because people are looking for a clear lead; but I am bound to sound some warning notes. I hope we shall not misuse an inevitably simple and direct appeal. Christians should not be concerned only to firm up old disciplines which were more palpable in a stable society; they should be eager to discover their appropriate expression in a society of much wider, more complex, and, yes, more human moral horizons than our fathers ever knew.

There is a cynicism about institutions, whether the

family, Parliament, or the Church. That is serious because institutions carry the conventions that undergird society, the things we take for granted; but there is much less cynicism, and more enthusiasm, for causes – and some of them very good causes. Perhaps the most serious need is for some realignment of the institutions of society with the causes they purport to serve. For this reason I am reluctant to see the church too easily hooked on to simple campaigns for remoralising the nation. It is not the primary duty of the church to go round telling people how to behave, but to declare and live by the Gospel we have heard – with all the implications that has for our understanding of the nature of man. The Pastoral Letter to be read in church is not meant to give satisfaction to the righteous, and we should see that it is not so interpreted.

There are many participants in a good debate on Christian initiation, and some serious voting. The synod faces up to a formidable budget, but it is one built on consultation. Several speakers say that any crisis is not one of money but of commitment.

Sunday: a rather rich diet of services around the diocese includes an inspiring Hertfordshire Guides' Service of Praise in the Abbey. It is a good example of imaginative and appropriate liturgy and it gives me some ideas for the next Youth Pilgrimage. In the evening I do some homework for a visit to one of my favourite spots in the north of the diocese. A church school is pioneering again, and I am to go to open the first nursery unit in the Bedfordshire programme which is part of the new buildings for Wymington School.

It is noticeable that in the course of recording those seven days he made no mention of taking a day off, and that was often the case. He found his relaxation in moving from one type of work to another. He did, however, try to play tennis at least once a week, usually with the chaplain of Napsbury Mental Hospital, Ted Norris, a man several years older than himself. When Runcie had an hour or so to spare he would ring up the hospital, Norris would be bleeped for, and they were usually able to meet within a quarter of an hour on the hospital court. 'It was very convenient,' remembers Runcie.

No doubt those who passed by would imagine that the two elderly gents on the court were patients, and that there was a coronary unit at the end of the corridor if we overdid it. But Ted was determined that I should keep up my tennis and relax with him for half an hour or so a week, and we did this wet or fine – and my memories are that it was usually wet! Although he was older than I was, he had been a sportsman all his life and was a very subtle tennis-player. He would talk to me about life in the hospital, and would listen to what was troubling me. So a certain amount of spiritual direction and tennis went together.

In the same issue of *See Round* in which he had described his week, the new Ministerial Training Course was announced. This was the joint brain-child of Runcie and Eric James whom Runcie had brought to the diocese with a broad brief as Canon Missioner. James's radicalism and outspokenness had caused such controversy in the Southwark diocese where he had been Canon Missioner that he had been out of a job when Runcie, who had a high regard for him as a man of ideas, invited him to St Albans. Runcie believed that 'it was worth having someone with a stronger sense than I possessed that progress is made by honest conflict'. It was a trait not always appreciated in the diocese, though he never had cause to regret his choice.

The Ministerial Training Scheme was a case in point. Runcie had been gripped by the idea that 'we could not afford so many full-time clergy as we had been used to, but I did not want to close churches because I never liked to ride rough-shod over local loyalties. I believed the way forward was with less but better-trained full-time clergy, supplemented by non-stipendiary ministries of different sorts.' So the scheme first put together by James was based on the belief that just as Christians have many different gifts and talents to offer, so there are many different forms of Christian ministry, though they all start from the same basis. What was unique about the St Albans scheme therefore was that a course of part-time training was offered in which, for the foundation year at least, all those training for any kind of Christian ministry would be trained together. Only at the end of the first year would potential priests be selected, while others carried on to become deaconesses or licensed lay-workers with different ministries in view.

The course was open to men or women whose spiritual commitment, resilience of character, and leadership potential were endorsed by a selection panel, and who would for the first year keep an open mind about what form their ministries would eventually take. Each student accepted on the course was assigned not only a tutor, but also a panel of four people who between them represented the student's home and work communities and would encourage and support him or her through the years of the course. The detailed work on the scheme was done by two ex-Cuddesdon clergy in the diocese, Robert Hardy (later Bishop of Maidstone) and Michael Bourke, who became course directors. They were later joined by Robert Langley, the ex-Warden of Brasted College. It was a tough regime, recognised by ACCM as providing training to the standards required for ordination, and the students were obliged to attend lectures and tutorials on two evenings a week, regular residential weekends, and a ten-day summer school.

The response was excellent with thirty students accepted for the first year, seven of them women, and among them the bishop's own secretary, Inez Luckraft, who went on to become a deaconess. At Michaelmas 1979 the first joint ordination and commissioning service was held; the new deacons trained on the MTS course were ordained – Mrs Luckraft with them – and the rest of the course graduates were commissioned as licensed non-stipendiary lay-workers in their parishes.

There were more changes in the diocese. Victor Whitsey

went to be Bishop of Chester, and in his place Runcie chose Peter Mumford, the Archdeacon of St Albans, to be Bishop of Hertford. After Whitsey's brusque northernness, Mumford was a popular choice, having been on the staff of St Albans Abbey and a much-liked vicar in Bedford. Then in 1976, to Runcie's great grief, his other suffragan, the Bishop of Bedford, died suddenly. He had loved John Hare as a man of rare holiness, humour and integrity, and feared that it was the work he had piled on him that had contributed to his early death at the age of sixty-four. A successor was necessary, and Runcie brought to the diocese the Warden of Lincoln Theological College, Alec Graham, whom he had got to know during his Cuddesdon days when Graham was Chaplain of Worcester College, Oxford. Graham had, Runcie considered, 'a lean, tough, rather rigorous mind, and was not afraid of following a saint in at Bedford'.

An important change as far as Runcie was personally concerned was the appointment of a new domestic chaplain. In 1975 Nicholas Coulton returned to parish life to be vicar of a church in the town centre of Bedford. In exchange Runcie chose a Bedford curate who had been one of the most difficult of his Cuddesdon ordinands. Richard Chartres, who was to be his chaplain for the next eight years (and would accompany him to Lambeth) was a young man of unusual intelligence and abilities who had given his tutors a hard time. Runcie had always appreciated his 'agreeably combative' conversation, the quickness of his wit, and the shrewdness of his observations, but Chartres had found it difficult to conform to the Cuddesdon pattern. Soon after Runcie left the college he had dropped out of his Cuddesdon training to spend a year doing odd jobs in Spain before succumbing once more to the pull of his vocation and finishing his theological training at Lincoln. He had none of Nick Coulton's orderliness of mind and method, but Runcie found him stimulating company, diplomatic, kindly, and immensely willing to take pains and anticipate needs. It was to become a very fruitful association.

In 1977 the diocese reached its centenary in a blaze of festivals and celebration. They called it FestAlban. From

April to November the diocesan diaries were filled with a multitude of events from lectures and historical exhibitions in the abbey to flower shows and picnics. Peter Mumford was the principal organiser. Special hymns were written, all-night happenings happened in the abbey, Runcie did a helicopter tour of the deaneries, festival Eucharists were held in many parts of the diocese, dramatic productions drew crowds. The Archbishop of Canterbury came in June, and the Queen Mother in November. In September the whole diocese had a 'day out' in Knebworth Park.

The day that Archbishop Coggan, accompanied by his wife, came to preach at an evening Eucharist in the packed abbey, the service was preceded by a garden party for 1,200 people in the Abbey Gate House garden. Garden parties, though not usually on such a grand scale, had become a feature of the Runcies' life at St Albans. From soon after their arrival clergy and their families from two or three deaneries at a time were invited in turn to these gatherings. Lindy did the baking and catering herself, and appeared as a sparkling hostess. She also catered for and entertained the ordinands and their families after each ordination service in the abbey, and the members of the Cell when they met in St Albans; and some of the major events were the annual cricket matches between the Bishop's XI and the diocesan clergy, when Runcie always captained his team, and Lindy summoned a great variety of helpers to lay on lunch and tea. These were some of her happiest years, with her piano pupils, the music column she wrote as correspondent for the local paper, and the busyness of life in and around Abbey Gate House. There were always people in and out, often for informal meals in the kitchen; with the family and visitors, according to Lindy's inflexible rule, washing up between each course.

Life at St Albans looked as though it could go on for ever, but Runcie was feeling in need of a break. He had long hoped to take a sabbatical and had come very close to arranging one from Cuddesdon when his move to St Albans had prevented him. Now he was planning one again for the first few months of 1979, but it suddenly came under threat when he was offered the bishopric of Oxford.

Lindy was adamant and in tears at the prospect, even though it would have meant going back to live in Cuddesdon. She feared that back in the Oxford environment Robert would once again become an academic, and she would find herself again in a country village, missing all the life she had grown to love in the centre of St Albans. In any case, she said, he would again lose his sabbatical, and it was quite clear that he needed a change and a rest. Oxford was turned down.

His original plans for a leisurely sabbatical of rest, reading, recreation, and a holiday in the sun turned into something more demanding. At a meeting of the Anglican–Orthodox Commission in Cambridge in 1977, the year following the Moscow Agreed Statement, the conversations broke down to such an extent that some members walked out. A new group of topics for discussion had been started, but the trouble was over the ordination of women. The Orthodox had suddenly become aware that in different parts of the Anglican Communion, in America, Canada, New Zealand, and Hong Kong, women were already being ordained; and in 1975 the General Synod of the Church of England itself had agreed that there were 'no fundamental theological objections' to women priests.

The Orthodox were appalled. The Anglicans, they said, had for years been assuring them that they were a true part of the Catholic church, and the Orthodox had so accepted their assurance that a special relationship had grown up between them such as the Orthodox had with no other church. Yet now the Anglicans were tampering with one of the three fundamental principles of the Catholic tradition, the three-fold ministry. They felt bewildered and betrayed, and the relationship was near collapse. It was all that Runcie could do to save the immediate situation and ensure a further meeting the following year in Greece.

They met at Pendeli near Athens in 1978, shortly before all the Anglican bishops gathered from all over the world for the Lambeth Conference being held in Canterbury. At the behest of the Orthodox the commission sent a message to the Lambeth Conference expressing grave concern at the effect the ordination of women would have on relations between the two communions. It was an anxious time, for the Orthodox were clearly waiting to see what response they got from Canterbury before they would agree to further meetings.

Runcie, of course, was at the Lambeth Conference, and spoke on behalf of the Orthodox in the debate on women priests. 'When the Anglican Church embraces such a fundamental change as to the nature and character of the ordained ministry without sufficient regard for those with whom we proudly aim to share the apostolic ministry, it registers itself as a different sort of church,' he said. But despite his warnings about ecumenical bad faith, there was no comfort for the Orthodox. The Conference acknowledged the plurality within the Anglican Communion, that some churches either did or were preparing to ordain women, and some were not prepared to do so, and urged that there should be mutual tolerance between the different points of view.

Almost immediately Archbishop Athenagoras of Thyateira, Runcie's co-chairman of the commission, threatened that the Anglican–Orthodox conversations would become 'simply an academic and informatory exercise, and no longer an ecclesial endeavour aiming at the union of the two churches'; and that in future, instead of the high-powered hierarchs, the Orthodox would probably appoint only laymen to the commission. For those who cared about Anglican–Orthodox relations as Runcie did, the situation seemed desperate.

He himself was by no means implacably opposed to women priests. While the issue came low on his list of personal priorities, he was prepared to admit in private that he found the arguments in favour of women priests more convincing and more compatible with his Christian instincts than the arguments against. But he was very conscious of carrying a responsibility on behalf of the Anglican Communion towards the Orthodox Churches and so, when the General Synod in the following November debated whether the time was right for it to start legislation to make the ordaining of women possible, he felt he had to speak against it.

> It is the Orthodox who have talked in the past about a special relationship with the Anglicans, and that has not been hollow, and it has been particularly concentrated on the history of the Church of England. That is why today is so important to them. They know that from the seventeenth century onwards the Anglicans, through this country, have particularly maintained the bridge between East and West – one of the only theological bridges between East and West. They are now coming out of their geographical isolation and winning the respect of many seekers for their witness to serious religion, particularly in Eastern Europe, along with Roman Catholics and Baptists. They believe that stand depends upon being rooted in tradition. They have even said to me, 'We only came into the ecumenical movement because we thought you were our friends,' and it seems that we are letting them down.

In speaking like this he was earning a certain amount of opprobrium among those liberals who would normally have regarded him as an ally, and putting himself out of step with most of his friends on the bench of bishops who were in favour of proceeding towards the ordination of women by a nearly two-thirds majority. But the move was resoundingly defeated by the clergy, and the whole matter thereby deferred for an indefinite number of years.

This was not enough to reassure the Orthodox whose confidence had been severely shaken, and Runcie saw his sabbatical as a chance to do what he could to rebuild the bridges. He had in any case been planning to visit the Soviet Union, a country which, by its very mysteriousness to Western eyes, has continued to fascinate him. But he now decided to visit all the Orthodox Patriarchates so that he could extend and renew friendships on a personal basis, and do all that was possible to restore amity and the 'special relationship'.

After spending three quiet weeks in Cambridge catching up on some rest and reading, he left for Istanbul in the middle of February where he had two meetings with the Ecumenical Patriarch. The Patriarch told him, 'You are stirring the waters so that God can act through us more effectively,' and enabled him to meet most of the members of the Holy Synod who assured him that they wanted the Anglican–Orthodox dialogue to continue on its old footing.

He had less satisfactory meetings with the Patriarch of Jerusalem and his advisers, but in Jerusalem he saw many old friends, including Murray Rogers whose *ashram* in India he had stayed in nearly twenty years before, and who now had an *ashram* in Jerusalem. He then went on to Damascus where the widely travelled Patriarch of Antioch received him warmly, but shrewdly remarked that the characteristics of Christian witness in the Middle East should be charity and steadiness, and theological conversations and innovations like the ordination of women did not immediately contribute to either!

From Damascus he went to Egypt, and in Alexandria he talked at length to an old Ethiopian friend, the Metropolitan Methodius of Aksum, who was one of the most active members of the Anglican–Orthodox Commission. Runcie knew well that he was vigorously opposed to the ordination of women, but found him keen that the dialogue should continue. Pleased, he went on to Cyprus where he was again warmly received by the Archbishop who arranged for him to meet all the Orthodox bishops and theological advisers in the Greek part of the island. He spent some days touring, including the Turkish sector, and was able to visit small groups of Orthodox Christians there, taking them blessings from their bishops in the Greek south who were not allowed in Turkish territory.

Lindy flew out to meet him at Athens to accompany him on a lecture cruise organised by the University of Pennsylvania, but before joining the ship Runcie had the most formidable encounter of his tour. The Archbishop of Athens had summoned from all over Greece the members of the official committee of the Holy Synod for Ecumenical

Relations, and they questioned him for four hours. The Greeks were blunt about their disappointment in the Lambeth Conference and the recent behaviour of the Anglican Communion, not only in the matter of the ordination of women, but in the instability that they saw in the writings of Anglican theologians. They were on the verge of saying that the continuation of the joint dialogue was now impossible, and Runcie found himself supporting the arguments for women priests and theological openness with a conviction he had never mustered before.

He lectured as usual on the cruise as it toured the eastern Mediterranean, and travelled home with Lindy to St Albans for a few days. He spent most of them writing a huge batch of 'thank-you' letters to his Orthodox hosts: a time-consuming task because so many of them needed to be couched in what he called 'the honorific periods required for patriarchs'.

He then set off again for the Eastern European countries, starting with Hungary where he stayed with the Ambassador, Richard Parsons, an old Oxford friend. From there he went to Yugoslavia where his welcome had an extra warmth because the Serbian Academy had been housed at Cuddesdon during the First World War, and the link remained. Discussions there were friendly and open, with an admission that the Orthodox Churches needed to look again at the deployment of women in the ministry; and the Patriarch went so far as to say that 'the ordination of women may lie ahead of us, but it is a matter that can only be decided by all who are loyal to the Catholic order'.

In Bulgaria the hospitality he had shown in St Albans to the Patriarch and some of the bishops was returned with interest and with enthusiasm for the continuation of the dialogue. In Romania his old pupil from Cuddesdon was unfortunately abroad, but Runcie was there in time to celebrate the Orthodox Easter at the convent of Dintr-un-Lemn which he had visited before with his friend, Bishop Josif of Rimnical Vilcea.

I arrived on Good Friday and stayed through the week of Easter. The long service of the *Epitaphion* was deeply moving, and there was a victorious note in the sacred procession at the end of the long vigil. And so through the following days I shared their worship and their life, welcoming many opportunities to join with them as one of the family, reading the gospel in English at the 'Second Easter'. The Great Service of Easter began at midnight. After dull wet days it was a still starlit night. A large party of tourists and other onlookers crowded into the court and filled the church to overflowing. The sisters who had so faithfully kept the fast and devotions of Lent might have been forgiven for resenting such an intrusion. Not at all! They had made special arrangements for the guests to be received, to attend the first hour of the service, and then to enjoy some Easter egg cracking in the refectory while the Liturgy flowed on gloriously and uninterrupted until we all emerged with the dawn.

The Patriarch of Romania was encouraging about the Anglican–Orthodox dialogue. 'Friends don't give up when they strike difficulties,' he said, and suggested that as the subjects of the ordination of women and the *filioque* clause had had everything said about them that could be said, it was time to move on to other topics of discussion.

The final fortnight of his tour was spent in Russia where Runcie found that the Patriarch of Moscow and All Russia had planned a three-week programme to fit into his two weeks. On his first day he was officially received by the Patriarch at Vespers in the cathedral, and that same evening was the guest of honour at a long and lavish banquet, such banquets being a feature of all Orthodox hospitality. He spent time in Moscow, Leningrad, and the diocese of Minsk – where he was taken round parishes and saw something of local church life well off the beaten tourist track – and he learned that the Russians were willing to carry on the dialogue, but were more interested in ecumenical relations with the Roman Catholics, the Lutherans, and the World Council of Churches in Geneva, than specifically with the Anglicans who had no presence in the Soviet states.

He returned home in the middle of May to write another pile of 'thank-you' letters, not only to his Orthodox hosts, but to the friends he had made among the locally based diplomats of the Foreign Office who had done much to smooth his path and make his contacts. He also wrote an official report for Archbishop Coggan, spelling out the Orthodox worries about what they saw as the theological instability of the Anglican Church, and their difficulty in discerning any seat of Anglican authority. 'They cannot understand,' he wrote, 'how we can be an episcopal church and stand with them in that succession while tinkering about with the operations of the episcopate in a unilateral way.' It was inevitable that they now found the authoritarianism of Rome and the confessional faith of the Lutherans easier to converse with. As for the official conversations, the Anglicans were left, he considered, a choice between a cosmetic repair that would enable the Anglican–Orthodox dialogue to appear to continue, or a radical review which might secure a fresh and more constructive start. He personally believed it should be the latter, and he suggested that a theological discussion of common pastoral problems – marriage and the family, evangelism in a multi-faith society, the spiritual life, church and state relations, etc. – might be the way forward. 'It would, of course, be only a step on the long haul towards Christian unity,' he concluded, 'but it might be a rather particular sort of step.'

He had barely finished writing these letters and reports when Archbishop Coggan announced his impending resignation. The secular and church press immediately began to discuss likely successors, and Runcie was amused to see his own name quoted so often. He was picking up his life at St Albans with fresh energy, catching up with the five months that he had been away, and slightly looking round for something new to do. The Ministerial Training Scheme had been going well, and the first batch of twenty-four students were nearing their ordination and commissioning. The two following courses were also doing well. His five-year term as chairman of CRAC had been extended by a year, but that also was coming to an end. He had just expended great effort on Anglican–Orthodox relations, and he now had to wait to see the outcome.

Nevertheless, he honestly had no expectation that the invitation to Canterbury would come his way. He still believed that the people who mattered considered him to be theologically too lightweight. That had indeed been said of him on the previous occasion when Canterbury was vacant, five years earlier – but it was the opinion of those who took him at his own valuation and saw only the spontaneous good humour, the pragmatic approach to pastoral problems, and the apparently natural gifts for communication, without knowing anything of the exceptional abilities and tremendous hard work that were behind all these. But he more than half believed it of himself. His profound respect for first-class theologians, his determination to raise theological standards at Cuddesdon and any other college where he had influence, his emphasis on theological education in the St Albans diocese, and his own continual reading of solid theology throughout his career, all suggest that some part of him never ceased to regret that he did not take a theological degree while at Cambridge; perhaps he had always felt some inadequacy because of it. He was thus able to hear his name being quoted in all quarters, confident that he knew better, especially since he had recently been offered the bishopric of Oxford which he saw as a certain indication that the new Crown Appointments Commission was not thinking of him in archiepiscopal terms.

At the General Synod in early July he had to speak in the debate on whether women ordained in other parts of the Anglican Communion should be allowed to function as priests in England, and he told the Synod of the Orthodox experiences so fresh in his mind.

Many have asked me, 'What on earth is the Anglican Communion up to?', and it is very difficult for them to know where to go for an answer – to the Lambeth Conference, to the office of Bishop Howe, or to the General Synod – and we keep clouding the issue of authority by creating yet more structures, and some wonder whether they should even go to the Diocese of Europe. Meanwhile, of course, the Orthodox are making really steady progress in the dialogue with the Roman Catholic Church with its clear, historic, and international claims, and also with the Oriental Churches deep in the Third World and against the important background of an inter-faith context, and also with the Lutheran Church with its traditions of theological scholarship and commitment to Europe and to the World Council of Churches. Therefore proposals that they should urgently share in the theological grounds for including women in the order of priesthood are not going to get a quick reply, and it is not necessarily because they are out of touch. Indeed there are, some would say, more urgent items on the agenda for Christian discipleship in places like Eastern Europe, the Middle East, Africa, and India, and we are no longer at the centre of the ecumenical position. Nevertheless, I can report a conviction that our theological conversations with the Orthodox should continue and, indeed, people will be coming from different parts of the world next Tuesday in order to start planning again the resumption of our dialogue in 1980, and that will be one of two meetings this year.

He then went on to say that if Synod pressed on with the recognition of women priests in England it would seriously disturb the delicate ecumenical situation that at present existed, and that 'synodical fidgeting' was the despair of the Orthodox partners in the dialogue. He added that while he himself believed implicitly in the ministry of women, and in his own diocese he had extended that ministry by every means possible, he believed that at that moment it was right to do nothing about recognising the women ordained overseas. It was a speech that came as a great disappointment to many Synod members who were hoping, on all other counts, that he would be chosen for Canterbury.

For the next few days he continued to be occupied with the Orthodox, planning a resumption of the dialogue at a meeting in Wales the following year. Then he returned to other long-standing engagements in a diary that seemed fuller than ever after his five months away. On Thursday 19 July he was to preach at the King's School, Canterbury, which meant he must leave St Albans very early in the morning, and that same evening he was to meet Lindy in London for dinner at the BBC.

It proved to be a very enjoyable day and evening. Both he and Lindy were in good form at the BBC, and he was chaffed about succeeding to Canterbury and laughed it off. In high spirits the Runcies arrived back at Abbey Gate House about half an hour after midnight to find Richard Chartres still up, in his dressing-gown, with a letter in his hand which had arrived that morning after the bishop had left. It was marked 'Office of the Prime Minister – Private and Personal', and Runcie saw it in a wave of shock. 'Now your troubles begin,' said his chaplain, handing it to him.

Runcie took it to his study to read it by himself. It was a simple and routinely worded letter from Mrs Thatcher: could she send his name to the Queen for appointment as Archbishop of Canterbury? His first thought was how could he get out of it; what good reasons could he give for turning it down? Despite all that had been said and written about him as a probable candidate, he had simply never visualised himself as Archbishop of Canterbury – a completely different job from being Archbishop of York. The responsibility and the exposure seemed terrifying.

Lindy, having guessed the implications of the letter, was aghast. She had been steadily telling everyone who asked that she, at least, had no intention of leaving St Albans, and had been quoted in the press a few days earlier that she would go only if she were carried out feet first. She could see the move completely wrecking what family life they had left to them. Both the Runcies went to bed in a state of panic.

The following day the bishop had arranged to drive north with a friend to Ripon to see John Turnbull, now a canon of Ripon, who was dying of cancer and very near his end. Runcie was a silent and preoccupied companion as his friend drove. He said nothing about what was so much on his mind until he reached John Turnbull's bedside and found his old friend a very sick man. Turnbull was not too sick, however, to be still the same affectionate and wise counsellor that Runcie had known in his curate days: when Runcie told him about the Prime Minister's letter and how much he wanted to say 'no,' Turnbull exerted all his energy to be reassuring. It was the church that had chosen him to be Archbishop of Canterbury, and if God was calling him through the church, then God would enable him to do it properly. After an hour's talk between them, and some prayers for each other, Runcie left, calmed, saddened that he would not again see on earth a man he had loved for thirty years, but resigned at least to thinking seriously about the archbishopric.

Meanwhile Chartres had been in touch with Colin Peterson, the Prime Minister's appointments secretary, and had made arrangements for the bishop to go and see Mrs Thatcher. Secrecy was essential. Any bishop seen at this time going anywhere near the front door of 10 Downing Street would immediately give the game away, and that was to be avoided at all costs until the appointment had been agreed and received royal approval. So the following Monday Runcie had a comically cloak-and-dagger meeting with Peterson under Admiralty Arch off Trafalgar Square, and was hurried quickly through a back door of Downing Street. He spent half an hour with the Prime Minister. They had not met since they had been at Oxford together, and the first few minutes were spent in renewing their old acquaintance. Then Runcie confessed his doubts, and they talked about the strains of the job. Mrs Thatcher was brisk but sympathetic, and said he could have until Saturday to make up his mind. If he wanted it, she would be willing to talk to him again in the next few days before she went to the Commonwealth Conference in Africa.

Still in immense secrecy, Lindy agreed to go and look at Lambeth Palace after dark on the Thursday evening. She, too, was smuggled in a back door, and Mrs Coggan showed her round the rambling building with its wide corridors, high and spacious rooms, and the upstairs flat for the archbishop's family. In Lindy's eyes an enormous amount of work needed to be done, but at least she felt that – unlike the palace at York – it could be turned into an attractive and comfortable home.

Next day it was Runcie's turn to visit Lambeth, looking as unobtrusive as any bishop paying a routine call on the Archbishop. Donald Coggan told him something of the work of the primacy as he saw it, and how to survive in it, and then Runcie went to have a medical check-up to make sure that his always excellent health and stamina showed no early signs of letting him down. But he still had not made up his mind. The following day he asked Colin Peterson for more time.

By Saturday he was saying to himself: 'How could I face an ordinand or a curate in the future and tell him that vocations sometimes involve the call of the church to an individual to serve in a difficult position, if I do not say "yes"?' – he had almost decided. On Sunday he wrote his letter of acceptance to the Prime Minister, but asked that the announcement should be delayed until after he and his family had had their summer holiday in Italy. His letter was acknowledged, and Peterson, because of the difficulties of keeping the secret so long without leaks, pressed urgently for an early release of the news. But Mrs Thatcher, on her return from Lusaka, sympathised with the Runcies' desire to have their holiday in peace, and the date for the announcement was fixed for 3 September.

They spent the middle weeks of August in a farmhouse in Tuscany and on their way back they heard the news of Lord Mountbatten's assassination in Ireland. It was obviously right to defer the announcement, and it was agreed that it should be at the end of the week after Mountbatten's funeral. Family and close friends had to be told, and press releases and photographs prepared; and on the Thursday night Runcie gave the news in confidence to the editor of the *Hertfordshire Advertiser* – a paper with whom he had had close associations, and for whom Lindy wrote a regular music column – certain that that week's edition of the paper had already gone to press. But he had not bargained for the resourcefulness of the editor who had it in headlines the following morning several hours before the official press conference and announcement.

All the family were at the press conference (Rebecca enquired anxiously whether she was likely to be asked any theological questions) and at the mercy of the photographers afterwards. John Miles, the church's chief information officer, provided much-needed refreshments in his room in Church House after the photographic session was over and while the bishop was still giving radio and television interviews. James and Rebecca came in and Rebecca dropped exhausted into a chair saying she simply could not smile any more at anybody. Miles was touched by the pride they both so obviously had in their father. 'The way he took that press conference was superb,' said James.

The news coverage was tremendous. The present writer saw it on American television within an hour. As had happened when he was appointed to St Albans, all the popular press seized on Runcie's war service, his interest in football, his lively family, and this time they had a new interest: his keeping of Berkshire pigs. It was a fairly peripheral interest. He had first taken a liking to Berkshires when staying with Kath during the war, and when he arrived in St Albans and met Jenny Boyd-Carpenter who kept pigs, he had a fancy for some of his own, which Mrs Boyd-Carpenter looked after for him. But the press were so delighted by the idea of an archbishop pig-keeper that those particular Berkshires became, for a year or two, the most notorious pigs in the world.

The more sober press paid attention to his plans for tackling his new job and, once the first news of the announcement was over, requests for serious interviews came thick and fast. Everyone wanted to talk to him and record his views on every matter of public interest, and everyone wanted to give him advice on what he should do as primate. Even *Gay News*, the newspaper for homosexuals, gave the whole of its front page to his appointment, acknowledging his personal kindness to many individual homosexuals 'while feeling some apprehension at his public unwillingness to declare at least a gesture of support for the past and present ministry of homosexuals in his church'. Many papers carried the welcoming comments made by other church leaders such as Cardinal Hume and the moderators of the Free Churches. The only sour notes came from a handful of Evangelicals who disliked his Anglo-Catholic churchmanship, deplored his ecumenical leanings, and had horrible visions of his effecting a closer relationship with the Roman Catholic Church. Most Evangelicals were more generous.

Among the more thoughtful reactions, Clifford Longley of *The Times* probably summed up the general view.

In an age that has acquired a taste for warmth in the personality of its church leaders, Bishop Runcie emerges as the man for the season. The job he will be moving to next spring, however, is likely to make more demands on him than on any of his predecessors in recent memory. More will be expected from him because he is a popular choice, but the actual levers of power and influence available to a modern archbishop are fewer and shorter than ever before. The problems facing the Church of England and the Anglican Communion, which he also has to lead, can hardly have looked so complex or so difficult . . . His inestimable advantage is undoubtedly that the modern world will not start for him beyond the walls of Lambeth Palace; it will be there inside, present in his family, present in himself. It will make for an easy relationship with the people, which is probably, in the end, why he was chosen.

Chapter Thirteen

Lambeth – I

Throughout his holiday Runcie had been thinking about his new role and, from the time that the news was announced, there was no shortage of well-meant advice. Much was said, both publicly and privately, about the need to lighten the burden on the new archbishop, not least by the Archbishop of York, Stuart Blanch, who had himself just been ordered by his doctor to take several weeks' rest. There were warnings that, unless something radical was done to relieve the load, the task of meeting all the expectations of church, state, and the Anglican Communion would drive a conscientious primate to a martyr's grave.

The message coming from those currently installed at Lambeth was much the same. Archbishop Coggan had so small a staff that he drove himself to the limits simply to survive. Runcie was determined to do more than survive, and he saw the key to the situation in a hand-picked team of staff with whom he could work, to whom he could delegate, and on whose briefing he could draw. When he spoke in public, as he would have to do incessantly, he wanted what he said to sound pertinent and well-informed, and so he would have to depend on others not only to do his research, but to write the first draft of his addresses. Not for him the hasty notes jotted on the back of an envelope at the last minute. He had been impressed to see Orthodox patriarchs being handed their well-written speeches in a leather folder as they took their place to preach or lecture, confident they could speak with unhurried authority. It was this sort of efficient organisation that Runcie required. Any spontaneous light touches, of which he was so much a master, would be but the decoration on a well-thought-out statement. His prime task, therefore, was to identify the areas of work and to get the right team together.

Meanwhile he had gradually to withdraw from his work in St Albans and to hand over to the suffragan bishops until such time as a new diocesan was appointed. He had regretfully to cancel a Swan lecture cruise in the Mediterranean booked for the following June. Farewell parties were arranged for him and Lindy all over the diocese, and at the end of January there was a festival Evensong in the abbey followed by a presentation of parting gifts. The city of St Albans also honoured him when the mayor delivered to him the freedom of the city at a ceremony in the City Hall attended by a thousand people.

Over 5,000 letters of congratulation poured in from all over the world. All those who had ever known him – or thought they had known him – wrote to say how delighted they were, many of them taking six closely written pages of family history to do so! Complete strangers wrote assuring him of their prayers. Hundreds proffered advice; and a good sprinkling of cranks and fanatics wrote to enlist his aid in their eccentric causes. Every letter which bore an address was acknowledged, and many were replied to at careful length.

He was in continual demand for interviews. The quality papers and the Sunday supplements asked for serious sessions, wanting to cover not only his life story but his views on all the theological and moral questions of the day. The popular papers were lighter-hearted in their approach, but he was equally willing to talk to them, seeing them as a means of establishing some relationship with a public that was rarely in touch with the church. When the members of the Church Information Committee, most of them professional journalists, invited him to one of their meetings in Church House to discuss how he might be helped to cope with the demands of the media, he left them in no doubt that he saw television and the popular press as the primary means of communicating with the non-church-going public, giving him the opportunity to preach – however lightly or indirectly – the church's message. He hoped, he said, that the religious newspapers would understand and forgive him if, when the demands were heavy, he gave priority to the mass-circulation secular press, even the *News of the World*, rather than addressing the faithful through the columns of the *Church Times*.

Among the many articles showing genuine interest and appreciation, there were the few that were snide and malicious. Richard Ingrams, for example, wondered in the *Spectator* how did 'a nice, inoffensive, but totally uninspiring bishop suddenly get lumbered with the top job', and supposed that it was silly to hope that the Church of England might be able to choose as its leader someone of real spiritual authority. The occasion of this particular article was Runcie's most controversial television appearance: a late night chat show with Michael Parkinson. The criticism had started some days before as soon as the programme was announced, and privately Runcie admitted that he had accepted Parkinson's invitation knowing that it was something he would not be able to do once he was actually archbishop. There were murmurs that he was being over-exposed in the media and should hold back, but to the *Daily Star* he said, 'Some will say I shouldn't trivialise my office. But I'll go where people are. People watch Parkinson, so I'll have a go.'

During the show he was easy and humorous, telling jokes against himself and joining in the banter of the occasion, but still able to use the opportunity to speak seriously for a few minutes about his beliefs. The result was that thousands of people who had never consciously paid heed to an archbishop before remembered for long afterwards that here was a new style of primate who could tell jokes, stand up to 'Parky', and still sound sincere about religion.

Plans were going ahead for his enthronement at Canterbury on 25 March, the feast of the Annunciation. It would be a far greater occasion than at St Albans, with many guests from overseas, including all the Primates of the Anglican Communion, the top leaders of other churches – patriarchs, cardinals, and moderators – the Prime Minister and members of the Cabinet, and, it was announced, Prince Charles and Princess Margaret.

An unexpected crisis blew up in the middle of January when the Chancellor, Sir Geoffrey Howe, announced that 25 March – which was a Tuesday – would be Budget Day. It was a surprising and insensitive *faux pas* by the Government, and the newspapers took it up in a big way. Runcie mildly admitted in public that he was disappointed that his friends in Parliament would not be able to come to his enthronement, and a number of leading politicians from both sides of the House declared that they valued their invitations to Canterbury more highly than listening to yet another Budget. There was some rapid work behind the scenes, including a fortuitous meeting on a train between a Church House press officer and a senior member of the Treasury, followed by some late night telephone calls in Downing Street. Eventually the Leader of the House, Norman St John Stevas, announced amid cheers that the Budget would be presented on a Wednesday, the day following the enthronement, instead of on the traditional Tuesday, so that Mrs Thatcher, many members of her Cabinet, and leading members of the Opposition would be able to go to Canterbury.

On 25 January Dr Coggan formally retired and left Lambeth for a cottage in Sissinghurst in Kent, and for a month there was no Archbishop of Canterbury. Then, on 25 February, Runcie once more went through the extraordinary ceremony of the confirmation of his election by the Canterbury chapter which had taken place a fortnight before. This time the confirmation was in the crypt of St Paul's Cathedral, in the presence of the Lord Mayor and Sheriff of London, invited friends, and a very large number of reporters. What made it different from his confirmation as a diocesan bishop was the presence of eight senior bishops as the Queen's Commissioners. They sat, dressed in their scarlet and white Convocation robes, at a long baize-covered table, while Runcie, in plain black and white, made his oaths before them. Susan Young described it in the *Church Times*.

There were officers called the Proxie; the Advocate; the Apparitor-General; the Principal Registrar; and the Queen's Royal Commissioners – the Bishops of London, Winchester, Lincoln, Salisbury, Worcester, Rochester, Southwark, and Derby; with the Bishop of London (Dr Gerald Ellison) presiding in the absence through illness of the Archbishop of York.

And then there was the central figure himself, Robert Runcie, looking awed and, for much of the ceremony, almost insignificant beside the sheer volume of the ritual formalities.

These consisted chiefly of people 'porrecting' (presenting), witnessing, signing and reading certificates, schedules, letters patent, public instruments, oaths and declarations – mostly long on words and short on punctuation. Periodically the documents lapsed into an endearingly human 'and so forth' as if the syntax itself had got fed up with its prosiness and repetition . . .

Most of the proceedings were designed to establish that the election had been correctly conducted, that any objectors had been given a fair hearing, and that the man sitting in the archbishop's chair before the glittering cross of Canterbury was who he purported to be. The climax came, after he had taken the oath of allegiance and made the declaration of assent, with a 670-word sentence pronouncing the election valid and the Archbishop-elect 'a man both prudent and discreet, deservedly laudable for his life and conversation . . .'

Runcie was now officially Archbishop of Canterbury and could sign his name Robert Cantuar: – the traditional abbreviation of Cantuariensis, meaning 'of Canterbury'. Susan Young described how he turned to give his first blessing as primate to a congregation. 'He asked among other things for courage "to strengthen us in all that lies ahead". He meant it for all who were present; but Archbishop Runcie, now visibly moved, gave it a poignantly personal ring.'

Immediately after the ceremony, and after meeting the

demands of the photographers on the steps of St Paul's, he was taken to a luncheon given by the Lord Mayor at the Mansion House. Later that same day he moved into Lambeth Palace to begin his new life in earnest. It was not a comfortable start. He was to camp out in the guest flat while work continued on decorating and refurbishing what would eventually be the family's spacious flat on the first floor. Lindy, most reluctant to move to London, was still packing up at St Albans. She was then to stay with a friend in Earls Court and supervise the work in the palace from there without having to live among its depressing chaos.

To ease the new archbishop into his role, Dr Coggan's senior chaplain and secretary remained temporarily at Lambeth, but it was time for Runcie to establish his own staff. Richard Chartres would continue as his chaplain and closest personal assistant. They had been together so long that they almost thought each other's thoughts, and Chartres more than anyone could draft addresses and sermons in the archbishop's own style and language. Mrs Luckraft, now a deaconess, would remain his personal secretary. Dr Coggan's lay assistant, Michael Kinchin-Smith, a former controller of staff administration at the BBC, would stay at his post to handle the archbishop's secular engagements, his involvement in social and political affairs, including his participation in the House of Lords, and to cope with much of the correspondence from the general public: letters which arrive at Lambeth in their hundreds every day, expressing views on every conceivable subject, asking help and advice on matters which are often heart-rending, praising or criticising almost every archiepiscopal utterance, or simply giving vent to crankiness and abuse – usually in block capitals and a rainbow of coloured inks.

Across the palace courtyard was the office of the Archbishop's Counsellors on Foreign Relations where Canon Michael Moore and the Revd Christopher Hill were responsible for the archbishop's ecumenical contacts, his visits to and from other churches at home and overseas, and all his official ecumenical correspondence, including the regular fraternal greetings which go between church leaders at the great Christian festivals. (When Canon Moore eventually left for another appointment, Christopher Hill was to take over as the Archbishop's Assistant for Ecumenical Affairs.)

To complement that part of the work Runcie had already found his Assistant for Anglican Communion Affairs. The name of Terry Waite had been suggested to him by the former Bishop of Bristol, Oliver Tomkins, in whose diocese Waite, trained as a Church Army captain, had once been director of lay training. Since then he had had a career which uniquely fitted him for the post that Runcie had in mind. He had spent three years in Uganda, organising leadership courses for senior clergy and lay people, and surviving some alarming times during Idi Amin's coup. While there, his work had brought him to the notice of one of the major Roman Catholic orders at a time when all the Roman Catholic communities were changing dramatically, and he had been engaged as a consultant. Based in Rome with his wife and four children, he had travelled extensively throughout the Third World for seven years visiting and advising the houses of the order. By that time he needed a change and a rest, and his twin teenaged daughters needed to return to England to finish their education. So they found a house in London at Blackheath and, despite the fact that Waite was hoping for a few quiet months, he was almost immediately asked to look after the African desk at the British Council of Churches on a part-time basis.

It was while he was settling in there that the invitation came from Runcie, still at St Albans, to discuss joining the Lambeth staff. His task was to handle the archbishop's liaison with the other churches of the Anglican Communion, keeping in touch with their affairs, dealing with correspondence from their members – including, quite often, those Anglicans living under oppressive political regimes and in trouble with their authorities – preparing the way for the archbishop's overseas visits, organising the meetings of the Anglican primates, and eventually preparing for the next Lambeth Conference to be held in 1988. Waite moved into Lambeth Palace two days after the archbishop and Richard Chartres. They made a formidable trio when they appeared together in public as they were often to do, with each of them more than six feet tall: the Archbishop, elegantly precise of movement, flanked on one side by the gravely-bearded Chartres, and on the other by the six feet six inches of black-bearded Waite – soon to be known to the press as the 'gentle giant' – who almost dwarfed the other two by his extra height and huge frame.

Already Runcie was being expected to speak authoritatively on public issues, such as the gaoling of an Anglican priest in South Africa for breaking a banning order imposed on him for his outspoken criticism of apartheid. He had again to take his seat in the House of Lords. He had been in the Lords as Bishop of St Albans since 1973, speaking occasionally on social issues or matters which particularly affected the well-being of the people of his own diocese. As archbishop he was sponsored in the Lords by the Bishops of London and Durham and, two days after he again took his seat, he made a speech on a Bill to help the disabled. He also felt bound to join in a current controversy over whether British athletes should boycott the Olympic Games – due to be held in Moscow that summer – as a protest against Russia's invasion of Afghanistan. Despite his personal relationship with the Russian Church, he joined several other of the bishops, in particular David Sheppard of Liverpool, in advising the athletes not to go. It was a stand which created difficulties among his Orthodox friends, and caused a partial boycott of his enthronement by the Russians. Four Russian hierarchs were to have been present at the service at Canterbury but, in the event, only the Archbishop of Volokolansk came to convey the Moscow Patriarch's dismay at the way the Church of England had been 'drawn into a political campaign against our country and our people.'

His enthronement was very close. To give himself space to prepare for his new spiritual responsibilities, he went away for a short private retreat with the contemplative nuns of the Community of the Sisters of the Love of God, and then spent the day before his enthronement in further prayer and meditation with all the Anglican primates who had come from overseas for the ceremony. He needed that quiet day, not only to keep the tremendous event with all its national and international implications in its spiritual perspective, but also to escape from the demands that were already being crowded upon him by distinguished overseas visitors hoping to seize an early opportunity to catch the ear of the new archbishop.

On the day itself it seemed as though the world came to Canterbury. It took nearly an hour for the official guests to process into the cathedral to a selection of music by the choir, organ, and an orchestra, some of it chosen by Lindy. The diocese of Canterbury was fully represented by its clergy and representatives from public life; the other churches were there in force with no less than five Roman Catholic cardinals, Orthodox patriarchs and archbishops, leaders from the Free Churches, and representatives from the Jewish, Buddhist, Moslem, Hindu and Sikh communities. The politicians who came included the Prime Minister, Lord Chancellor, the Speaker of the House of Commons, the Leaders of the Labour and Liberal Parties, and even Sir Geoffrey Howe who was prepared to neglect his preoccupation with the Budget for a few hours. From the royal family came Princess Margaret and – by helicopter – the Prince of Wales.

There was a reception beforehand in the deanery for the distinguished guests – at which James and Rebecca stole a good deal of the limelight – and then the family lunched quietly together. Then the archbishop dressed in his robes, his rochet with its wide lawn sleeves and, over it, the cope of wild white silk, lined with yellow, its wide gold-thread orphreys matching the gold on his mitre. His friend Jenny Boyd-Carpenter, a self-taught embroidress, had been making his vestments – and looking after his pigs – almost ever since he first went to St Albans, and she had cut this cope in slim panels instead of the traditional extravagant half circle so that its plain white elegance made him look even taller than usual. It would be in dramatic contrast with the gorgeously elaborate robes of the clergy who would surround him in the cathedral.

With Richard Chartres carrying a cross before him, the archbishop walked to the closed west doors of the cathedral and, taking his staff, struck three times for the doors to be opened. He was greeted by the Dean of Canterbury, Victor de Waal, and by the immense congregation. Then, with fanfares and with glorious music, he was enthroned twice: first by the Archdeacon of Canterbury in the throne of the cathedral as Archbishop of Canterbury, and then by the dean in the twelfth-century marble chair of St Augustine behind the high altar, looking down upon the vast array of people, as Primate of All England and Metropolitan that 'by God's grace you may govern and guide this See to which the eyes of all Anglican Christians look as the centre of their Communion and fellowship'.

Philip Potter, the black General Secretary of the World Council of Churches, and Cardinal Hume read passages of Scripture; prayers were offered by the Moderator of the Church of Scotland, by the Orthodox Archbishop of Thyateira, and also by the first woman ever to take part in the enthronement of an Archbishop of Canterbury, Dame Betty Ridley, the Third Church Estates Commissioner. No detail that could involve other churches and other lands was overlooked. The Archbishop of West Africa gave a blessing, a hymn was sung to a Hebrew melody, the Creed was said without the much-disputed *filioque* clause which distresses the Orthodox Churches, a Marian hymn (of sound Anglican theology) was sung before Cardinal Hume read a lesson, and, as saints and martyrs were remembered, the name was added of Oscar Romero, the Roman Catholic Archbishop of San Salvador who had been murdered while celebrating Mass only the day before.

The *Te Deum* was sung, and then the new Archbishop of Canterbury preached in his clear light voice on the authority of Christ's church which begins 'not in the assumption that we possess all the answers, but in our recognition of our poverty of spirit. From that can come a real longing to hear God speak . . .'

I had a dream [he said] of a maze. There were some people

very close to the centre; only a single hedge separated them from the very heart of the maze, but they could not find a way through. They had taken a wrong turn right at the very beginning and would have to return to the gate if they were to make any further progress. But just outside the gate others were standing. They were further away from the heart of the maze, but they would be there sooner than the party that fretted and fumed inside.

I long to be able to speak while archbishop with men and women who stand outside the Christian Church. I would like to say to them, 'You can teach us so much if together we could look for the secret of the maze-like muddle in which the world finds itself.' I ask for your prayers that I may be given the grace to speak like that and to listen . . .

The way of Jesus means reverencing people whether they belong to our party or not. The strategy of Jesus means changing lives with love. This is a hard way and people tend to want it only in theory. The cry is 'the Church must give a firm lead'. Yes, it must – a firm lead against rigid thinking, a judging temper of mind, the disposition to over-simplify the difficult and complex problems. If the Church gives Jesus Christ's sort of lead it will not be popular. It may even be despised for failing to grasp the power which is offered to it in the confusion and fears of our contemporaries. But it will be a Church not only close to the mind of Jesus, it will find itself constantly pushing back the frontiers of the possible – 'For, with God, nothing is impossible.' And it will be a Church confident with the promise of Jesus, 'Lo, I am with you always, even to the end of the ages.'

With more splendid music the service came to an end and the archbishop processed to the great west door to greet and bless the people waiting outside. A tea-party followed, and then dinner at the University of Kent just outside the city; and the following morning there was a reception at the university – the only place where there was enough room – for all the people who wanted to come and see him.

In his sermon he had compared his enthronement to one he would shortly be going to in Africa on his first overseas visit as archbishop. There would be no cathedral, let alone trumpets, there.

This service in Canterbury, so carefully prepared, so magnificently beautiful, speaks eloquently of the glory of God and the dignity which God gives to men and women by loving them. Its pageantry speaks, too, of English tradition of which we are rightly proud – countries like individuals only thrive if they are loved, and I am proud of a religious tradition which, in attempting to blend freedom and religious conviction, has coloured a nation's life and sometimes been paid for in blood. But it may be that the simple service to which I shall go in Africa will prove more eloquent about the uncluttered way in which the Church should live now, about the unpretentious character of real Christian authority. There is no place in our understanding of authority for the Archbishop of Canterbury to visit Africa like some reigning monarch descending on a viceroy. I will be there to share what we have in England with our brothers and sisters, and to learn what they have to teach us about personal discipline and self-sacrifice, and about the fresh joy of being a new follower of Christ.

His promise to be at the enthronement of Archbishop Bezaleri Ndahura when the new French-speaking Anglican province of Burundi, Rwanda, and Zaïre was inaugurated, dated from before his own appointment to Canterbury. Only five years before he had ordained Ndahura as a curate in Luton when the outstandingly able African had been sent to him by his bishop to gain experience of the church in England. It was Terry Waite's first major task to plan that journey.

As he set about it, Waite learned that the Pope would be visiting Africa at the same time. It seemed to offer an excellent opportunity for the archbishop and Pope to meet for the first time on neutral ground, far from the old rivalries of Europe. The Pope was approached and agreed to adapt his programme, and it was organised that the two should meet in Accra two days before Archbishop Bezaleri's enthronement.

Runcie flew to Ghana on 8 May taking Waite, Christopher Hill, and Richard Chartres with him. They stayed with the High Commissioner in Accra and, very early the next morning, were driven to the papal nuncio's house where they were met in the garden by a variety of senior Roman Catholic clergy. Then the Pope came out of the house and greeted them all: a vigorous, attractive figure with a good command of English. After introductions and a few minutes' pleasant conversation he led Runcie indoors, and they spent three-quarters of an hour alone together. It was a very private conversation in which two warm and naturally friendly men established a personal relationship, and in the course of it the archbishop invited Pope John Paul II to be the first Pope to visit England and, in particular, to come to England's most historic shrine at Canterbury. 'We have a martyr there who would appeal to you,' said Runcie, speaking of his predecessor Thomas Becket. 'I know,' said the Pope. 'We have one very like him in Poland – Stanislaus.' He went on to say that he knew very little about the Anglican church, and had never really met any Anglicans before. He was certainly looking forward to coming to England, a country that he admired, but he had not yet been officially invited by his own people. It was a very promising and happy meeting and, at the end of it, they issued a joint statement saying that it had been a joyful and moving occasion, and that time was too short and the need too pressing 'to waste Christian energy pursuing old rivalries'; the talents and resources of all the churches must be shared if Christ was to be seen and heard effectively.

When they parted Chartres and Hill returned to England and Runcie and Waite flew on to Zaïre, the pious pilot slightly unnerving his passengers by praying that they would have a safe journey 'if it be Thy will'. The open-air enthronement was in Bukavu, and Runcie was received with enormous enthusiasm. It was the first of many such overseas tours: a rigorous programme of constant travelling, official welcomes, incessant speechifying, unfamiliar and excessive meals; fêted all the way, and yet constantly having to give out instant interest, sympathy and charm to hundreds of strangers briefly introduced, each one expecting their few moments with this Very Important Person to be made memorable. He had before him a way of life shared only by a select company of world figures: Popes, Prime Ministers, heads of state, and the British royal family. Like them, he would need all his very considerable physical and mental stamina if he were to survive.

Back at home he immediately told Cardinal Hume the details of his meeting with the Pope and urged the Cardinal to make haste with the official invitation. He then returned to his daily round of public engagements, private interviews, and correspondence, always getting up very early in the morning and spending some time in his office before joining his staff in the palace chapel for morning prayers at seven thirty, followed, on Tuesdays and Fridays, by a celebration of Holy Communion. His early start notwithstanding, Mrs Luckraft, who had a flat in one of the wings of the palace, often saw the light still on in his study as she was going to bed at midnight.

To cope with the work load two more appointments were made. Bishop Ross Hook of Bradford was to be brought later in the year from his northern diocese to be chief of staff at Lambeth. He would not only run the organisation of the palace, but would also deal with all routine business with the bishops, and with those disciplinary matters among the clergy which are normally referred to the archbishop.

The other appointment was made in the Canterbury diocese. Runcie knew it was quite unrealistic to imagine he could administer the diocese properly as he had been used to doing in St Albans, and he arranged to delegate most of the responsibility for its affairs into the hands of Richard Third, the Suffragan Bishop of Maidstone who was moving to be Suffragan Bishop of Dover. For all ordinary purposes Third would be diocesan. However, Runcie had no intention of becoming an absentee bishop, or of denying himself the diocesan duties that he enjoyed so much. Like his immediate predecessors he determined to spend as many weekends of the year as he could at the Old Palace in Canterbury, the eccentrically rambling flint and stone house in the cathedral close, which was rebuilt from its ruined state by Archbishop Frederick Temple late in the last century.

Lindy, who was re-establishing her musical life in London and abhorred the thought of trying to live in two houses at once, seldom wanted to visit the Old Palace with its vast rooms and cavernous kitchen quarters, so the running of it was left in the hands of the newly appointed steward, Christopher Igglesden, and his wife, who were ready to cosset the archbishop and to ensure him a peaceful weekend whenever he could escape there. So Runcie established a pattern, which he has maintained, of being driven to Canterbury on about half the weekends of the year, and using the opportunity not only for some quiet reading, but to get about his diocese, holding confirmations, presiding at the synod, and getting to know his clergy and people. For this purpose he appointed David Maple to be his chaplain in Canterbury, filling much of the role that had been Coulton's and Chartres' in St Albans.

At his first Whitsun as archbishop he was in controversial hot water. While still at St Albans he had promised to lead the enormous pilgrimage which annually converges on Walsingham, the shrine in Norfolk which is the centre of Anglican devotion to the Virgin Mary. The shrine had originated in the eleventh century when the lady of the local manor had, in response to a vision, built a replica in Walsingham of the house of the Holy Family at Nazareth. The original shrine was destroyed at the Reformation, but rebuilt by Anglicans fifty years ago (with a Roman Catholic shrine built nearby shortly afterwards). Though some of the Anglo–Catholic trimmings to be found there were not entirely to Runcie's personal taste, his reverence for Our Lady was real and had led him to be quite willing as Bishop of St Albans, to lead the annual pilgrimage. However, in his present role he would be the first Archbishop of Canterbury to do so, at least since medieval times, and such authoritative countenance of the shrine brought strong disapproval from the extreme Protestants who made it clear they would demonstrate against the pilgrimage. Because of the controversy the Duke and Duchess of Kent who had intended to join in the procession were reported to have dropped out. Nevertheless, 15,000 people gathered at Walsingham on that Whit Monday together with television cameras and a large contingent of press men. The Duchess of Kent briefly mingled with the pilgrims almost unnoticed. Runcie, flanked by the Bishops of Truro and Chichester, went in procession through the village past groups of demonstrators with banners: 'Howl Ye Shepherds And Cry And Wallow Ye Principal of The Flock', and 'Keep Yourselves From Idols'. He celebrated the Eucharist in the open air among the ruins of the medieval priory, and even some of the newspaper reporters, bewildered by this unfamiliar face of the Church of England, confessed themselves moved by the occasion.

The archbishop's diary was now full of all manner of engagements. One part of his new role which took him by surprise was the extent of his involvement with the royal family. As primate and first peer of the realm he (with Lindy) was commanded to all state banquets, and had usually to escort one of the royal ladies in to dinner. After the first three or four he pleaded a prior engagement, thinking in any case that 'they won't want this chap turning up *every* time', only to be told that a royal command was exactly that. His more personal relationship with individual members of the family, and the private invitations to him and his wife to Windsor and Sandringham, are not a matter for discussion, but his first public royal occasion was the celebration of the Queen Mother's eightieth birthday when he preached at the service of thanksgiving in St Paul's Cathedral on 15 July in front of the whole of the royal family and the television cameras. From now on he would be expected to officiate at all the royal and state religious occasions; at the weddings, baptisms, funerals and thanksgivings, all of which would expose him to public scrutiny and the ruthlessness of the press, not all of whom were well-disposed. Certain newspapers and individual journalists were prejudiced against their own image of him from the beginning. It was only gradually that he grew a thick enough skin not to be hurt by them.

Meanwhile he and Terry Waite were to be in the headlines for a considerable period over their concern for three English missionaries and a number of other Anglicans who had been taken prisoner by the Ayatollah Khomeini's revolutionaries in Iran. The imprisonment of church members was a not unfamiliar anxiety for the staff at Lambeth. In many parts of the world where Christians stand for human rights against tyranny or prejudice they have risked their freedom and often their lives and, when those Christians have been Anglicans, the Archbishop of Canterbury has felt a special responsibility for them. But no archbishop had tackled a case in quite the same direct way that Runcie tried on this occasion, nor had any of his predecessors had such an experienced 'special envoy' as Terry Waite, willing to walk with delicacy into the lion's den.

The Iranian revolution was two years old, and the small Anglican community in Iran had been under persecution since the Ayatollah's return from exile and the takeover of the country by Moslem fanatics. One Iranian clergyman had been hacked to death; Bishop Dehquani-Tafti and his wife had been attacked in their own home and his lists of church members stolen; church property, including a hospital, had been taken over by the revolutionaries; and all the missionaries were being accused of espionage. When Bishop Dehquani-Tafti came to England for Runcie's enthronement, he was persuaded for his own safety not to go back, and he considered for the time being setting up his headquarters in Cyprus. Then he was horrified to hear that his Scottish secretary, Jean Waddell, had been shot and seriously wounded by revolutionaries who had burst into her flat in Tehran; and a few days later he had the yet more terrible news that his only son had been murdered while driving home from work.

In the middle of August Jean Waddell, having partially recovered from the bullet wound in her lung, was arrested on a charge of spying. At the same time two other British missionaries, John and Audrey Coleman, disappeared. Other missionaries were turned out of the country at a few hours' notice, and a number of Iranian Anglicans were arrested. The radio in Tehran broadcast wild accusations about the diocese being in the pay of the CIA, and incriminating letters, quite ludicrously obvious forgeries purporting to come from the British Embassy, were published.

At this time the saga of the fifty-two American hostages held in their embassy in Tehran had been going on for more than a year, overshadowing any world concern about the handful of persecuted Anglicans. Nevertheless Runcie, keeping closely in touch with the Foreign Office, was sure that mild-mannered diplomacy would be a wiser course than denunciation; a few days after the arrests were known, and routine Foreign Office protests had produced no results, he sent the first of a series of personal appeals to the Ayatollah Khomeini as one religious leader to another.

As there was no response he tried again towards the end of November, asking the Ayatollah to allow him to send a member of his personal staff – Terry Waite – to visit the missionaries over Christmas to take them greetings from their families. 'I want you to be fully assured,' he wrote, 'that this visit would be made on purely pastoral and humanitarian grounds.' There was still no reply, though Waite was patiently doing all he could in London to obtain a visa to Iran.

Shortly before Christmas Runcie's appeal was published in the Iranian newspapers, and Lambeth let it be known that a flight ticket to Iran was being held in readiness in the hope that Waite could get his visa. From then on, all over Christmas, the archbishop and his 'special envoy' were headline news. Would Waite be allowed to visit the missionaries? On the day before Christmas Eve it looked like a definite 'no'; and then suddenly and dramatically on Christmas Eve the fifteen-day visa was granted and, on Christmas Day itself, the archbishop waved off his envoy in front of the television cameras.

News came of a courteous reception in Tehran, but Waite was kept kicking his heels in a hotel. As well as presents and family greetings for the prisoners, he carried another letter from the archbishop to the Ayatollah conveying personal thanks to the Iranian government for allowing the visit, and sympathy with the Iranian people in their 'trials and tribulations'. Patiently Waite tried to make contact with the authorities who could take him to the prisoners. He also telephoned leading members of the Christian community to try and arrange a Christmas service in a local church at which he could convey the archbishop's blessing. Permission was obtained, and the papal nuncio lent his car and driver to take Waite to an Anglican church where he met 'a marvellous group of people'. They prayed together, and he had just started to give an address with a message from the archbishop when a group of revolutionary guards burst in and sat down in the front row with a tape-recorder. The gentle giant in his long black cassock carried serenely on, saying of the captive missionaries that if they were innocent they would be set free. He then gave the blessing from the archbishop and walked up to the guards and shook hands with them. One of them said, 'I like what you say. I will take you to see the Colemans.'

Waite asked to be allowed to hurry back to his hotel to fetch the Christmas presents, and he was then taken to one of the Shah's summer palaces where the Colemans were held. John Coleman, a priest and doctor, celebrated Communion, and Waite was able to give them the photographs and presents he had brought after the guards had first opened and examined them. The following day he was able to see Jean Waddell and one of the Iranian priests in a different prison.

Back at home the newspapers waited with impatient headlines. Would he be able to negotiate their release? It was more than a week before the news came that he had seen the missionaries (but not Andrew Pyke, a British businessman) and was flying home confident that they would be released 'in a matter of weeks rather than months'.

He arrived back in London to a belated family Christmas and a hero's welcome, but it was by no means the end of the story, even though the Iranian authorities had virtually admitted that the charges brought against the missionaries could not be substantiated. The American hostages were released towards the end of January after nearly fifteen months' detention, but there was a sudden alarm about the missionaries as the Iranian militants began to talk about bartering them for two Iranians being held in London in connection with a bombing incident. Waite again applied for a visa so that he could go back to Tehran, and the archbishop asked the press at an editors' luncheon to restrain their indignant headlines so as not to exacerbate the situation.

On 28 January Waite received an assurance from the Iranian embassy in London that the government in Tehran was 'working hard for the release of the missionaries', and a few days later the Iranian President assured *The Times* newspaper that all four Britons would definitely be freed. Waite got his visa and flew out again on 5 February and was able to see Jean Waddell, and then the Colemans three days later. Hopes were raised of an early release, and several times they were expected to be 'returning tomorrow'. Then there was a fresh alarm that they might, after all, be put on trial. The cat-and-mouse game went on for a further three weeks.

By now the General Synod was in session in London, and it turned out to be a triumphal week for the archbishop. At the two sessions that had so far been held since he had been primate he had kept a low profile, but this one was different. From the moment that he took the chair on Monday afternoon, and was able to announce that the missionaries and the Iranian Anglicans really had been released and the Britons were hoping to fly back on Wednesday night, he stepped into the limelight and stayed there the whole week.

Until that session he had not revealed his hand on a number of important issues, but this was a Synod that forced him to show it. There were three really major debates: on marriage and divorce; on homosexuality; and on the latest and most extensive church unity scheme, the proposal that Anglicans, Methodists, the members of the URC, the Churches of Christ, and the tiny Moravian Church, should enter into a covenant together to recognise each other's ministries and sacraments, and to grow towards organic unity.

The archbishop spoke on all three subjects. About marriage he stressed that the church needed to provide much better marriage preparation for the couples who came to it for their weddings, and he remained consistent with the views he had expressed years before in St Albans. 'Some of the strongest marriages I have known have been second marriages, because the teaching about marriage as a life-long bond is communicated sometimes in the most fertile soil; that is, to people who come to church with a sense of failure, longing for forgiveness, and with a hope of building on realistic foundations.' He did not share the view that remarriages in church would 'open the floodgates' to divorce, for the floodgates were already open. The church's marriage discipline must retain a reasoned theology, more accurate biblical scholarship, and a firm hold on the best pastoral traditions of the Catholic Church, then, 'with a strong and firm doctrine of marriage you can afford to be generous about the occasional exceptions which need special treatment'.

On homosexuality he was compassionate but less liberal than the Gay Christian Movement would have liked. He saw it 'neither as sin nor as sickness, but as a handicap; a state in which people have to cope with limitations and hardships, in which the fulfilment of heterosexual love and marriage is denied. If you take this view,' he went on, 'it has a very important consequence for your attitude. We are learning to regard the handicapped not with pity but with deep respect and an awareness that often through their handicap they can obtain a degree of self-giving and compassion which is denied to those not similarly afflicted.' It was known that he had, while at St Albans, ordained admitted but not practising homosexuals, and he added: 'One of my rule-of-thumb tests for ordination would be if a man was so obsessive a campaigner on this subject that it made his ministry unavailable to the majority of church people; then I would see no justification in ordaining him.'

It was on the Covenant proposals that he had kept even

those who knew him well guessing which way his vote would go. He was known to be critical of its Catholic orthodoxy in proposing that senior ministers of the Free Churches should be recognised as bishops by a 'service of reconciliation' rather than by a consecration within the apostolic succession. He said,

I think it is no secret that I have had very mixed feelings about the proposals. I was a supporter of the Anglican–Methodist scheme, and I am eager to see the wounds in English Christianity heal so that we can grow into the church of the English people again . . . but what sort of bishops would we have? Clusters and committees of them, undermining the very notion with which I have been reared . . . What sort of energy-consuming quagmire lies in store behind the easy phrase 'common decision-making' when we long for a church to be energy-creating in the life of a nation, not energy-absorbing?

But he did not think, as most of the opponents of the scheme were asserting, that to enter into the Covenant would be a serious set-back in Anglican relations with the Roman Catholic and Orthodox Churches who were having their own reunion conversations with Protestants in Europe. The real issue was the means of receiving the Free Church ministers into the historic episcopate and, after a tightly argued theological discussion of the difficulties he concluded:

The act of reconciliation and blessing of ministers must be seen as a positive sacramental act of the church approached with the specific intention of incorporating the Free Church ministers into the historic threefold ministry of the Catholic Church; and the positive spirit I am looking for is expressed powerfully in the most ancient Orthodox rite of ordaining a priest. Listen: 'The divine grace which always heals what is wounded and makes up what is lacking, elevate this deacon to become priest. Let us pray for him that the grace of the all-holy Spirit may come upon him.' That is the sort of prayer and trust we need – the divine grace which heals what is wounded and makes up what is lacking – not a churlish sense that God's grace can only act provided there is nothing in the small print to prevent it.

Once again he had turned to Orthodox doctrine to find a way out of a theological impasse that could be acceptable to those who shared his traditional Catholic conscience. But perhaps it was too subtle, for many were disappointed at what they saw as his lukewarm support for the Covenant: they had hoped for a whole-hearted commitment, brushing aside the theological ambiguities in a passionate desire to be united with fellow Christians. But Runcie was too much of a theologian, and too honest, not to voice his unhappiness at the doctrinally unsound means of reconciliation. He voted on that occasion for the provisional approval of the scheme, making it clear that he was still hoping that something could be done to make it theologically more acceptable. But eighteen months later, when the critical and final vote was to be taken, there was little change either in the scheme or his views. 'I am prepared to go forward even with my hesitations,' he said, and hoped that the service of reconciliation would be marked by 'an intense but unaffected love of our Christian neighbour'. Nobody had been willing to predict how the vote would go. There were large contingents in Synod clearly for and against it, and it all depended on the floating voters who had not yet declared themselves. Some say the combination of the archbishop's authority and his hesitation influenced some of those who might otherwise have voted for it. The result – as on other major occasions in the General Synod – was an insufficient majority in the House of Clergy, and the failure of yet another reunion scheme.

It seemed, during that Synod of February 1981, that he was hardly off his feet; and the television lights and cameras seemed to be continually on him. He had several important announcements to make, and one of them was about the Pope. Since shortly after their meeting in Accra it had been known that John Paul II was planning to visit England,

Scotland and Wales in the early summer of 1982, and there had been all sorts of speculation about what form his ecumenical visit to Canterbury would take; it was even suggested that he would celebrate a Roman Catholic Mass in the cathedral. Runcie was able to allay any Protestant fears on that count. 'When (the Pope) comes to Canterbury he will want to come to something specifically Anglican. I hope we may have an ecumenical devotion at the Shrine of the Modern Martyrs in the cathedral. Maximilian Kolbe, who is held in special affection by the Pope, is commemorated there, and we talked of these things when we were in Accra.' He went on to say that after the service in the cathedral he hoped that there would be an opportunity for the Pope to have 'some significant discussion' with the leaders from all the main British churches, and he and Cardinal Hume were sharing the hope that the visit would enhance relations among all the churches. 'In welcoming Pope John Paul to our country and to Canterbury,' he concluded, 'we do so as Anglicans on our own terms. The Pope would be the last person to want us to sacrifice our own theological integrity. But our welcome is sincere, warm, and from the heart.'

Then, appropriately enough, in the middle of the debate on marriage, he was able to make an announcement for which the whole country had been waiting, and the Synod members were almost the first to hear it. Getting to his feet just after eleven o'clock that Tuesday morning he said, with a gentle dig at members who had been gloomily deploring the divorce statistics:

The Archbishop of Canterbury feels a heavy sense of responsibility for keeping the Synod in touch with wider events in the world, and also from time to time a sense of responsibility for cheering the Synod up. Therefore I am sure you will all wish to know that at eleven o'clock this morning the engagement was announced between His Royal Highness The Prince of Wales and Lady Diana Spencer. I am sure the Synod will want to express its happiness at this news and send its best wishes to them;

and also to express how greatly encouraged we are here by the respect in which the marriage bond is held and the witness to it in the life of the royal family.

There was loud and loyal applause, and the archbishop disappeared from the assembly hall to spend the rest of the day in the Church House studio giving endless television and radio interviews as the clergyman who would marry the royal couple. During that week his views were constantly demanded on every subject in the news and, despite the national euphoria about the royal engagement, the plight of the Iranian-held missionaries was still in everyone's mind. They were staying in a hotel in Tehran with Terry Waite, and the cliff-hanging was still going on. They had even been driven to the airport to catch a flight to England and then taken back to their hotel again.

It was while the situation was still so tense that the archbishop was asked for an interview by the Iranian radio service. He had no time to prepare what he would say, and yet he knew that if he put a foot wrong he could still jeopardise the safe return of the missionaries. Never had he had to think so fast and carefully on his feet, for every question was loaded. Why, he was asked, did he think the detainees had been so well treated, and what did he think of Iranian revolutionary justice? He replied that the missionaries were religious people who loved their Iranian friends and had served the Iranian country, and this had been understood and appreciated by their captors. He had been grateful that, even before the evidence against them had been found to be forged, the Ayatollah Khomeini had seen that they were well looked after. He was asked for his view of the Iranian struggle, and he said that he had always supported the struggles of people trying to show obedience to God so that justice, mercy and truth should prevail. Then the real googly was bowled: what did Dr Runcie think of the Ayatollah? He hit it back cleanly if obliquely. In time of revolution, he said, a great deal of spiritual energy was released, and charismatic leaders emerged. It was therefore a matter for gratitude when such a charismatic leader had a devotion to God the All Merciful.

His skill was rewarded. On the last morning of the Synod he was able to announce, in the middle of the debate on homosexuality, 'I am sure the Synod will be pleased to know that I have just heard in the last few minutes that the plane has taken off from Tehran carrying Jean Waddell, John and Audrey Coleman, and Terry Waite; and I am looking forward to welcoming them home tomorrow.'

The room provided at Heathrow airport that Saturday morning for the press conference was packed to the walls with reporters, photographers, and television cameras. As soon as they landed, Jean Waddell and the Colemans were met by the archbishop and their families in a private lounge before coming through to meet the press. The three missionaries were shining with happiness at being home, and they told of their experiences. But nothing that the press could ask could persuade them to speak of their Iranian captors with anything but love and understanding. Jean Waddell sounded almost grateful that the men who attacked her had strangled her unconscious before they shot her. Dr Coleman and his wife said that their worst time was the weeks when they were separated and did not know if the other was alive or dead. But Mrs Coleman had knitted slippers for the guards, and her husband said that he had come to look upon them almost as sons. All three of them declared that they were ready to return to their work in Iran if they were permitted. The newsmen were bewildered. They had never met this sort of love before; and the archbishop was not the only one with tears in his eyes.

Chapter Fourteen

Lambeth – II

Terry Waite continued to work for the release of Andrew Pyke (the British businessman left behind in an Iranian gaol) for the next few months, but his more immediate task was to prepare the way for the archbishop's three weeks' visit to America during April and May. The main purpose of this visit was to preside at a conference of the Anglican primates, a gathering of the archbishops and senior bishops of all the Anglican provinces around the world at a five-day meeting in Washington. But, having in the past been only briefly to the United States, Runcie wanted to use the opportunity to see as much as possible, to meet as many of the people as he could, and to try to understand more of that powerful country from the inside.

He started in the South, at Atlanta; went on to Chattanooga; and at the University of the South, Sewanee, was given an honorary doctorate in divinity. (He had acquired his first honorary DD at Oxford soon after his enthronement, which – to the relief of journalists and headline writers – enabled him to be referred to as Dr Runcie.) He saw something of Maryland before going on to Washington, where on the first evening he preached in Washington Cathedral at a service broadcast on the national television network across America. The next five days were given to chairing the discussion of world problems by the primates, interrupted by an engagement to give an address to the National Press Club, and a lunch with the President of the World Bank. On his final day in Washington he preached again in the cathedral, and the Prince of Wales, who happened also to be visiting America at the time, read one of the lessons.

Throughout this time, Bobby Sands, MP, of the IRA, was on hunger strike in the Maze Prison in Northern Ireland in an effort to induce the British Government to recognise gaoled IRA members as political prisoners. It was apparent that he was near death, and Runcie was under constant pressure from American reporters to comment on the intransigent attitude of Mrs Thatcher's Government. He pleaded that he did not want to say much about the general situation in Ulster until he had been there the following month and had learned more at first hand; but on the ethics of the hunger strikers' position he was firm. He had great sympathy for their families, he said; 'nevertheless, I believe in the Christian ethical tradition that taking your own life is itself an act of violence.' His words were widely reported on both sides of the Atlantic.

Lindy flew out to join him in Los Angeles where she was to give a charity concert, and another in New York. On their way back across the continent they stopped in Iowa where the archbishop visited a hog farm and was given a young Berkshire gilt to add to his small herd of pigs. While he was there in 'the great bread-basket of the world' he challenged 600 well-fed diners on the need to be more deeply committed to feeding the world's hungry. That speech also was widely reported.

In New York he visited Harlem and some of the poor black community, and then he flew home to be greeted by news of the attempted assassination of the Pope: news which came to him as a deep personal shock. He joined other church leaders in calling for prayers for the stricken Pope. But those who surrounded him became suddenly extra conscious of the vulnerability of public figures, and how Runcie himself could be the target for such an attack – not that he would allow any extra precautions. But the alarm was sufficiently widespread for a number of Fleet Street editors anxiously to look out the archbishop's obituary and to have it brought up to date.

His four-day visit to Ireland was an exercise in Christian

diplomacy among the religious factions. He went to talk and to listen to as many of the key figures as he could reach, and in his sermons he made it his mission to remind each side that the other was also Christian. 'We are actually told,' he said, 'to pray for our enemies; and it is a peace strategy. I offer that, with some humility, as a visitor from outside.'

On his first evening he consecrated the new north transept which marked the completion of the Anglican cathedral in Belfast begun eighty-two years before. The Revd Ian Paisley had intended to bring 10,000 Free Presbyterians to protest against Runcie's willingness to talk with the Roman Catholics, but he called off the demonstration when he learned from a confidential source that Princess Alexandra would be at the service, and in doing so he leaked to the public and the press the news that she would be there – to the great consternation of those responsible for her safety.

The following day the archbishop addressed the Presbyterian General Assembly unaware that about fifty members had walked out in protest at his Roman Catholic connections before he began. He again talked about the need to build bridges between the two sides, and received a standing ovation from those members who remained. Most of the feeling against him had been stirred up by Paisley's misinterpretation of what Runcie had said in America about his sympathy and prayers for the families of the hunger-strikers; he translated it into a declaration that he was praying for the now dead Bobby Sands' soul – a notion which offended against both the nationalistic and the doctrinal stance of the Paisleyites. He also protested that Runcie had kissed Cardinal O'Fiaich when he had met him – to which Runcie replied, via a press conference, 'If Mr Paisley is not careful, I will kiss him as well!'

The archbishop talked and prayed with Cardinal O'Fiaich and, on his way south to Dublin, met the clergy of the border parishes, all of whom had buried parishioners murdered in the violence. In Dublin he met both political and church leaders, and finished by preaching at Evensong in St Patrick's Cathedral with leading Roman Catholic clergy present. All of his visit and all that he said was warmly reported in both Irish and English papers. The *Baptist Times* with ecumenical generosity commented that 'since his appointment he has shown himself to be forthright, honest and courageous enough to tackle the many hot potatoes served up to him.'

The time for the royal wedding was drawing near, and on 9 June Runcie had lunch with Prince Charles and Lady Diana and a long discussion about the service. It was Richard Chartres who was principally concerned with working out the details with St Paul's Cathedral and the engaged couple: the hymns, the music, the readings, and the prayers; but public and international interest in every aspect of the event was obsessive. The archbishop was overwhelmed with requests for interviews; so much so that it was the advice of his press officer, John Miles, that he should hold one major press conference on 13 July.

Facing an enormous crowd of journalists from all over the world he answered questions about the form the service would take: an updated version of the *Book of Common Prayer* service with some prayers from the new *Alternative Service Book*. 'It will be basically the same form of service that could be used at any Church of England wedding, however small the church or simple the occasion,' he said. There would, however, be considerable ecumenical involvement, with the Moderator of the Church of Scotland and Cardinal Hume taking part, and the Speaker of the House of Commons, the Methodist George Thomas, reading the lesson. Runcie's old friend from Westcott, Harry Williams, who had been chaplain at Trinity, Cambridge, when Prince Charles was there, would be composing a special prayer for the occasion.

He refused to say precisely what he had discussed with the couple. Such a question put him in difficulties, he said, as it left him poised 'between the cliché and indiscretion'. So he was asked how he usually prepared people for marriage, and replied that it had always been his practice to talk to any young couple about the reasons for matrimony, the bringing up of children, the creation of a new family, and sex. 'There has been in the church a rather distorted attitude to sex,' he said, 'but in the true Christian tradition sex is a good thing given by God which, nevertheless, like all God's gifts, needs to be directed aright.'

For once he had misjudged how the popular press would pounce on his innocuous words. The more serious papers reported what he had said in the spirit that he had said it. But the tabloids were ablaze with headlines about 'Charles and Di's chat on sex', 'Archbishop's sex advice', and 'What I told Di and Charles'. Then next day the inventive *Sun*, never a friend to the archbishop, splashed across its front page: 'WE WERE BETRAYED – Charles and Di in a rage at Runcie'; and in what they called a 'red-hot *Sun* exclusive' reported that 'the Prince was horrified when details of their private conversation were given to the world newspapers and TV yesterday. He told friends "Diana and I feel betrayed." I understand he is unlikely ever to confide in the archbishop again.' The *Sun*'s rival, the *Daily Star*, came to the rescue the following day. 'Honest Runcie was right!' it proclaimed, and went on, 'After all, what *did* he say? As the man who will marry the couple he chatted to them about marriage, sex, and life in the way the Church of England instructs all couples about to be married in its churches.' Sanity was vindicated, and also truth. Prince Charles had indeed been taken aback when he first saw the inflammatory headlines but, with his own wealth of experience of how the more sensational newspapers behaved, he had quickly seen what had happened and wrote a reassuring note to the archbishop. In no way was their growing friendship affected.

While all the preparations for the wedding were going on, Runcie's life was still full of its usual variety. He was visited at Lambeth by the royal family of Hawaii; and by the Dalai Lama, successor of Buddha and exiled god-king of Tibet. He was more than usually involved in the House of Lords speaking against the Nationality Bill on several occasions, on the grounds that it would leave large numbers of Commonwealth citizens stateless and would increase the sense of alienation felt by the immigrant communities in Britain. He managed to annoy a World Council of Churches conference on the status of women by speaking of women's complementary role in the church rather than of their equality.

But early in July he had the satisfaction of seeing the General Synod agree in principle – though detailed legislation would still have to be passed – to the remarriage of divorced people (under circumstances to be defined) in church. There was also a family triumph when his son James, reading English at Trinity Hall, the Cambridge college where his father was once a don, gained a First Class degree. A happy photograph of James with both his delighted parents took pride of place on the front page of *The Times*.

For a year the BBC had been making a television profile of the archbishop. A camera crew had followed him on his visit to America, and was still following him, even into his bedroom as he was dressing for the great day of the wedding. They piled into a car and pursued him as he drove discreetly to St Paul's.

While half the world settled down in front of its television sets to watch the processions make their way to London's cathedral, and waited all agog for its first glimpse of the bride, Runcie put on his new silk cope and mitre made by Mrs Boyd-Carpenter specially for the occasion and in which he had been photographed by Lord Snowdon a few days before. With Dean Alan Webster and the canons of the cathedral he waited at the great west door of St Paul's to greet the Queen and other members of the royal family, and to say a reassuring word to Prince Charles as he arrived with his two brothers. Then he made his way up the side aisle to the chancel to await the bride.

In essence it was like any other wedding, and he conducted it with the same calm and kindly reassurance that he had shown to all the couples he had married in the past. When first the bride, and then the bridegroom, made a nervous slip in the vows they were taking, Lady Diana getting Prince Charles's names in the wrong order, and the Prince getting confused about whose worldly goods he was to share, Runcie hesitated for a moment, and then let it go. He blessed the ring and then, when Richard Chartres as his chaplain brought him the primatial cross of Canterbury, he blessed the couple.

His sermon began: 'Here is the stuff of which fairy tales

are made: the Prince and Princess on their wedding day'; but he said that those who lived happily ever after were those who persevered in the royal task of creating each other and creating a more loving world. 'A marriage which really works is one which works for others. Marriage has both a private face and a public importance. If we solved all our economic problems and failed to build loving families it would profit us nothing because the family is the place where the future is created good and full of love – or deformed.'

To preach briefly and pertinently at such a wedding, speaking directly to the young couple yet conscious of the eyes and ears of the world, was a formidably daunting exercise. The iconoclastic Clive James was cruelly critical in the *Observer*. The archbishop 'drivelled', he said, 'adding further fuel to the theory that he's the man to hire if what you want at your wedding is platitudes served up like peeled walnuts in chocolate syrup: he's an anodyne divine who'll put unction in your function'. The readers were furious and bombarded the paper with protests. 'To millions of Christians the archbishop's sermon was a timely reminder of the fact that happy marriages and loving families have to be won by perseverance . . .' was a typical comment.

Very tired after his most taxing few months, Runcie escaped with his wife on a cruise to the Greek islands, not lecturing this time. Then Lindy came home for a concert and to see a play that James was directing for the Fringe Festival in Edinburgh, while the archbishop went on to Malta for a solitary week of silence and recuperation in a friend's villa put at his disposal. After the wedding he had been, in his son's words, 'knackered', and desperately in need of a rest; but three weeks in the sun restored his resilience. Despite his approaching sixtieth birthday he was still, given a break, able to bounce back from a state of exhaustion.

Among his visits later that year was one to the Low Countries which included the EEC in Brussels where he talked about the English church and the role of Great Britain in Europe. He spoke of the communication problem that the European Community still had in Britain. 'It is going to be hard to make progress if there is no vision of where we are going sufficiently strong to harness the energies which are easily diverted into mutual suspicions and the selfish kinds of nationalism.' He reminded them that Eastern Europe was still culturally and historically part of Europe. 'The Iron Curtain is not a totally insurmountable barrier; our aim must be to re-establish that freedom of travel and mobility of ideas which was possible in medieval Europe'; and he went on, as he did on almost all international occasions, to speak about the world's poor. 'You cannot build any kind of community if you are always harping on your own individual and sectional interests. There are people within our own European community, the handicapped, the unemployed, and the old who need support; but there are also the unimaginably poor in the hunger belts of Asia and Africa who have a claim on our fellow-feeling and compassion.'

He had spoken in Brussels about the need to search for peace, but he surprised many during a debate on disarmament at the General Synod that followed that November by his endorsement of the current policies of the Foreign Secretary, Lord Carrington.

The private member's motion before the Synod was calling on the Government to appoint a cabinet minister as a Minister of Disarmament to work for the control of the arms race. It was supported by most of the speakers, but the Archbishop did not see the point when Lord Carrington was already working to that end.

I speak as someone who has recently found himself at odds with the Government in another place on the Nationality Bill and on a cluster of questions surrounding the Brandt report which seem in danger of promoting insular policies. But I believe at this moment we should welcome and support the statesmanlike way in which the Foreign Secretary wins respect as a genuine seeker for peace and international justice within the present political realities. It may be better to recognise this and his significance in the Cabinet rather than divert our attention to

271

a proposal which might be merely cosmetic, or might seem to be another contribution on the part of the church which is predictably carping and complaining . . .

We should not always assume that we are dealing with a Government which lacks all moral sensitivity in these questions, even though we may well disagree with specific defence policies based on updating the terrible weapons designed to enable us to maintain the balance of a deterrent. While I sympathise with the spirit of those who wish to express themselves and make a specific proposal in this area, I do not find it possible to vote for this motion, and I remain to be convinced that any specific amendment has captured my support.

There was a moment of astonished silence at the unusually blunt authority with which he spoke, and then the debate collapsed. The Bishop of Norwich got to his feet and moved that the 'question be not now put', and that was virtually the end of the matter.

He spent the first three weeks of 1982 in the Far East, starting with six days visiting the church in Burma. There he was the first religious leader to have been admitted into the country since it had closed its doors to foreigners in general, and missionaries in particular, two decades before. He found a small church surviving bravely, deprived of all its privileges, and the once grand episcopal residence housing about twenty families. His next stop was Hong Kong, an area where the Anglican church was growing substantially in numbers with 120,000 children in its schools. From there he became the first Archbishop of Canterbury ever to set foot in China for, at short notice, he received a permit to accept an invitation from Bishop K. H. Ding to visit him in Nanking.

Bishop Ding Guangxun, an Anglican bishop, was the recognised leader of China's one million Protestants who were, under the relaxing regime, again being allowed to come out into the open. The structures of the churches had been destroyed in the Cultural Revolution, and so had denominationalism: the Chinese church's priority was to rebuild Christianity with a Chinese face, not in the old patterns of Europe. It was a fruitful meeting. The archbishop visited a thriving seminary, had an opportunity to speak at a tea-party held in his honour, and took part in a celebration of Communion in Bishop Ding's house. It was a strictly informal visit, but plans were laid for a more extensive and formal one in the not too distant future.

From China they returned to Hong Kong, and then Runcie and Chartres went on to Sri Lanka where they were delighted with the Sri Lankan liturgy with its drums and dancing at the offertory, and its flowers and incense. That, said the archbishop later, was what he believed Anglicanism was all about – the translation of the Catholic and reformed traditions into local culture.

They arrived home in the middle of January with the papal visit very much on their minds. It had been confirmed the previous October that the Pope had recovered sufficiently from his gun-shot wounds to be able to keep to his plans and the date for the start of his visit had been fixed for 28 May. At the General Synod in February, therefore, the archbishop announced some of the detailed thinking about the service at Canterbury.

We should first of all welcome John Paul II on a simply human level. He has been educated both in the most rigorous academic disciplines and by hardship in the war-ravaged Poland of his early years. When I first met him in Ghana soon after becoming archbishop I was astonished by the depth and spiritual quality of his listening, and from many stories and pictures we all know him to be a person of quick sympathy and deep affection. These personal qualities are part of his equipment as a very powerful world Christian evangelist. We welcome a great teacher of the Christian faith and life and a global focus for loyalty who is also potentially a focus for unity . . .

Welcome, then, is the first note of the service. We shall then move into a celebration of our common faith reading the Gospel together, the congregation reaffirming

273

baptismal vows and reciting the Creed. In our attitude to the visit also, I hope that the accent will be on the faith that unites us – the faith that unites not only Roman Catholics and Anglicans, but the other Christian traditions in these islands as well.

The service is designed to ensure that the representatives of the Free Churches are participants, not guests. In addition to the members of the General Synod and representatives of many other facets of national and church life, the congregation will, I hope, include the whole of the Free Church Federal Council – more than a hundred strong – while the Moderator and other key Free Church leaders will have a prominent part in the liturgy . . .

The third aspect of the service takes up the theme of the world-wide church. The Pope will lead a representative group of Christians to the Chapel of the Twentieth Century Martyrs and we shall honour people like Maximilian Kolbe, the Polish priest who died in Auschwitz, Oscar Romero, the Archbishop of San Salvador who was assassinated the day before my own enthronement, and the Revd Martin Luther King, martyr for human rights. Followers of Christ are, like him, still prepared to lay down their lives for their friends. This is our common hope for the future . . . Christians live with this dynamic sense of time which, remembering our beginnings when Jesus Christ walked this earth, and looking towards our hope for the future, has a powerful, transforming effect on the present. The present is more likely to be changed if we are, as churches, looking together in the same direction rather than trapped by staring obsessively at each other.

Four weeks later he paid a two-day visit to Liverpool with a sense of real pleasurable excitement at returning to his boyhood home. He was to celebrate the Eucharist in St Faith's Church in Crosby where he had first learned his Christianity, and even to meet his old primary school teacher, Jessie Gale. However, he was also going to a part of the country where, with a large population of Irish origin,

Catholic–Protestant feelings traditionally ran high, and some demonstrations against the papal visit were expected.

With Richard Chartres and John Miles he went to Liverpool on the Wednesday morning and that day had a familiar round of engagements: he addressed the Liverpool Luncheon Club, met the staff of the diocesan offices, and then all the Merseyside church leaders. The following morning he had breakfast with the Bishop of Liverpool, David Sheppard, and all the clergy from the area of Toxteth, recently made notorious by its riots, and heard at first hand about its many social problems and about the encouraging initiatives that were being taken by the local churches. He then went on to St Faith's where, with a full choir, he celebrated at the altar where he had so often served as a boy. It was a very happy occasion as he met a number of friends from his distant past, and he went on cheerfully with the bishop to meet the Mayor and Mayoress of Liverpool before his address at St Nicholas's Church in the city centre.

There were already demonstrators outside the church when they arrived. When they went in they found that every seat was filled with people who genuinely looked as though they had come to hear the lecture. But the side aisles were crowded with demonstrators who had smuggled in their placards and were now brandishing their anti-Pope and violently Protestant slogans: 'REVIVE THE REFORMATION', 'ROME RULES RUNCIE', 'CALVARY NOT POPERY', 'THIRTY PIECES OF SILVER – HOW MANY FOR RUNCIE?', and crude pictures of the Pope with 'NEVER' scrawled across them.

The archbishop, dressed in his cassock (for this was not a formal service but a simple lunch-hour address) took his place in the pulpit. He was alone in front of the crowd; Bishop Sheppard and the mayor and mayoress were sitting in the congregation, and Chartres and Miles were at the back of the church with the police where they could keep an eye on the trouble-makers. It had been Runcie's express wish that, whatever happened, no force was to be used against the demonstrators, and no one was to be ejected from the church.

He started to speak, and his first few words were about St Nicholas in compliment to where he was. But then, his theme being Church and State, he touched on the church's earliest history and mentioned Pope Gregory. That started the jeers and cat-calls. He asked for calm and tried to carry on, but the boos and hisses grew louder, and there were shouts of 'Judas' and 'traitor'. After another paragraph or so it was clear that he would not be allowed to speak from his script, so he picked up a Bible and said he would read from it, choosing to read the Beatitudes from the Sermon on the Mount, but was interrupted by jeers. Then the demonstrators started singing an anti-Roman Catholic song, beating time with the Bibles they carried. Rapidly the archbishop announced a hymn and, with the help of the organ and lusty singing from the congregation, managed for a few minutes to drown the protestors.

Keeping extraordinarily calm, but feeling that he was in the presence of an evil – all focused on him – that he had never met before, he tried to lead the congregation in the Lord's prayer. Even that was raucously interrupted, though one elderly woman among the demonstrators tried to quieten her fellows. He then said, with sad authority, that Christian discussion had become impossible and that all he was now concerned about was that the church should not be further desecrated by such disobedience to the Lord's will. He left the pulpit to further jeers from the placard-bearers and applause from the congregation, many of whom, including the mayoress, were in tears. He walked up to the altar and knelt before it in silent prayer for several minutes and then, to ever more vindictive abuse, he walked slowly down through the church with members of the congregation reaching out to him all the way to shake his hand.

He had to be protected by the police as he made his way out of the church, running the gauntlet of the jostling and vociferous demonstrators who had not been able to get inside. The bishop and the mayor and mayoress followed him to the vestry, and the bishop suggested that they said a prayer together. Reporters were surging round the door, and John Miles permitted one of them to ask one question:

Would the archbishop be able to forgive those who had so abused him? 'I am trying my best to find forgiveness for them,' he replied. 'But it has been very upsetting.'

His car was brought round to a side door and he got straight into it and was driven to the station. After some lunch and a large brandy he went alone to a first-class compartment to get some rest, and the reaction began. Having kept calm and in tight control of his emotions in the face of violent hatred such as he had never before experienced, he now began to shake and feel terribly cold. For a while he sat there exhausted and trembling, and eventually was able to fall asleep.

At Euston station a BBC television reporter was waiting for him, complete with camera; so were two plain-clothes police officers. For some unexplained reason his aides were unable to find the archiepiscopal car which should have been ready for him, and so they took a taxi to get back to Lambeth. Meanwhile Terry Waite, at Lambeth, who had heard about the fiasco at Liverpool on the radio, had an urgent call from the chauffeur still at Euston saying he had been unable to find the archbishop, and when the three turned up in their taxi they found Waite convinced that Runcie had been kidnapped.

There were yet more television cameras waiting at Lambeth and, getting away from them as quickly as he could, the archbishop went indoors for an hour's brief peace. Such was his life, that an hour was all the time he could allow himself before going out to give another important lecture on Anglican–Roman Catholic relations that same evening in Croydon.

During these months leading up to the Pope's visit all the old Protestant–Roman Catholic sensitivities and bigotries were being brought out of the nation's cupboards, dusted down, and given an airing such as they had not known for generations; and into the middle of these tensions there came at the end of March the publication of the final Agreed Statement of the Anglican–Roman Catholic International Commission. It was a dense and theologically technical document, but it included the suggestion that, in any forthcoming union of the two churches, the Pope would be the 'universal primate'. As a concept it fuelled both the old prejudices and the new ecumenical hopes, and the newspapers made much of it. The archbishop welcomed the statement in general terms as a valuable discussion document, and the Vatican took a cooler view; but it provided a generous gift of ammunition to those who were agitating against the papal visit and Runcie's part in it.

But by this time a new crisis was preoccupying the nation. On 2 April the Argentines invaded the Falkland Islands and within a few days the British Task Force had sailed for the South Atlantic. It was Holy Week, and the archbishop composed two prayers to be used in churches on Easter Day. One was for the Task Force: 'give them gifts of judgment and courage; restore them safely to their loved ones'; and the other was for the people of the Falklands: 'protect them in danger, encourage the fearful, recover their freedom and peace'. He used them himself when he preached his Easter sermon in Canterbury Cathedral. But that same day the Pope for the first time spoke publicly about the threatening conflict, carefully not taking sides between a Roman Catholic country and the country he was shortly to visit. He appealed both to Britain and Argentina to seek 'a peaceful and honourable settlement of the dispute while there is still time to prevent a struggle involving bloodshed'. It was at this point that people suddenly became aware that the crisis could affect his visit. If, by the time the visit was due, Britain and Argentina were actually at war, it would not only be very difficult for the Vatican to be seen to maintain its tradition of neutrality, but it would give great offence to the Roman Catholic stronghold of South America.

Then the plans for his visit to Canterbury were abruptly thrown into confusion by a flying visit to Britain by Archbishop Marcinkus, the Pope's personal bodyguard and security chief. An American one-time footballer, he appeared to have learned his diplomacy among the charging-bull tactics of the American football pitch, and bluntly demanded from the police a number of changes in the Pope's programme at Canterbury which would have virtually eliminated his long-planned ecumenical meeting with the Anglican and Free Church leaders. The first the Anglicans at Canterbury heard of it was from an embarrassed senior policeman.

The news reached Lambeth just as the archbishop was about to leave for a fortnight's tour of Nigeria, and it was he who had to break the news to Cardinal Hume. There followed some very urgent telephone calls between the Cardinal's House in Westminster, the Vatican, and Lambeth Palace before the stormy ecumenical waters were calmed and the now-suspicious Free Churches could be assured that they would have their opportunity for dialogue with the Pope.

But fears were growing stronger every day that if war with the Argentines really came to pass – as looked increasingly likely – the Pope would find his visit impossible. Cardinal Hume said as much at a press conference on 20 April, and the Pope used every opportunity in Rome to call for an end to the conflict. The Anglican bishops themselves were reported to be at odds over the sending of the Task Force. There were those, such as the Bishop of Manchester, Stanley Booth-Clibborn, who thought that Britain would have done better to have accepted a loss of face rather than to risk the loss of many lives; and there were those, like the newly-appointed Bishop of London, Graham Leonard, who used the arguments for a just war to oppose the aggression of a military dictatorship. Runcie inclined more to the latter view and said tentatively that 'within the complexities of an imperfect world, self-defence and the use of limited force in defence of clear principles can sometimes be justified'. Then, as ships were sunk and lives were lost, he wrote an article for *The Times* in which he expressed himself more strongly.

The recent losses to both sides are sickening and they make it all the more important to remember that certain vital principles are at stake. In the House of Lords on April 14 I said, 'the need to ensure that nations act within international law is the bulwark on which the future peace of the world depends. We would be gravely in breach of

279

our moral duty if this country had not reacted as it did in this matter.' This still applies. It was wrong then and it would be wrong now to give any encouragement to those in many parts of the world, not simply in South America, who attempt to pursue territorial claims with armed force.

At the same time we must continue to stand by the interests of the Falkland Islanders to ensure that they and other similarly exposed groups of people in the world do not have to live in continual fear of aggression by more powerful neighbours. Nevertheless, it remains a cardinal principle of the 'just war' tradition of thinking about conflict that the cost of every action should be counted. It is possible for a war to be waged at such a high cost and to entail so much suffering that this would outweigh any attainable good . . .

Churchmen are in no better position than anyone else to judge precisely what actions are or are not necessary for the prosecution of our military pressure. They are not in possession of all the facts; they are not professional strategists; and they do not have to carry the responsibility for the political and military decisions that are made. There has to be some basic presumption that the commanders in the field or in the air or on the ocean will pursue their goals with the minimum necessary force. The retaking of South Georgia [which the British had regained with only one seriously wounded Argentine, and one killed by accident the next day] was an exemplary case. Christians have the responsibility to urge that the force deployed must be subservient and proportionate to clearly defined and morally justifiable political objectives.

During the first week in May, with little more than three weeks to go before the visit was due, Cardinal Hume and Cardinal Gray from Scotland went to Rome to see the Pope and came back on 11 May with the news that the visit would definitely not take place 'if the crisis continued'. There was extreme dismay, not only over the Canterbury visit, which in many ways would be the easiest part to cancel (though it was felt that if it were cancelled it would be very hard to revive the same ecumenical impetus on a future occasion), but because more than three million pounds were being invested in the five-day visit by the Roman Catholics, not to mention the many commercial companies busy producing souvenirs.

Time was getting very short and on 17 May the Roman Catholic Archbishops of Liverpool and Glasgow flew to Rome to try their persuasiveness on the Pope despite the fact that he was reported almost daily to be saying that, though he still wanted to come, he did not think it would be possible. Two days later Mrs Thatcher, to ease the situation, said that she would not be offended if the Pope did not include a meeting with her during his visit, and it was hoped that this gesture would appease Argentine feelings. Then Cardinal Hume was called to Rome again to take part in a special 'Mass for peace', concelebrating with the Pope and three Argentine cardinals. The ecclesiastical battle was nearly won and, on 22 May – with less than a week to go – the Cardinal arrived back in London saying that the visit was '99 per cent certain'. That very day the British reinvaded the Falklands, but three days later it was announced as certain that the Pope was coming. Three days after that he arrived.

His first full day included a meeting with the Queen, and he flew by helicopter to Canterbury the following morning. The archbishop was waiting for him as he landed in a local park and together in the 'popemobile' they drove through the modest crowds in the streets of Canterbury to the cathedral close. They had met as friends, and each was delicately careful not to upstage the other. Runcie found John Paul an older, frailer man than the one he had met in Africa before the nearly-fatal assassination attempt, and throughout that momentous morning he appeared to guide and hover protectively over his white-robed guest as he first showed him the sights of Canterbury from the popemobile, and then, when they reached the cathedral, introduced him to the Dean and canons who were waiting. Then Mrs Runcie and other guests were introduced before the archbishop led the Pope into the deanery to meet the Prince of Wales.

For an hour the congregation had been streaming into the cathedral. Security was extremely high; electronic passes were issued, and plain-clothes policemen posted at almost every pillar inside the great church. The whole event was broadcast live on television, and the congregation already seated in their places could watch on the television screens inside the cathedral the slow informal progress of the archbishop and Pope towards the west door; the Pope having posies of flowers pressed into his hands at every step while the security men watched every movement of the crowd.

Then they entered the cathedral, the Pope and the archbishop together, and, with a fanfare of trumpets, the whole congregation burst into applause. As he walked up the aisle with the Pope at his side, the choir singing a glorious introit, Runcie was mentally pinching himself in an effort to believe what was happening. He, Robert Runcie, with Karol Wojtyla, as Archbishop of Canterbury and Pope, were healing many hundred years of bitter history. The lineal descendants of St Gregory and St Augustine were at last together – in Canterbury – in love and charity.

With hearts full and overflowing with all that the occasion meant they both knelt before the nave altar in silent prayer. And then the archbishop helped the Pope to his feet and said, 'Your holiness, beloved Brother in Christ, in the name of the Lord we greet you.' And before the altar they clasped hands and embraced, and the crowd again broke into applause. The archbishop reminded the people that Pope Gregory had sent Augustine to preach the word of God to the English race, and that Augustine had been the first Archbishop of Canterbury. 'I rejoice that the successors of Gregory and Augustine stand here today in this great church. But our unity is not in the past only, but also in the future.'

The service continued as had long been planned, and Clifford Longley wrote of it in *The Times*:

The Church of England has never paid a more remarkable compliment to anyone than its service in Canterbury

Cathedral for Pope John Paul. And it covered itself with glory in the process; neither demeaned nor diminished nor upstaged by its illustrious guest, it did its very best for him, and he for it.

No Pope has ever paid another church such a compliment either. There he was, not the man in charge, doing what the order of service said he had to do, accepting whispered hints from the Archbishop of Canterbury at his side, and so obviously moved and impressed by this unique encounter with another system's beating heart.

They let him preach to them, and he did not fail them; then let him bless them, move them to tears, lead them in profound reflection, and survived with their dignity and integrity enhanced . . .

Anyone who tried at any point in that service to explain it as the Bishop of Rome meeting an assembly of heretical laymen, whose only duty was to return individually to the one true fold at once, would have found it just could not be done; every moment contradicted such a hypothesis.

So that neither Pope nor archbishop should take precedence over the other, the ancient Canterbury Gospels, said to have been brought to England by Augustine fourteen hundred years before, were enthroned on St Augustine's Chair, and the Dean brought them to the Pope and archbishop for them to kiss. Then the representatives of the different churches prayed for the world and the church, the Pope spoke to the people, and all who were present renewed the baptismal vows that they all held in common.

All the bishops of the Church of England, the Primates of the Anglican Communion, and cardinals and senior clergy from the Roman and other churches were crowded round the altar, and the Pope greeted them all with the kiss of peace while the choir sang the church's ancient hymn of praise, the *Te Deum*. Then a quiet procession of seven people, including the Pope, archbishop, an African bishop, and a black woman from a Pentecostal church in Brixton, went to light candles for the six named modern martyrs and all the unknown martyrs of our own time. The service was nearly over. The congregation sang 'For all the saints' with all the fervour they could muster; the archbishop and Pope together blessed the people and embraced once more, and then together and alone they left the church, the television viewers having a last glimpse of them as they walked side by side, deep in conversation, through the cloisters.

It was indeed the high point of Robert Runcie's first three years as Archbishop of Canterbury, and it is difficult to see what in the future could match it. But – please God – it will be many years before the story of his archiepiscopate can be written in full, and it is far too early to try to assess what his place will be in history, though all the indications are that he will be accounted an outstanding archbishop of the present century.

He has learned to play his present role with confidence. He frankly enjoys mixing with statesmen, politicians, and men and women of affairs, just as he genuinely delights in getting back to Canterbury, or among local church gatherings, and doing the things he would do, and meeting the people he would meet if he were still a diocesan bishop or a parish priest. Politically he has been both approved and disapproved of by both sides. There are those on the Left, particularly on the CND Left, who see him as a figure of the Establishment with friends in the Thatcher Government, supporting hawkish policies by the very fact that he will not espouse the cause of unilateral nuclear disarmament. But he has also been complained of as a wet and trendy cleric, not least over what may prove to be one of his greatest sermons: that at the Falklands service in St Paul's after the fighting was over and the British had won back the islands. For though he did praise the courage – and the restraint – of those who fought, he angered some Conservative members of Parliament by not sounding a fanfare of triumph:

> While giving thanks we also mourn for grievous losses. Thank God so many returned, but there are many in this cathedral who mourn the loss of someone they love, and our thoughts go out to them. We must not forget: our

prayers for remembrance will not end this day.

They remind us that we possess the terrifying power for destruction. War has always been detestable, but since 1945 we have lived with the capacity to destroy the whole of humankind. It is impossible to be a Christian and not to long for peace. 'Blessed are the peace-makers for they shall be called the sons of God.' This was one of the themes to which the Pope repeatedly returned during his visit to this country. His speech in Coventry was particularly memorable when he said 'war should belong to the tragic past, in history. It should find no place on humanity's agenda for the future.' I do not believe that there would be many people, if any, in this cathedral who would not say amen to that. War is a sign of human failure, and everything we say and do in this service must be in that context . . .

War, demonstrably irrational and intolerable, has left a terrible mark on this century, it has claimed tens of millions of victims and even now occupies some of the best talents and resources of the nations. The great nations continue to channel their energies into perfecting weapons of destruction, and very little is done to halt the international trade in arms which contributes so much to the insecurity of the world . . .

Our hope as Christians is not fundamentally in Man's naked goodwill and rationality. We believe that he can overcome the deadly selfishness of class or sect or race by discovering himself as a child of the universal God of love. When a man realises that he is a beloved child of the creator of all, then he is ready to see his neighbours in the world as brothers and sisters. That is one reason why those who dare to interpret God's will must never claim him as an asset for one nation or group rather than another. War springs from the love and loyalty which should be offered to God being applied to some God substitute, one of the most dangerous being nationalism . . .

People are mourning on both sides in this conflict. In our prayers we shall quite rightly remember those who are bereaved in our own country, and the relations of the young Argentinian soldiers who were killed. Common sorrow could do something to reunite those who were engaged in this struggle. A shared anguish can be a bridge of reconciliation. Our neighbours are indeed like us.

He deeply offended those who had come hoping to applaud the successful defeat of the enemy; instead, he reminded them – as he had reminded both the warring factions in Ireland – that Christ commands that our enemies are among those we must specially pray for. But what else, as a deeply conscientious and compassionate Christian, could he say?

He remains an intelligent Christian pragmatist, with an observant eye and a thorough knowledge of human nature, and with a political sense – in the widest meaning of that phrase – which takes into account the whole context and the many ramifications of any situation. He is well equipped to be a wise, resolute and compassionate archbishop amid the complexities of the modern world, but not a charismatic leader in the sense of a Pied Piper leading the church into an absolutist position. Neither will he entice it to pursue quixotic visions. That is not his style. He does not have the single-mindedness of the great campaigner, for he has never lost his compulsion to listen to all arguments and to acknowledge that the other side (unless it is an obvious evil) might also have a case. He will not be the sort of leader demanded by those looking for a schoolmaster to tell them – or, more often, to tell others on their behalf – what to do. He accepted in his enthronement sermon that the church had a duty to give a firm lead, but 'a firm lead against rigid thinking, a judging temper of mind, the disposition to over-simplify the difficult and complex problems'. His own thinking is not rigid and, judging from what he has recently said about all the best arguments about the ordination of women being in favour of women priests, it will be surprising if he ever again votes against them.

He has been charged with ambition as though ambition in a man of God is *ipso facto* reprehensible. But of what does it consist? When a man is blessed with both great ability and great energy he seeks to use them, meeting challenges head on. Once one job is successfully grappled with, he looks for another. And though his own high standards may cause his confidence to falter in the face of some large new task, it is those same standards that drive him on to further achievement. Each job he has done in the church, starting with his brief curacy, he has done to the best of his formidable ability, but always with capacity to spare. Even when he was a diocesan bishop those working close to him felt that he needed and was unconsciously looking for a wider canvas.

This natural progression has taken him to the top job in his particular career structure, and it is only now that he really seems at full stretch. The real danger is exhaustion, physical and spiritual. The alarms that were raised at the time he was appointed about the sheer weight of demands made on any man who becomes Archbishop of Canterbury were justified, but set in the wrong key. Robert Runcie was one of the few men with the energy and resourcefulness to meet those demands, but a Parkinson's Law is now operating. The fact that he has built up an able staff and has organised his working life so as to delegate much of his routine work simply means that he takes more on.

It is his positive attitude towards his role that enlarges and enhances it. He still thinks strategically. He believes, for instance, that as a world religious leader he has opportunities to play a part in national and international affairs; in particular in relating to other religious leaders – as in his approaches to the Ayatollah Khomeini – and also in conversations with many of the world's secular leaders. He has no papal pretensions. His authority among the autonomous churches of the Anglican Communion is as difficult to define as the *esse* of Anglicanism itself; but he remains a focus of unity and affection. He welcomes the indigenisation of the overseas Anglican churches, seeing it as a particular Anglican gift to translate the ancient catholic faith into local cultures; but he knows that that does not altogether answer the question of what is distinctive about Anglicanism.

To grapple with these issues, and also to meet the frequent criticism that one does not have to believe anything in particular to be an Anglican, he has pulled together the Doctrine Commission after its interlude on the wilder shores of radical theology, and has set before it an agenda that should lead to a clearer and more authoritative statement of the belief of the Church of England. He himself cherishes the freedom that his church allows to explore the truth, but that exploration needs the tools of sound theology. Just as, when he was principal of Cuddesdon, he insisted that his students should have good theological teaching, and as Bishop of St Albans he initiated the same high standard of theological training for his laity, now he wants it for the church at large.

He is still a teacher himself. He tries to be selective and discriminating about his preaching and speaking engagements, and his staff who keep his diary struggle to keep them under control, but there are so many of them that his diary is filled two years in advance. Each one of those engagements is thoroughly prepared for. Though one of his staff might write the first draft of what he will say, and though some of the material in it might have been used more than once, he makes it his own; going through it, adding his own touches, having it revised and revised again. Then, when he is in the car or train travelling to where he is to speak, he will go through the script yet again, worrying with his chaplain whether the opening passage is 'too jokey', whether the local allusions are scrupulously accurate, and making marginal notes in handwriting that only he can decipher. And if the occasion is a service or some other ceremony, he will also study the service sheet or programme in close detail so that he knows precisely what will be expected of him, where he will put on or take off his mitre – or his microphone – where he will sit, at what point he will rise to speak. It is this attention to detail beforehand which makes his public appearances seem so relaxed and spontaneous.

He demands the same sort of briefing and puts the same sort of work into the time he gives to the administration of the Church of England, though here he has also delegated many of his routine responsibilities to other bishops; for instance he only attends the Board of Governors of the Church Commissioners two or three times a year, having delegated the regular chairmanship to a senior bishop. At Church House he has a close and trusting relationship with Derek Pattinson, the Secretary-General and chief bureaucrat of the Church of England, who in his own and different way matches Runcie in ability. There is no one who knows the General Synod so well, or has his finger so accurately on the pulse of ecclesiastical politics as Pattinson and he performs the same sort of briefing function for the archbishop in these areas of his expertise as do the key members of the Lambeth staff.

But it is not only on these public and administrative fronts that the archbishop operates. He is still a deeply pastoral bishop and an affectionate human being. His pigs have gone to a residential farm for mentally retarded teenagers, and he will always find time to visit those teenagers just as he takes an enduring interest in another home for emotionally disturbed young people. His enjoyment of pastoral occasions is genuine and trouble-taking. A word in his ear that some person present is in special need of comfort – or of congratulation – and he will, with instant sympathy and sensitivity, give that person the whole of his attention until he or she is left glowing with the reassurance the archbishop has been able to bestow. On more ordinary social occasions, however, this charm and immediate rapport has its dangers. It can mislead people into thinking he has adopted them into a more personal friendship than he intended, with the occasional embarrassing result that they have thereupon felt themselves at liberty to turn up to tea at Lambeth or Canterbury.

In part he finds his relaxation in moving from one type of work to another, but he also conscientiously tries to play 'geriatric' tennis on the public courts adjoining the Lambeth Palace gardens or with the King's School boys at Canterbury. He also enjoys a weekly swim. He occasionally reads a novel and on a rare free evening dozes in front of the family television set, or he and his wife have dinner with friends. Their holidays are important, but always in danger of being eroded or broken into, as one was by a royal baptism. They are, however, the one time he and his wife can spend together, some compensation for the way so much of their daily relationship has been sacrificed to the incessant demands of his job.

Lindy Runcie has now settled at Lambeth, though she spends one day a week at the small house they have bought in St Albans where she gives piano lessons to her St Albans pupils. (The house also gives her the security that all clergy wives need who know that sudden widowhood would deprive them of their homes as well as their husbands.) Now that her children are grown up (James, trained as a drama director, works for the BBC, and Rebecca is at university) her music has virtually taken over her life and she practises for several hours every day. Since her husband was appointed to Canterbury she has also become a media personality in her own right, and her outspoken repudiation of the traditional image of a clergy wife occasionally makes ecclesiastical hairs stand on end. But this has also led to her being discovered as a pianist of sufficient calibre to be in great demand for charity concerts. It is to her everlasting regret and frustration that, great though her dedication as a pianist is, her performances will always be limited by the small size of her hands, but in three years her concerts have raised nearly £100,000 for a range of good causes. With her passionate and fiery personality she has not been an easy person to be married to, but neither has her workaholic husband. It is a triumph for both that they have managed so well, and that they are still able to have fun and happiness together.

Robert Runcie has been spoken of by many people as an enigmatic character whom nobody will ever really know because there is some great guarded citadel at the centre of his being. This has not been my impression. Complex, yes: one has to accept that here is a man whose instincts as a romantic traditionalist are always in tension with his highly-trained critical and sceptical mind. Temperamentally he is a conservative, not least in his Catholic concept of the church; but intellectually he is a liberal, keeping his eyes fixed on the Christian truths while accepting that the road towards them can have its rough places made smooth in new and modern ways. In this his fixed faith and pragmatic approach become compatible and understandable. As for this secret centre that some of his friends have referred to, it seems more likely that what was once a reserve about his origins as he made his way in the world has now become a defence mechanism to preserve some space and sanity in the face of the voracious demands being made upon him. His instant friendliness and sympathy could lead him to being eaten up by other people if he did not keep some distance between them and his private self.

Having accepted these tensions between his instincts and intelligence, and between his sympathy and self-preservation, I believe he is a consistent character, exceptionally able, with qualities remarkably adapted to his present role. He has never ceased to drive himself hard and, whether or not that is the result of the pressures upon him as the youngest child in that family in Crosby so many years ago, it is a trait that God can use to his own purpose. Robert Runcie is a very remarkable man, and is well on the way to becoming a great archbishop.

April 1983

Postscript

Nearly two years further on the pressures are no less. The more the archbishop does, both at home and abroad, the more hopes and expectations are raised and invitations come flooding in. His diary is filled with official engagements two years in advance, and even a personal luncheon date can take six months to arrange. And this is despite a new staff at Lambeth Palace dedicated to trying to keep the demands made on him under control.

At sixty-three he is as resilient as ever. Extreme tiredness can make him red-eyed and talkative and more than usually self-disparaging. But a day's rest enables him to recover his acute and trouble-taking grasp of the multifarious concerns that confront him. Almost obsessively he talks of the amount of time it takes to sort out his priorities. He says he has tried to become 'brisker' with people so that they do not take up so much of his time, but this is something one hesitates to believe because it goes so much against the grain of his personality. The personal and pastoral sides of his work, such as the weekends he spends in Canterbury confirming and visiting and meeting local people like any other diocesan bishop, are not only important to him for their human contact, he finds them a relaxation. His way of life demands that he keeps to timetables; his instinct is not to leave until he has talked to every person in the room.

It was this instinct, the desire to establish personal relationships, which led to his committing himself to visit as many as possible of the provinces and dioceses of the Anglican Communion before all the Anglican bishops should again converge on Canterbury for the Lambeth Conference in 1988. It was an extravagantly generous undertaking because the thirty Anglican Churches and provinces (not to mention the individual overseas dioceses still under the personal jurisdiction of the Archbishop of Canterbury) cover half the countries of the world with a great variation in both climatic and political temperature. In addition to these taxing journeys there were a growing number of ecumenical invitations to visit other churches abroad which could not be refused, as well as overseas meetings of the World Council of Churches and the Anglican Consultative Council. From the autumn of 1982 to the spring of 1984 he made ten overseas visits, several of them very extensive tours; and in the twelve months following April 1983 he spent no less than 118 nights out of the country on these journeys.

Having paid a flying visit to Bermuda in the autumn of 1982 to sort out a diocesan crisis, he went to Singapore for five days where he enthroned Moses Tay Leng Kong as Bishop and met all the Anglican bishops of South-East Asia. The following spring he spent five colourful days in Hawaii on his way to New Zealand as a guest of the New Zealand Government. He met Mr Muldoon, the Prime Minister, with his Cabinet and Opposition Leaders, and travelled widely over both islands to meet bishops, clergy, and local people, to visit schools, and to spend a night in the Maori campus. At the Anzac Day ceremonies he gave the main address and laid a wreath on the Auckland war memorial in company with the Prince of Wales who happened to be visiting New Zealand at the same time. That evening he dined privately with the Prince and Princess.

While in Auckland he came up against a problem that continued to dog him on his travels. New Zealand is an Anglican province that has been ordaining women priests for some years, and he was to take part in an outdoor Eucharist on the Ellerslie racecourse at which two of the celebrating priests would be women. He was saved the embarrassment of finding himself actually celebrating communion with them by being asked to preach while Archbishop Paul Reeves of Auckland presided at the altar. In a press interview Runcie said he would not refuse to take communion at a service in which women priests were involved, but it would not be honest for him to concelebrate with them because 'it would not reflect the situation' that actually existed in the Anglican Communion and that, as Archbishop of Canterbury, he had to take into account the views of all the other Anglican Churches including his own.

However, at the Sixth Assembly of the World Council of Churches which met in Vancouver for two weeks at the end of July he did find himself celebrating in company with women at the altar, but they were not Anglican priests. Nine hundred Christians of all colours, nationalities and churches (with the notable exception of the Roman Catholic Church which was not a member but sent a handful of observers) had gathered under the banner 'Jesus Christ is the Life of the World'. By many accounts the archbishop was the outstanding personality among them, and it was he who was asked to preside at the great Eucharist that was the highlight of the Assembly's worship. The liturgy used was the 'Lima rite' which had been drafted by the WCC Faith and Order Committee when the WCC met at Lima in Peru in 1982. The archbishop celebrated at an open-air altar before this huge crowd of Christians, and was flanked by a row of assisting ministers, two of whom were women, each representing a different church and a different nationality.

Predictably, many of the Assembly's debates had a clearly left-wing, anti-nuclear, anti-American bias which caused some difficulties for the English delegates who felt that the one-sidedness of the political prejudices being shown did little to contribute to the causes of justice and peace which were the Assembly's main concern. It was left to the archbishop, whose friendship for the Russian and other Orthodox Churches was well known, to try to adjust the anti-American bias by speaking more firmly than any other church leader was prepared to do in criticism of the Soviet Union's treatment of Russian dissidents and the invasion of Afghanistan. He used the occasion to make a strong public appeal to the Soviet Government on behalf of Father Gleb

Yakunin, a Russian Orthodox priest then serving a five-year sentence in a labour camp.

Very shortly afterwards he was off to Nairobi for a meeting of the Anglican primates, a gathering of twenty-five of the archbishops and presiding bishops of the Anglican Communion. Between them they represented many of the small and threatened countries of the world, and they had fears to share about the spread of injustice and oppression, the growth of nuclear weaponry, the increase of hunger, and the 'sense of helplessness which drives us to declare unequivocally that there is no solution without God'.

The main item on the agenda was a discussion of plans for the 1988 Lambeth Conference, but many of them also had domestic worries. The Primate of Japan wanted more training for new bishops; the Archbishop of Armagh was concerned about the difficulties of mixed Anglican–Roman Catholic marriages in Ireland. Some archbishops were wanting advice on exorcism, while the exiled Bishop of Iran was worried about how his people could be confirmed without his presence and ministry. (The solution suggested was that they should be anointed with oil specially blessed by the bishop. This ceremony later took place in Lambeth chapel, and the oil was taken to Iran by Terry Waite.) The archbishops of Africa wanted a full discussion of what it was that held the Anglican Communion together in unity, and it was agreed that this should be considered by the Inter-Anglican Theological and Doctrinal Commission.

After less than a fortnight back in England the archbishop, accompanied by Christopher Hill, went to Germany, both West and East, for the celebrations of the five hundredth anniversary of Martin Luther's birth. He was glad of this excuse to give emphasis to Anglican–Lutheran relations. The two churches in the course of their history had never unchurched each other, but relations had been distant and, in recent years, overshadowed by the growing Anglican interest in unity with Rome. Yet the Lutheran and Anglican Churches had much in common, and the archbishop was particularly asked to speak to the Lutheran Synod in West Germany about the Church of England's abortive attempt to enter into a covenant of shared ministries with the other non-Roman churches of England.

Across the border in East Germany he was determined not to be manipulated by the Government. At the state ceremony for Luther held in the state opera house he declined an invitation to sit in the official box, but took his place with the German church leaders. In Leipzig he preached in the church of St Thomas where Bach is buried. He spoke warmly of Anglican–Lutheran relations, and of the courage and integrity of his friend Bishop Hempel, the presiding Bishop of East Germany who was also a president of the World Council of Churches. On Remembrance Day he preached in Dresden, the town – now twinned with Coventry – that was almost completely destroyed by British bombing during the Second World War. His text was 'blessed are the peacemakers', and he made it clear that, while he supported the churches' work for peace, he did not associate himself with the East German Government's 'peace movement':

> There is much Utopian talk about Peace, Peace, where there is no Peace. This talk is shallow and promotes cynicism. Christians believe that the truth is that this world is in rebellion against God. There is a profound egoism in individuals and a demonic complexity in the relations between groups and states which make easy talk about peace impossible . . . The Christian church cannot just lament the evils of the day; we must work urgently and strenuously for a new way. We must fight against complacency and any callous acceptance of the present reality as anything but madness. A number of so-called developed societies are spending their best brains and a very large proportion of their resources planning for lunacy and destruction. This is a world where children are dying of hunger while we continue to pour our best efforts into preparing for Armageddon.

On 1 December he began another visit to a communist state. With Terry Waite, Richard Chartres, and a delegation from the British Council of Churches, he flew to Peking for three weeks in China. He had received a personal invitation for such a visit in 1982 when he had briefly crossed the border from Hong Kong as the first world Christian leader ever to step on Chinese soil. In the meanwhile, as part of the opening up of the churches in China, a group from the China Christian Council had visited Britain and had invited the BCC. As the archbishop was President of the BCC it seemed logical to combine the two tours. Further contacts had been made as Runcie met the Chinese Prime Minister and Foreign Minister when their paths had crossed in New Zealand.

In China they were able to see some of the newly-revived church life. Two thousand worshippers came to a thanksgiving service in Shanghai, and there were opportunities for groups of delegates to visit local churches, bible study classes, factories, and farming communities. The archbishop, with Dr Philip Morgan, Secretary of the BCC, was treated as a state guest. He met Madam Chou En Lai and various political leaders, and he had an hour's conversation with China's President Li Xiannian. Runcie expressed his gratitude for China's new 'open-door' policy, but asked what were the implications of the 'spiritual pollution campaign' he had heard about. He received assurance that the campaign was not directed against the churches but against pornography and other immoral influences. 'We protect normal religious activities by our constitution,' said the President, and added that if religion had been regarded as spiritual pollution 'we would not have had you here, Archbishop!'

Runcie had also been invited to give two lectures. In Shanghai he talked to the Academy of Social Sciences about the place and influence of Christians in British society. In Peking his audience wanted to hear about the British Christians' experience of China. He spoke of his appreciation of the Chinese churches' Three Self Movement: self-support, self-government, and self-propagation. 'Far from wishing to see any foreign mould imposed upon the church in China,' he said, 'my companions and I have been delighted by every sign that the worship and the spiritual life of the Christians is becoming more deeply rooted in your rich and ancient culture.'

Early in 1984 there were two more major overseas visits. At the end of January the archbishop went to preach at the enthronement of Yona Okoth, the new Archbishop of the Province of Uganda and successor to the murdered Archbishop Janani Luwum (now regarded as a Christian martyr) with whom Okoth had spent time in the notorious Luzina gaol. By this time Runcie had a new chaplain to accompany him and Terry Waite. Richard Chartres, having been his personal aide for eight years, had left to become vicar of a parish in Westminster, and his place had been taken by John Witheridge, a tall, dark, neat man, with a wife and three children and a Double First in English and Theology.

Witheridge was chaplain and head of religious studies at Marlborough College when he received the archbishop's invitation to join the Lambeth team. He had come from the St Albans diocese and had been one of the last men Runcie had ordained but, since leaving the diocese, he had only met the archbishop on one occasion and was not at all aware that he had made any particular impression. Yet Runcie had noticed him at the time of his selection for ordination, had (unknown to Witheridge) argued on his behalf when ACCM had hesitated about whether the young man had had a wide-enough experience, and had kept an eye on him. Within months of receiving the archbishop's invitation Witheridge had found himself installed with his family in one of the houses in the grounds of Lambeth Palace, learning to adjust his own academic style in the preliminary drafting of archiepiscopal addresses to the archbishop's easier tone of voice. He also, almost immediately, found himself accompanying the archbishop on one of his less comfortable overseas journeys.

Three days before they were due to leave for Uganda there had been a fresh outbreak of guerilla killings and four Europeans had been shot when driving not far from Kampala. Under President Obote's hard-pressed left-wing Government the country was in a state of deteriorating security. But the archbishop refused to consider postponing his visit, and his wife agreed. 'He's been in dangerous places before,' said Lindy to the *Daily Express*. 'I assume there's a certain Gent looking after him.'

His visit was welcomed by the Ugandan Government as a show of confidence which could help persuade the World Bank to approve further development loans. The archbishop used the opportunity of a conversation with Obote to press for better conditions for the one hundred and thirty thousand people – mostly women and children – in Uganda's refugee camps. Then he preached to five thousand people at a joint service in the Roman Catholic Cathedral in Kampala where he appealed for unity both in the churches and the nation. Tragically, that same day, which was the eve of the enthronement, there was a new atrocity. A village outside Kampala was attacked by guerillas and thirty people were massacred and many more savagely wounded. At the enthronement the archbishop assured the congregation that 'the world has not been deaf to the stricken cries of the people of Uganda. We have heard the screams of a people subjected to appalling suffering at the hands of godless and cruel men . . . if, together, Christians in this land would stretch across the chasms which separate you, and take hold of the hand of fellowship, what a powerful witness that would be to all your people!'

Their next tour was in very different circumstances. The archbishop, with Waite and Witheridge in attendance, spent March extensively touring the Anglican Province of the West Indies. After the first three days in Belize where they visited the local churches and the British troops stationed there, the main part of their journey round the Caribbean islands was made easier by the loan of a private aeroplane. John Shearer, an old Scots Guards friend with a house on the Caicos Islands, not only gave them the use of his plane but accompanied them on what was virtually a triumphal progress among the West Indian churches. It was still gruelling as they flew among the eight dioceses, meeting bishop after bishop and prime minister after prime minister, with the archbishop finding appropriate things to say on each occasion. But the pattern was broken at their last port of call when they found no one to greet them at the airport at Guyana. There was no official welcome from that left-wing Government still deeply resentful of Guyana's colonial past, and the atmosphere only thawed when the archbishop paid a visit on President Forbes Burnham. But the church offered its own warm welcome in the world's biggest wooden cathedral in Georgetown, and the visitors had a memorable day at a theological college for Amerindian clergy deep in the Guyana rain forest on the Brazilian border where the students supported themselves by their traditional hunting.

From there the archbishop came straight back to host an unprecedented meeting of church leaders at Canterbury. With only a single day between his arrival home and the gathering at Canterbury he had even less time than usual to draw breath before plunging into the incessant round of meetings and correspondence that was always waiting for him back in England. However, this was a meeting with a difference, and was an illustration of the way that ecumenical relations had been developing since the watershed summer of 1982 which had seen the triumph of the Pope's visit as well as the Church of England's rejection of the Anglican and Free Churches' Covenanting scheme all within a matter of weeks.

The Covenant Proposals had been a follow-on from the abortive attempt at Anglican–Methodist unity ten years before in 1972. But this time the Church of England, the Methodist, United Reformed and Moravian Churches, and the Churches of Christ, were all involved. The intention was that they should enter into a solemn agreement to work closely together and to recognise one another's ministries as a major step towards eventual unity.

After two painful years of debate the scheme was adopted – though in some cases narrowly – by everybody except the Anglicans. Just six weeks after the Pope had shared in an Anglican service in Canterbury Cathedral, the House of Clergy in the General Synod blocked this major ecumenical movement towards the Free Churches. The principal arguments against it were the problems of recognising Free

Church ministers on the same sacramental footing as Anglican clergy who had been episcopally ordained; the fact that the Free Churches had women ministers who would also have to be recognised in the same way; and a deep concern that to enter into this sort of relationship with the Free Churches would hinder the rapprochement with Rome. In the crucial Synod debate in July 1982 the archbishop had spoken powerfully in favour of the scheme. But, while most of his fellow-bishops supported him, as did sixty-eight per cent of the laity, the clergy vetoed it.

At the General Synod the following November, Runcie announced a 'two-pronged strategy' for church unity to follow the failure of the Covenant. Increased encouragement was to be given to the many local ecumenical projects where people in individual parishes were spontaneously learning to live and share with their neighbours of other churches. New initiatives were to be taken on the theological level to reconcile the doctrines of the several churches on the basis of the work done by ARCIC, the Anglican–Roman Catholic International Commission, and the World Council of Churches' report on *Baptism, Eucharist and the Ministry* which covered much of the same ground from the other churches' point of view.

On the Roman Catholic front things were suddenly moving fast. The Roman Church had made it clear that they were still not ready to join the British or the World Councils of Churches because the Councils were structured in too Protestant a way, their business being done by elected members who were not necessarily church leaders in the sense that Roman Catholics understood church leadership. However, it was no sooner announced that a group of British church leaders were going to take up the Pope's invitation for talks at the Vatican than the RC bishops of England and Wales invited representatives of other churches to a formal conference. At the same time Runcie announced that a new ARCIC would be set up to examine the doctrinal differences that still separated Anglicans and Roman Catholics. The Anglican co-chairman would be Mark Santer, by this time Bishop of Kensington; and Canon Christopher Hill, the archbishop's Secretary for Ecumenical Affairs, would be its Anglican secretary.

The meeting initiated by the Roman Catholics took place in January 1984 when Runcie and John Habgood, now Archbishop of York, together with the Archbishop of Wales and leading members of the BCC, spent twenty-four hours with all the Roman Catholic bishops in Chelmsford, worshipping together and discussing 'the Catholic Church and church unity – the present position and future plans'. The three-day meeting at Canterbury which immediately followed Runcie's return from the Caribbean was almost entirely given to prayer and reflection. There was a deepening of trust and mutual understanding, and all concerned were looking forward to a major conference of the churches in 1987 – significantly the year before the Lambeth Conference – when they would consider together the ARCIC and WCC doctrinal statements. That meeting could be a major step forward in unity for the whole Christian church.

While relationships with other churches were moving to a deeper level of understanding, those with Mrs Thatcher's government were rather less than sweetness and light. Nor did the national media refrain from stirring the situation. From the time of the controversy which surrounded the archbishop's sermon at the Falklands service they had begun to find that the Church of England was not nearly so boringly in tune with the Establishment as they had assumed.

Hard on the heels of the Falklands furore came a prepublication leak of the contents of *The Church and the Bomb*, a report produced by a Board for Social Responsibility working party under the chairmanship of Bishop John Baker of Salisbury. Its more controversial recommendations were that Britain should unilaterally renounce nuclear weapons, cancel its order for Trident missiles, and refuse to allow American nuclear weapons to be based on British soil.

The Church and the Bomb went off like a bomb. Its explosion caught the archbishop unprepared. He had just been having a lot of media pestering over some unauthorised new words to the National Anthem which had appeared in a recently-published hymn-book, and he now found himself in the middle of another uproar over something he had not yet had a chance to read. He replied rather testily to newspaper questioning that the report had not yet been debated by the General Synod and had 'no more official sanction than the so-called alternative National Anthem'. But that did not stop furious letters pouring into Lambeth Palace as well as highly approving ones from supporters of the Campaign for Nuclear Disarmament.

The archbishop made nuclear warfare the subject of his sermon in Canterbury Cathedral that Christmas, and sparked off yet another burst of political controversy when he spoke – as he did in East Germany – of the madness of employing so many of the world's best minds and precious resources on preparing for 'the lunatic unthinkable'. His expressed sympathy 'with those who have a pain in the mind and will not let the subject drop', and for those who demonstrated against nuclear weapons, was taken out of context by the media as support for the 'peace women' camping at the Greenham Common nuclear base and an indication – quite a wrong one – that he shared their unilateralist stand. He was again under attack by several Conservative Members of Parliament; but it did not stop him being asked, a month later, to speak on the moral issues of nuclear armaments to the Royal Institute of International Affairs.

The church was as divided over *The Church and the Bomb* as the nation. The book was all but disowned by the Board for Social Responsibility which wrote its own report for the Synod to debate and attached *The Church and the Bomb* to it as an appendix. The Conservative Party took the whole matter badly, and the newspapers collected many cross remarks from various members of the Government, including Mrs Thatcher. Labour Party members and the Campaign for Nuclear Disarmament warmly approved. For weeks there was non-stop correspondence on the subject in nearly every national newspaper, and there was much huffing and puffing – made the most of by the press – about disestablishing the church.

The Synod debate on nuclear weapons was during the February session of 1983. By this time the public interest was so great that the day-long debate was actually broadcast live on television. The quality of speeches was high, and after a large number of amendments – both unilateralist and multilateralist – had been worked through, the Synod finally came down in a 'no-first-use' position, saying that even a small-scale first use of nuclear weapons could never be morally justified.

With the possible exception of the two or three Members of Parliament who were also members of Synod, the archbishop was probably in closer contact with political reality than anyone else present. He had close contacts (and friendship) with politicians of all persuasions and was used to meeting world leaders. His perspective was that of a statesman as well as a churchman. He argued for 'the moral seriousness of the multilateral approach'. He said he did not find the recommendations in *The Church and the Bomb* either coherent or convincing. He had no confidence that a unilateralist stance on the part of Britain would have any of the effect on the other nuclear powers that the working party had suggested. It might even undermine the disarmament negotiations then going on:

It would be a tragedy if the Soviet will to make progress, for example in eliminating the most threatening weapons in Europe, were to be weakened by the spectacle of NATO in disarray and the tempting prospect of gaining great diplomatic advantage by consolidating nuclear as well as conventional superiority in Europe. Too often this country has appeared to send misleading signals to those who have been tempted to pursue aggression. Make no mistake. An announcement of the United Kingdom's carrying out 'a phased disengagement from active association with any form of nuclear weaponry' would have a traumatic effect on the NATO alliance. I have seen very little evidence that those responsible for policy in other NATO countries would regard renunciation of nuclear weapons as anything other than a repudiation of NATO's defence policy.

On the contrary, I have heard much to suggest that such a step would put a new strain on the alliance on which the peace and stability of Europe has rested since World War Two by strengthening the advocates of isolationism in the United States.

He did not confine his arguments purely to such pragmatism. Alliances, he said, depended on a willingness to share responsibilities. 'Is there not some moral inconsistency in seeking to remain within an alliance which accepts a policy of nuclear deterrence while declining to take one's share in the means by which that policy is sustained?'

Shortly afterwards his involvement in politics took a slightly farcical turn when he confessed that he had cast his vote as an ordinary citizen in the General Election that June, and it appeared that he was the only bishop in the House of Lords to have done so. He had voted as he had done in all elections since his St Albans' days when a constitutional lawyer had assured him that bishops in the House of Lords were not peers of the realm but spiritual peers and therefore the voting disqualification did not apply. His polling card had arrived at Lambeth Palace in the usual way, and he had gone with Lindy to the polling station in the safe Labour stronghold of Vauxhall. In the storm in a legal tea-cup which followed, the archbishop agreed not to put the ruling to the test but, in future, to accept the precedent that bishops should not exercise their vote so long as they remained spiritual peers. He was not entirely convinced.

The House of Lords is a place where, even more than most, he is determined not to speak in platitudes. When he feels he can make a useful contribution in a debate he depends for a detailed briefing on the research coordinated by his Secretary for Public Affairs, the role filled by Michael Kinchin-Smith until he moved to become the archbishop's Appointments Secretary at the end of 1983. Kinchin-Smith's place was taken by Wilfrid Grenville-Grey, a layman with a degree in theology, a wide experience in foreign affairs, a Zulu wife and three children. With a background in the Overseas Civil Service and seventeen years in Africa,

Grenville-Grey was Director of the Centre for International Briefing at Farnham Castle before representing the International Defence and Aid Fund at the United Nations. With the help of Lambeth Palace's residential researcher, Andrew Acland, and a whole range of outside resources, he keeps the archbishop up to date on social and political matters, and handles a large part of his enormous correspondence from the public on those issues.

A piece of legislation which exercised Runcie a good deal, and on which he and several other bishops spoke a number of times, was the Nationality Act which he considered a defective blunt instrument causing great insecurity among many new British citizens. He also opened an important debate in November 1983 on violence in society. A year previously the General Synod had voted overwhelmingly against the reintroduction of capital punishment and, more recently, the House of Commons had once again reached the same conclusion. Speaking as a cross-bencher, the archbishop emphasised the complete unacceptability of such a penalty for even the most serious crime. In an influential and wide-ranging speech he considered the roots of violence to be found in the home – 'in Britain there is not so much an absence of parental love as a failure of parental nerve' – in the schools, and in the community. He pointed to the violent effects of alcohol and a 'daily diet of mayhem and murder' on television and video screens.

He also told the Lords that he had recently set up an Archbishops' Commission on Urban Priority Areas to discover ways in which the church could do more in the inner cities, the notorious breeding grounds of violence. This commission, expected to report in September 1985, was composed of a distinguished collection of people chaired by Sir Richard O'Brien. In the words of Canon Eric James, whose gad-fly tactics had done much to prompt the archbishop to take this initiative, it was hoped that they would 'articulate questions about public policy at the national level of both church and state'. It was expected to be one of the most important and influential reports that the Church of England had yet produced.

1984 was the year of the miners' strike. On a Saturday in September the Archbishop went to preach in Derby Cathedral where he warned of the 'bitter harvest' the strike would bring both to the miners and the country. He then visited the village of Creswell which had been the scene of violent picketing. The local vicar, Peter Bowers, had arranged that the archbishop should meet a cross-section of the villagers, even though he had to talk to working miners and striking miners in different rooms. Before returning to London Runcie held a press conference in which he talked further about the need for reconciliation in the mining communities.

By this time the public were only too ready to listen to fresh voices on the subject which had been dominating their television screens for months. Arthur Scargill, President of the National Union of Mineworkers, and Ian MacGregor, Chairman of the National Coal Board were at loggerheads, and the country itself was deeply divided. So all the more attention was paid when, just after the archbishop had been in the news for his views on the strike, the new Bishop of Durham, David Jenkins, made some rather more contentious remarks in his enthronement sermon in Durham Cathedral.

Since just after the announcement of his appointment, Jenkins had been at the centre of controversy for making ambiguous theological statements in a television programme in which he appeared to contradict the traditional doctrines about the Virgin Birth and the Resurrection. Though his views would scarcely have raised an eyebrow in a theological college, they caused a public storm and much opposition to his consecration as a bishop. The result at Lambeth was a flood of letters – a hundred a day over a considerable period – from many deeply distressed people imploring the archbishop to reassure them that the doctrines were true and that Jenkins should be brought to heel. This latter was beyond the archbishop's powers for he and his predecessors had never claimed a Vatican-style authority over other bishops. But he was irritated by what he saw as episcopal irresponsibility in the way that Jenkins had carelessly upset those of simple faith by using phrases that could so easily be misinterpreted by the media. He was not prepared to condemn what Jenkins had actually said because such speculation had been common currency among radical theologians for a generation. Questioned both by the media and by the General Synod, Runcie steered a careful path without committing himself theologically other than in general terms to a belief in the Incarnation and Resurrection. It meant that he left dissatisfied a good many who had hoped for a firm restatement of belief in the biblical details of each event.

Meanwhile Jenkins, who had spent most of his life in universities as an academic, appeared to have a taste for rocking ecclesiastical boats, and lost no opportunity to expound his views further. And, with the media watching his every word, he began speaking his mind on the miners' strike. His enthronement sermon was described by Runcie as 'a robust statement about reconciliation', but in the course of it he said that 'the miners must not be defeated', and he referred to MacGregor as 'an important elderly American'. Both remarks were taken out of context and assumed to imply he was wholly on the miners' side (which was not true for he had also said that *neither* side must be allowed to win). But the sermon made headlines and once again the Government was in a rage.

At this point the archbishop made one of the very few political ineptitudes of his career out of the best of motives. Afraid that Ian MacGregor had been personally hurt by Jenkins's remarks, he wrote a kindly letter of sympathy (which he later strongly denied was any sort of apology), completely on impulse, in his own hand, with no copy, and posted by himself.

By this time he had acquired on his staff at Lambeth a highly experienced Secretary for Broadcasting, Press and Communications in Mrs Eve Keatley, an ex-BBC producer and a former director of broadcasting in Church House. The first she knew of this letter, which the archbishop had confidently assumed would be a private matter between himself and MacGregor, was when she was rung up late at night from Fleet Street because the editor of another paper had seen it splashed across the front of the *Daily Mail* as RUNCIE REPENTS. It was made to look as though he had completely repudiated what one of his own bishops had been saying, and Mrs Keatley and the archbishop shared a nerve-racking twenty-four hours with newspaper and television interviews in an attempt to recover the situation.

All that was forgotten when, a few days later, the archbishop was interviewed at length by Clifford Longley in *The Times* on the Government's current policy. It was a thoughtful interview with Runcie characteristically struggling to see every issue in perspective and to make reasoned judgments taking all arguments into account. But there was one point on which he was not tentative. While economic growth with all its benefits would seem to be self-evidently worth aiming for, he said, 'if the human consequences of such aims mean unemployment on an unprecedented scale, poverty, bureaucracy, despair about the future of some communities, and the inequitable sharing of the sacrifices called for, then the objectives must be called in question.'

It took the popular papers to put it into the simplistic terms in which most political statements are made. RUNCIE LASHES TORIES was the *Sun*'s version; and that evening in London the *Standard* declared on its front page, VOTERS BACK RUNCIE, as it had been learned from a MORI poll that there was growing concern about Government policy among Tory voters.

Members of the Government, including his old friend Lord Whitelaw, accused him of being politically naïve and talking of things about which he knew nothing. But the public were delighted. Quite by chance, because *The Times* interview had been delayed for a week, it had been published just before the start of the Conservative Party conference. With a number of other bishops, notably David Jenkins and Hugh Montefiore, joining in the criticism of the Government, the Tories were obviously shaken. In the first few days of their conference they and their press observers were constantly referring to what 'the bishops' had said. But it happened to be the conference which ended tragically with an IRA bomb in the hotel at Brighton where Mrs Thatcher and her Cabinet were staying, and which resulted in five deaths. For some days the wave of support and sympathy which came from church and nation wiped out all other considerations.

Exactly a fortnight after *The Times* interview the archbishop was due to speak to the Coningsby Club, a stronghold of right-wing Conservatism. It was a private meeting, but such a turn-out of members had rarely been seen. Many had come to savage this turbulently waffling priest who talked such nonsense about government, and they had some merciless questions prepared. But so was Runcie prepared. He made an exceptionally well-informed and incisive speech which those who heard it say was superbly delivered. He talked of the church's 'critical solidarity' with the state, and its obligation to be both a uniting and a critical force in society. He was equally incisive as he dealt with the questions, and scored a significant personal triumph in the way he turned some of his fiercest critics into grudging admirers.

But though he has the ability to win the admiration and usually the affection of his audience, it does not always mean that he gets his way in the church's Synods. He spoke strongly for the Covenant scheme, but it was defeated by the clergy. Remarriage in church for those divorced people who sincerely want to make a religious commitment to their second marriage – something for which he has been arguing during the whole of his episcopate – seems to be steadily slipping away as more dioceses vote against it. On the ordination of women he remains equivocal in action if not in principle. In November 1984 when the issue was once again before the General Synod he gave a number of people – including the present writer – the impression that this time he would vote for it. But his shift was more subtle than that. He accepted the existence of validly ordained women in the Anglican Communion, but pleaded for a policy of gradualism on the part of the Church of England. 'I cannot conceal my conviction,' he said, 'that we have a duty not to be seen acting in abrasive and unfraternal disregard of very large Catholic bodies with whom we share the very fundamentals of the faith.' However, in an unexpected swing in the mood of the Synod, the motion was passed to start the necessary legislation to allow women to be ordained.

His major disappointments have been more personal. One was that the church's official doctrine commission had not yet proved to be the body which produced any clear formulation of faith in language that the common people of England could understand – a need which has been highlighted by the controversy surrounding Bishop Jenkins. He would also have liked to be able to create a House of Bishops with more time and opportunity for talk, theology and friendship, with time to discuss at leisure more of the major issues before the church in the way that he persuaded them to do before the Synod debates on nuclear weapons and the Covenant. He has sensed this close relationship between bishops in other parts of the Anglican Communion where circumstances are very different. But the bishops of the Church of England are, like himself, too busy for their own good, and he does not feel he can call on them for support in the national matters which occupy so much of his own time.

However, he is deeply grateful for two recent appointments. Dr John Habgood, the new Archbishop of York, is a scientist and academic theologian, and has a gift for logical clarity in his increasingly-regarded comments on national affairs as well as a clear grasp of the church's needs. He is a cooler personality than Runcie, but the two men complement each other and form a distinguished partnership. The other appointment that has meant much to him is Dr Samuel Van Culin as Secretary-General of the Anglican Consultative Council. Canon Van Culin, from the diocese of Hawaii, travels widely throughout the Anglican Communion and keeps in close touch with its many constituent parts. He is a most valuable link and colleague for the archbishop, as well as a personal friend.

He has also built up a first-class team at Lambeth Palace headed by Bishop Ronald Gordon who gave up his diocese of Portsmouth to replace Bishop Ross Hook as Chief of Staff (though he prefers the more ambiguous title of 'Bishop at Lambeth'). Ronald Gordon is a quiet, orderly man who coordinates the growing staff and undertakes much of the archbishop's routine archiepiscopal work with other bishops, with clergy under discipline, with legal matters, and also with the archbishop's unique privilege of bestowing his own degrees or diplomas on those who have earned them or have served the church in some special way. The fact that Lambeth Palace is now such a friendly, cooperative and efficient place, and is a pleasure for outsiders to deal with, owes not a little to Bishop Gordon's unobtrusive deputy leadership.

The work goes on unabated, trying to keep the archbishop's diary under control and the hundreds of letters answered – by return of post if humanly possible. The overseas visits continue to be scheduled and, in the latter months of 1984, the archbishop visited Yugoslavia, Nigeria, and France where he was the first Archbishop of Canterbury to preach in Notre Dame Cathedral. People suffering from injustice, particularly those who believe themselves to be wrongfully imprisoned, write from all over the world to ask the archbishop's help, and at Christmas 1984 Terry Waite made another of his dramatic journeys to plead with Colonel Gadaffi for the release of four Britons held in a Libyan gaol. Christopher Hill works away at ecumenical relationships, and the archbishop goes on trying to meet all the expectations he has raised, and fretting about having to give so much of his time to the machinery of church government.

It is legitimate to ask whether all the work that Robert Runcie undertakes is properly the role of the Archbishop of Canterbury as the leader of a world-wide church. What is clear is that he could work no other way. There is a force within him that drives him on and never lets him rest or be satisfied. His great talent and good fortune is that he attracts the same commitment from those who work with him.

When the earlier chapters of this biography were published in November 1983, a number of critics with well-known views used the opportunity for cynical mockery of the church in general and of Runcie in particular. But a few among the many sympathetic reviewers were disappointed that the emphasis had not been on the archbishop's own spirituality. What they had wanted were revelations about the religious insights and the relationship with God of a spiritual leader.

But Runcie is not – and has never thought of himself as – a profoundly-thinking spiritual giant like his last predecessor but one, Michael Ramsey. His strengths are very different. He is a deeply and privately religious man who has never pretended to be an original Christian thinker, but has, nevertheless, a coherent theology of God's relationship with the world which is revealed in his collection of sermons and addresses, *Windows on to God*, published by SPCK, also in 1983. Now, in his life of living sacrifice to his job, he knows himself to be very dependent on other people's prayers, and he deeply values the circle of friends who regularly pray for him with sympathetic understanding of what he is trying to do.

His early mornings in chapel are his own precious times for reflection and waiting upon God. He always spends Good Fridays in silence with an enclosed religious community, seizes such other brief times for retreat when he can, and wishes he could manage them more often. But he has accepted that, if he is to do what he feels called to do, he must live with this tension in his personal life. With pragmatic realism he can say: 'When I was at a theological college I used to tell my students "the busier you are the more time you must find for prayer – a priest's priorities should be rest, prayer, and work", but, frankly, the epigrams of a secluded theological college are not always helpful beyond giving you a guilty conscience,' and he adds the revealing remark, 'I have too often seen clergy use spirituality as an excuse for idleness.'

His three predecessors, each in their very different styles, began exploring what it was to be a modern Archbishop of Canterbury, but it is Runcie who has really developed a pattern of leadership which focuses the attention, loyalty and affection of all sorts and conditions of men and women of half the nationalities of the world. It has required a very special stamina, commitment, and vision; and Robert Runcie will be hard for another archbishop to follow.

Index

Abbott, Eric, 166
ACCM, 176, 195, 221, 298
Acland, Andrew, 306
Aksum, Metropolitan Methodius of, 227
Alexandra, Princess, 266
Allchin, A. M., 150
All Saints' Church, Gosforth, 118,
  122–4, 125, 127
Alternative Service Book, 44, 267
Anglican Consultative Council, 29, 215,
  293
Annan, Lord, 210, 211
Anselm, Archbishop, 17
Antioch, Patriarch of, 227
ARCIC, 277, 301, 302
Armytage, Duncan, 109
Ashton, Sir Hubert, 174
Athenagoras of Thyateira, Archbishop,
  225, 247
Athens, Archbishop of, 227
Augustine, Archbishop, 13, 14, 15, 247,
  282, 283
Ayer, A. J., 76

Baker, John, 302
Balfour, Colonel 'Bill', 79
Balfour, Peter, 85, 100, 101, 175
Baptist Times, 267
Barker, Marjorie (sister of RAKR), 50,
  51, 52, 56, 62, 63, 64, 69, 72, 73, 76,
  117, 120, 121, 124, 135, 182
Barkway, Lumsden, 166, 169
Barne, Michael, 125–6
Basil, Archbishop, 206, 207
Bateman-Champain, J. N., 166
BBC, 64, 76n, 208, 210, 233, 243, 269,
  277, 290
Becket, Archbishop Thomas, 9, 18, 250
Bede, Venerable, 14
Beeson, Nigel, 90

Benson, Ann Edna, 'Nancy' (mother of
  RAKR), see Runcie, Ann Edna
Benson, Henry, 'Paddy' (grandfather of
  RAKR), 54
Berlin, Isaiah, 107
Betjeman, Sir John, 113, 171
Bezzant, J. S., 128
Bhutto, President of Pakistan, 38
Bible, Authorised version of, 22, 36
Bird, Anthony, 147, 149, 150, 151, 162
Birley, Sir Robert, 106
Blanch, Archbishop Stuart, 30, 45, 46,
  216, 238
Blomfield, Bishop, 25
Blunden, Edmund, 78
Book of Common Prayer, 20, 21, 22, 27, 32,
  34, 36, 37, 267
Booth-Clibborn, Stanley, 279
Bouquet, A. C., 113
Bourke, Michael, 221
Bowers, Peter, 307
Bowlby, Ronald, 31
Boyd-Carpenter, Jenny, 236, 246, 269
Braithwaite, R. B., 115
Brasenose College, Oxford, 75, 76, 100,
  102, 103
British Council of Churches, 244, 297,
  301, 302
Britten, Lord (Benjamin), 119
Broady, Maurice, 161
Brooks, John, 147, 149
Browning, Wilfrid, 147
Burnaby, John, 128
Burnham, Forbes, 300

CACTM, 108, 160
Callaghan, James, 28, 45, 187
Campaign for Nuclear Disarmament,
  303
Carey, David, 185

Carey, Kenneth, 110, 112–13, 114, 116, 117, 127–8, 130, 131–2, 146
Carpenter, Harry, 141, 173, 177, 205, 206
Carrington, Lord, 174, 271
Cathcart, Lord, 85
Cell, The, 166–70
Chadwick, Henry, 148, 158
Chadwick, Owen, 128, 131, 133, 137, 139, 140, 141, 144, 157
Chandler, Maurice, 105, 106
Charles V, Emperor, 20
Charles I, King, 10, 22
Charles II, King, 22
Charles, Prince of Wales, 241, 261, 265, 267–8, 269, 282, 293
Charteris, Hugo, 109
Chartres, Richard, 47, 222, 233, 234, 243, 244, 245, 247, 250, 267, 269, 273, 275, 296, 298
Chase, George, 136
Christ Church College, Oxford, 75–6, 77
Christian Newsletter, 106
Church Commissioners, 41, 174, 182, 183, 289
Church House, Westminster, 30, 41, 47, 195, 236, 239, 241, 262
Church Times, 30, 40, 165, 215, 240, 241
'Clapham sect', 24
Cocks, Frank, 185
Coggan, Archbishop Donald, 30, 33, 38, 44, 46, 48, 76n, 215, 223, 230, 235, 238, 241, 243
Coggan, Jean, 234
Coleman, Audrey, 255, 257, 263
Coleman, John, 255, 256, 257, 263
Coleman, Peter, 113, 128
Coningsby Club, 310
Convocations, 25, 130
Cornwell, Peter, 145, 150, 158, 162
Coronation Road Primary School, Crosby, 59
Costin, W. C., 140, 141
Coulton, Nicholas, 164, 198–9, 215, 222
CRAC, 208, 209, 210, 211, 230
Cranmer, Archbishop Thomas, 20, 21
Cromwell, Thomas, 20
Crosland, Anthony, 77
Crown Appointments Commission, 28, 31, 44, 45, 46, 231
Cuddesdon Theological College, 113–14, 119, 132, 139–40, 141, 142, 143, 144, and passim
Culin, Samuel Van, 311
Cunningham, B. K., 110–11, 112, 113
Cupitt, Don, 133

Cuthbert, S. J., 90

Daily Express, 109, 299
Daily Mail, 109, 309
Daily Star, 240, 268
Daily Telegraph, 79
Dalai Lama, 268
Dalziel, Catherine (gt-gt-grandmother to RAKR), 53
Davey, Colin, 206
David, A. A., 64
Dehquani-Tafti, Bishop, 254
Deusdedit, Archbishop, 14
Ding, Bishop K. H., 272–273
Dodds, Neil, 124, 126
Dunbar, C. I. H., 99

Eadsige, Archbishop, 16
Ecclesiastical Commissioners, 25
Edward the Confessor, King, 16
Edwards, David, 158
Elfric, Archbishop, 16
Elizabeth I, Queen, 21, 23, 35
Elizabeth II, Queen, 106, 187, 194, 281, and passim
Elizabeth, Queen Mother, 223, 253
Elliott, David, 217
Ellison, Gerald, 242
Enabling Act, 27
Erasmus, 20
Erskine, David, 91
Ethelbert, King, 13, 14
Evening News, 40

Farmer, H. H., 128
Fellowes, Charles, 83
Fisher, Alexander, 52
Fisher, Michael, 128
Fitzalan Howard, Michael, 85, 93
Fleming, Launcelot Scott, 136
Fletcher, Archie, 97–8, 100, 188
Fordham, Emily, 61

Gadaffi, Colonel, 312
Gale, Jessie, 59, 274
Gay News, 236
General Synod, 28–9, 41, 42, 43, 44, 192–4, 200, 225, 231–2, 257–63, 269, 271, 273, 300, 301, 303, 304, 306, 308, 310, 311
George I, King, 23
George III, King, 24
Ghandi, Indira, 38
Godwin, Earl, 16
Gollancz, Victor, 71
Gordon, Ronald, 311–12
Graham, Alec, 222

Graham, Billy, 128
Graham, Eric, 172
Gray, Cardinal, 280
Great St. Mary's, Cambridge, 135, 180
Greenacre, Brigadier, 97
Greer, W. D. L., 108, 111
Gregory the Great, Pope, 13, 14, 15, 276, 282
Grenville-Grey, Wilfrid, 305–6
Gresford Jones, Michael, 166, 178, 182, 191
Gunning, Elizabeth (Great-aunt Leily), 50, 57
Gunning, Sarah (grandmother of RAKR), 54

Habgood, John, 31, 112, 132, 156, 302, 311
Hanson, R. P. C., 206
Hardy, Archie, 117
Hardy, Robert, 221
Hare, John, 191, 222
Hare, Richard, 135
Harrison, John, 55
Hawaii, Royal Family of, 268
Heaton, E. W., 113
Hempel, Bishop, 296
Henry II, King, 9, 18
Henry VIII, King, 19, 20, 21
Hertfordshire Advertiser, 46, 47, 179, 235
Hill, Christopher, 243, 244, 250, 295, 301, 312
Historic Episcopate, The, 130
Hodson, Mark, 166
Holroyd, Michael, 104, 110
Honest to God, 156, 157–9, 167
Honest to God Debate, The, 158
Hood, Sinclair, 174
Hook, Ross, 251, 311
Hook, Ruth, 190
Howe, Sir Geoffrey, 241, 246
Howe, John, 215
Howley, Archbishop William, 25
Hudson, Noel, 119, 123, 127, 157
Humble, R., 90
Hume, Cardinal Basil, 40, 49, 237, 247, 251, 261, 279, 280, 281

Igglesden, Christopher, 252
Independent Broadcasting Authority, 208
Inglis, Angus (brother-in-law of RAKR), 68, 69, 71, 73, 75, 101, 102, 107, 108, 117, 124, 135, 139, 140, 142, 184
Inglis, Kathleen (sister of RAKR), 50, 56, 58, 61, 65, 67, 68, 72, 73, 75, 87,
101, 109, 117, 124, 135, 143, 174, 176, 181, 183, 236
Inglis, Robin (nephew of RAKR), 87, 109
Inglis Rosemary (niece of RAKR), 73, 87, 109
Ingrams, Richard, 240
Innocent III, Pope, 18
Islip, Archbishop Simon, 18

Jackson, Jill, 199
James II, King, 22, 23
James, Clive, 270
James, Colin, 44
James, Eric, 220, 306
Jenkins, Bishop David, 148, 158, 307–8, 309, 311
Jenkins, Roy, 77
Jerusalem, Patriarch of, 227
John I, King, 18, 24
John, Ernest, 154
John Paul II, Pope, 40, 250, 260, 265, 273, 278, 281–4, 285, 300, 301
Johnson, Hewlett, 87
Jones, Penry, 209
Josif, Bishop of Rimnical Vilcea, 228
Justinian, Patriarch of Romania, 206

Katharine of Aragon, Queen, 19
Keatley, Eve, 308, 309
Kennaby, Noel, 213
Kent, Duke and Duchess of, 253
Khomeini, Ayatollah, 254, 255, 262, 287
Kinchin-Smith, Michael, 76n, 243, 305
King, Martin Luther, 274
Kirk, Kenneth, 77
Knapp-Fisher, Edward, 140, 149
Knowles, David, 128
Kolbe, Maximilian, 261, 274

Labilliere, P. F. D., 166
Laing, Sir Hector, 85
Lamb, Kenneth, 209
Lambeth Conference, 32, 224, 225, 228, 231, 244, 293, 295, 302
Lambeth Quadrilateral, 129
Lang, John, 208, 209, 210
Langley, Robert, 221
Langton, Archbishop Stephen, 18
Laud, Archbishop William, 10, 22
Leo III, Pope, 15
Leonard, Graham, 31, 279
Lewis, C. S., 106–7
Li Xiannian, 297
Lightfoot, R. H., 115
Lloyd, Henry, 108
Lloyd, Roger, 157

Longley, Clifford, 237, 282, 309
Luckraft, Inez, 199, 221, 243, 251
Luther, Martin, 19, 295
Luwum, Janani, 298

MacGregor, Ian, 307, 308
Maclean, Sir Charles, 85
Mann, John, 93, 99
Maple, David, 252
Marcinkus, Archbishop, 278
Margaret, Princess, 116, 241
Martin, Christopher, 209
Mary I, Queen, 21
Mary II, Queen, 23
Marx, Karl, 36
Mascall, Eric, 148
Mathieson, D. G., 92
McKellar, Isabella (grandmother of
   RAKR), 53, 56
Meacham, Joy, 47
Meakin, Tony, 123, 128
Mepham, Andrew, 150
Merchant Taylors' School, Crosby, 55,
   56, 61, 62, 63, 66, 70, 72, 75, and
   passim
Miles, John, 47, 236, 267, 275, 276
Milford, T. R., 103
Miller, Powell, 64
Molyneux, David, 64, 76
Montefiore, Hugh, 111, 117–18,
   119–20, 127, 128, 130, 131, 156, 157,
   180, 309
Montgomery, Lord, 84
Moore, Michael, 243, 244
Moore, Peter, 213
Moorman, J. R. H., 110
Morgan, E. R., 166
Morgan, Philip, 297
Mortimer, Robert, 77
Moscow, Patriarch of, 229
Moule, Charles, 128
Mountbatten, Lord, 47, 235
Muldoon, Roy, 293
Mumford, Peter, 222, 223

Ndahura, Archbishop Bezaleri, 249, 250
News of the World, The, 240
Norman and Beard, 54
Norris, Miss, 115
Norris, Ted, 219–20
Norwich, Bishop of (Maurice Wood),
   272

O'Brien, Sir Richard, 44, 45, 306
Obote, President, 298, 299
Observer, The, 156, 270
O'Fiaich, Cardinal, 266

Okoth, Yona, 298
Oldham, J. H., 106
Otter, Tony, 73
Owen, Leslie, 166
'Oxford Movement', 25, 66

Paisley, Ian, 266
Parker, Archbishop Matthew, 21, 22
Parkinson, Michael, 240
Parr, R. F., 72
Parsons, Richard, 228
Pattinson, Derek, 289
Paul, Leslie, 159, 160
Pears, Sir Peter, 119
Pembroke College, Cambridge, 74
Pepys, Christopher, 166, 167, 169
Peterson, Colin, 234, 235
Philip of Spain, King, 21
Phipps, Simon, 111, 115, 116, 118–19
Picken, Sarah, 53
Pinochet, President of Chile, 38
Piper, John, 172, 182
Pitt, William, 24
Plunkett, Patrick, 186
Pole, Archbishop Reginald, 21
Potter, Philip, 247
Prayer Book – see Book of Common Prayer
Price, Christopher, 66, 67
Pritchard, A. J. W., 148
Pusey House, 77, 103
Pyke, Andrew, 256, 264

Quick, Oliver, 77
Quinn, Captain, 100

Ramsey, Ian, 207, 208
Ramsey, Joan, 185
Ramsey, Archbishop Michael, 38, 128,
   158, 180, 185, 196, 200, 207, 209, 215,
   313
Ratcliff, E. C., 113, 128
Reeves, Paul, 294
Reid, George, 85, 86
Reyntiens, Patrick, 172
Riches, Kenneth, 177
Ridley, Dame Betty, 247
Robert of Jumièges, Archbishop, 16
Roberts, Margaret – see Thatcher,
   Margaret
Robinson, J. A. T., 128, 130, 156, 157, 158
Rodger, Patrick, 111, 215
Rogers, Murray, 154, 227
Romania, Patriarch of, 229
Romero, Oscar, 247, 274
Runcie, Ann Edna, 'Nancy' (mother of
   RAKR), 50, 51, 52, 54, 56, 57, 63, 68,
   73, 87, 117, and passim

Runcie, Catherine (aunt of RAKR), 53
Runcie, Florence (aunt of RAKR), 53
Runcie, James (gt-gt-grandfather of
    RAKR), 50
Runcie, James (grandfather to RAKR),
    53
Runcie, James (son of RAKR), 47, 49,
    138, 141, 143, 151, 162, 177, 179, 216,
    236, 246, 269, 270, 290 and passim
Runcie, Kathleen – see Inglis, Kathleen
Runcie, Kenneth (brother of RAKR),
    50, 51, 54, 57, 58, 62, 63, 64, 69, 73,
    109, 116, 117, 135, 182
Runcie, Marjorie – see Barker, Marjorie
Runcie, Rebecca (daughter of RAKR),
    47, 49, 151, 162, 177, 184, 216, 236,
    246, 290 and passim
Runcie, Robert, Dalziel (father of
    RAKR), 50, 51, 52, 53, 54, 56, 57, 63,
    68–9, 72, 75, 87, 101
RUNCIE, ROBERT ALEXANDER
    KENNEDY, 9–12, 13, 15, 16, 17, 21,
    30, 42, 43, 45, 46
Career
childhood, 9, 50–62; at Merchant
    Taylors' School, 63–74; at Oxford,
    75–81, 102–10; in Scots Guards,
    81–101; at Westcott House, 110–21,
    127–31; curacy in Gosforth, 122–7; at
    Trinity Hall, Cambridge, 131–42;
    Principal of Cuddesdon, 142–83;
    Bishop of St Albans, 178–237;
    Archbishop of Canterbury, 237–313;
    –marries, 135–6; son born, 138;
    daughter born, 151, 162;
    – baptism, 52; confirmation, 64; first
    communion, 65; ordained deacon,
    120; ordained priest, 124–5;
    celebrates first communion, 125;
    consecrated bishop of St Albans,
    185–6; enthroned as bishop of St
    Albans, 187–8; 'short-listed' for
    Canterbury, 42–6, 230; appointed to
    Canterbury, 47, 235–6; enthroned at
    Canterbury, 245, 247–8
Overseas tours
India via Holy Land (1962), 151–4;
    Swan cruises to Eastern
    Mediterranean (from 1968), 174–6,
    227, 239; Eastern Europe, Middle
    East, and Russia (1979), 227–9;
    Ghana, Zaïre, Nairobi (1980), 250–1;
    United States (1981), 264–5; Ireland
    (1981), 265–7; Low Countries (1981),
    270; Far East and China (1982),
    272–3; Bermuda (1982), 293;
    Singapore (1982), 293; Hawaii

(1983), 293; New Zealand (1983),
    293–4; WCC, Vancouver (1983),
    294–5; Nairobi (1983), 295; Germany
    (1983), 295–6; China (1983), 297–8;
    Uganda (1984), 298; West Indies
    (1984), 299–300; Yugoslavia (1984),
    312; Nigeria (1984), 312; France
    (1984), 312
Pastimes
cricket, 58, 63, 76, 173, 179, 223; sport
    and athletics, 61, 63, 70–1, 106, 173,
    175, 179, 219; mimicry and acting, 60,
    64, 82, 101, 115, 118, 175; Berkshire
    pigs, 48, 236, 265
Involvement with
Anglican-Orthodox Conversations,
    30, 43, 205–7, 224–30, 232, and
    passim; broadcasting, 209–11, 239–40,
    263; Falklands Islands conflict,
    278–86, 302; Iranian prisoners,
    254–7, 262; Liverpool demonstration,
    275–6; politics, 71–2, 77, 105–6,
    302–6, 309, 310; Pope John Paul II,
    49, 250, 260, 261, 300, 301;
    reorganisation of theological college,
    194–7, and passim; Royal Family, 106,
    116, 187, 223, 241, 246, 253, 261–2,
    265, 267–70, 281–2; Walsingham
    pilgrimage, 252–3
Views on
abortion, 48; disarmament, 271–2,
    296, 302–5; homosexuality, 48, 49,
    236–7, 258; marriage and divorce, 48,
    201–4, 258, 269, 310; ordination of
    women, 43, 44, 48, 225, 228, 231–2,
    286, 294, 310; prayer, 48, 165–6, 313;
    theological training, 148–9, 150, 156,
    159–61, 164–6, 220, 221, 231, 288,
    and passim
Runcie, Rosalind, 'Lindy' (wife of
    RAKR), 46, 49, 133, 135, 136, 137,
    139, 141, 142, 143, 145, 146–7, 162,
    173, 177, 178, 182, 184, 186, 198, 204,
    216, 223, 224, 227, 233, 234, 235, 239,
    243, 251, 265, 270, 281, 290, 298, 305,
    and passim
Russell, Charles, 70, 74
Ruston, John, 147, 149

St Albans Review, 46
St Benet's Church, Cambridge, 135
St Faith's Church, Crosby, 65, 66–8, 69,
    74
St John Stevas, Norman, 241
St Luke's Church, Crosby, 52, 64, 67, 74
St Mary's University Church, Oxford,
    77, 102, 103, 108

Sancroft, Archbishop, 22, 23
Sands, Bobby, 265, 266
Santer, Mark, 162–3, 183, 301
Saumarez Smith, William, 178
Saye, David, 45
Scargill, Arthur, 307
Schofield, John, 67, 68
Scott, Archbishop Ted, 33
Sea Round, 202, 216, 217, 220
Semant, Professor, 119
Shah of Iran, 38
Shaw, Denis, 113
Shearer, John, 299
Sheppard, David, 31, 245, 275
Smythe, Charles, 149
Snowdon, Lord, 269
Soundings, 156–7, 169
Spalding, K. J., 76, 104
Sparks, H. F. D., 147, 148
Spectator, The, 240
Standard, The, 309
Spencer, Lady Diana – see Wales,
    Princess of
Stevenson, A. R. G., 82, 84, 85
Stigand, Archbishop, 16
Stockwood Mervyn, 135, 180
Storey, Graham, 136
Street, George Edmund, 144
Stylianos, Archbishop, 207
Sun, The, 268, 309
Surtees, Tim, 170
Sutton, Archbishop Charles Manners,
    24
Sykes, Norman, 115, 128

Talbot, Neville, 68
Tate and Lyle, 53, 54, 69
Tay, Moses Leng Kong, 293
Temple, Archbishop Frederick, 252
Temple, Archbishop William, 40, 41,
    70, 88
Templeton, Jean, 61
Thatcher, Margaret, 45, 106, 233, 234,
    235, 241, 265, 281, 302, 303, 309 and
    passim
Theodore and Tarsus, Archbishop, 15
Third, Richard, 251
Thirty-Nine Articles, 34, 185, 206
Thomas, George, 186, 187, 267
Thoresby, Archbishop John, 18
Thornton-Duesbery, J. P., 108
Tiffin, Mrs, 122
Till, Barry, 130
Times, The, 237, 267, 279, 282, 309, 310
Tod, Marcus Niebuhr, 76
Tomkins, Oliver, 244
Townsend, Mr, 171

Tremlett, A. P., 86, 136, 140, 141
Trillo, John, 191, 192, 200
Turnbull, John, 118, 122, 123, 124, 127,
    233–4
Turner, J. W. Cecil (father-in-law of
    RAKR), 133, 135
Turner, Jill (sister-in-law of RAKR),
    133, 184
Turner, Marjorie (mother-in-law of
    RAKR), 133
Turner, Rosalind – see Runcie,
    Rosalind

Vanstone, William, 111, 130
Verney, Stephen, 111, 118
Vidler, Alec, 156
Vitalian, Pope, 15
Volokolansk, Archbishop of, 245
Vorster, Prime Minister of South Africa,
    38

Waal, Victor de, 247
Waddell, Jean, 254, 256, 257, 263
Waine, John, 44
Waite, Terry, 244, 245, 249, 250, 254,
    255–7, 262, 263, 264, 277, 295, 296,
    298, 299, 312
Waldock, Sir Humphrey, 100
Wales, Prince of – see Charles, Prince of
    Wales
Wales, Princess of, 261, 267–9, 293
Ward, Adrian Somerset, 166
Ward, Reginald Somerset, 166
Warham, Archbishop William, 19, 20
Warner, Charles, 77
Waters, Dr Charles and Mrs, 77–8, 82,
    83, 86, 109, 116, 117, 151
Waters, Derek, 77–8, 82, 83–4, 85, 86,
    151, 213
Webster, Alan, 31, 111, 127, 130, 151,
    269
Wesley, John, 24
Westcott, Brooke Foss, 110
Wescott House, Cambridge, 108, 110,
    127, 140
Westcott House Chronicle, 116, 130,
    131–2
Wheeler, Sir Mortimer, 174
Whitelaw, William, 85, 86, 88, 90, 92,
    309
Whitgift, Archbishop John, 22
Whitsey, H. V., 111, 200, 221
Wickham, Lionel, 149, 162
Wigram, D. R., 195
Wilberforce, Samuel, 140, 144
Wilberforce, William, 25, 140
William I, King, 16

William II, King, 17
William III, King, 23
Williams, Harry, 112, 156, 157, 167, 185, 267
Wilson, Sir Harold, 178, 187
Wilson, Roger, 187
Witherage, John, 298, 299
Wolsey, Bishop Thomas, 19
Woods, G., 128
Woollcombe, Kenneth, 130, 195, 215

World Council of Churches, 229, 232, 247, 268, 293, 294, 296, 301, 302
World Interdenominational Missionary Conference, 27
Wright, Butler, 74
Wynn, Harold, 74, 75

Yakunin, Gleb, 294-5
Yates, Dennis, 191
Young, Susan, 241, 242